THE PROFESSIONAL **DESIGN GUIDE** to
Green Roofs

THE PROFESSIONAL **DESIGN GUIDE** to
Green Roofs

Karla Dakin, Lisa Lee Benjamin & Mindy Pantiel

Photography edited by
Lisa Lee Benjamin

TIMBER PRESS
Portland | London

Published in 2013 by Timber Press, Inc.

The Haseltine Building
133 S.W. Second Avenue, Suite 450
Portland, Oregon 97204-3527
timberpress.com

2 The Quadrant
135 Salusbury Road
London NW6 6RJ
timberpress.co.uk

ISBN-13: 978-1-60469-312-6

Printed in China
Book design by Breanna Goodrow

Library of Congress
Cataloging-in-Publication Data

Dakin, Karla.
 The professional design guide to green
roofs / Karla Dakin, Lisa Lee Benjamin,
Mindy Pantiel ;
photography edited by
Lisa Lee Benjamin. -- 1st ed.
     p. cm.
 Includes bibliographical references and
index.
 ISBN 978-1-60469-312-6
 1. Green roofs (Gardening)--Design and
construction. I. Benjamin, Lisa Lee. II.
Pantiel, Mindy. III. Title.
 SB419.5.D35 2013
 635.9'671--dc23
                    2012015965

A catalog record for this book is also
available from the British Library.

To my son, Dakin Alexander Platt, whom I love more than anyone or anything in this world.
—Karla Dakin

To Jewels and Annabel Downs for the boldness to pursue beauty.
—Lisa Lee Benjamin

To Shaina and Zak, the lights of my life.
—Mindy Pantiel

Contents

Foreword

I first met Karla Dakin and Lisa Lee Benjamin while speaking at a green roof conference in Denver. Since then our friendship and my admiration of these creative spirits have bloomed along with the many green roofs they have designed, planted, visited, and studied. Each honored time I spend with these zealots is filled with tales of green roofs they have admired throughout the world, green roof gurus with whom they have collaborated, and ideas they have to improve the sustainability and design of vegetated roofs.

This book is a compilation of their exuberant creativity, experience, and knowledge and is a must-read whether you are a seasoned green roof professional or a curious novice. Wherever you fit on the green roof curiosity spectrum, there are three reasons this book stands out from previous publications.

First, it astutely combines pragmatic advice with beautiful, high design inspiration. Through the authors' words and gorgeous photography, this book provides sound counsel for all phases of a green roof project, from predesign through construction and often-neglected maintenance. It also transcends previous green roof books by offering thoughtful design inspiration that will awaken even the most latent biophilia.

Second, this book adds an extremely important fourth dimension to sustainability: sophisticated design. Throughout my twenty-year career in environmental sustainability, I have always thought refined and thoughtful aestheticism have been lacking in sustainable architecture, landscape, and green roof design. The authors of this book completely get this and have succeeded, through words and photographs, in presenting design that is both ecologically benevolent but also, just as important, compositionally splendid.

Third, this book will quickly become the "go to" resource for every design professional, developer, urban planner, and evolved bureaucrat. I know I will be using it daily as I consult with developers and designers working on green roof projects in the city of Chicago. Whether it is providing advice on how to create relief from wind on the forty-second floor of an office building or bring color, texture, and movement to a condominium rooftop garden, this will be the book I have at my side.

Michael Berkshire
Senior Planner
City of Chicago

Preface

We wrote this book to explore the design aspect of planting on the roof. The field of green roof garden design was expanding in new, provocative, and inspiring ways, and we saw an opportunity to illuminate all the intriguing branches of the same tree.

Our intent was to take a holistic look at as many projects as we could from all over the world. Rather than presenting case studies with a lot of statistical analysis, we aimed to illustrate through the lens of design.

It is our goal to expose the reader to a broad spectrum of exciting and innovative work in the hope of providing clear, educational information about a world of possibilities. We encourage people to look at designing in a new way.

We hope this book inspires designers, landscape architects, architects, contractors, landscapers, scientists, horticulturalists, and anyone wanting more nature, beauty, and green around them.

PART

Inspiration—Form and Function

1

Sources of Inspiration

Inspired by the mountains surrounding it, a residential rooftop meadow bursts into color each spring in Steamboat Springs, Colorado. Designed by Lisa Lee Benjamin.

nspiration is generally defined as being an unconscious burst of creativity, and if you accept that explanation, you know it's not going to be an easy topic to pin down. Inspiration is a universal concept, but it plays out differently for every individual, and what sparks one person might not stimulate another.

Harvard business professor Rosabeth Kantor, often cited as one of the most influential and innovative business thinkers in the world, has compared creativity to looking through a kaleidoscope. "You look at a set of elements, the same ones everyone else sees, but then reassemble those floating bits and pieces into an enticing new possibility," she says.

Historically, the impetus for designing and building green roofs has come from a variety of sources. For a famous king in Babylonia, it was the vegetation of his wife's native country—she was homesick, which propelled him to order the creation of the Hanging Gardens. On a more practical level, early settlers in northern Scandinavia added sod roofs to their houses and barns primarily to absorb rainfall and provide thermal protection from cold winters. In both instances the motivations behind these actions were immediate and obvious—the king wanted a happy wife and the Scandinavians wanted to keep warm—but as you are about to discover, the pathways are not always so clear.

Observations of the Physical World

In the realm of design, including the frontier of green roofs, inspiration often starts with a purpose or desire followed by a plan of action enriched with observations of the world around us. Each of us (the authors of this book) has a kaleidoscope filled with fragments of art, architecture, nature, and whatever else the senses absorb. Our goal is to share what informs our design process and, in turn, encourage you to consider the obvious and the not-so-obvious pathways to inspiration.

When Practicality Rules

Sometimes form has no choice but to follow function, as evidenced in Portland, Oregon, in 1991 when a lawsuit filed by Northwest Environmental Advocates put pressure on the city to address stormwater mitigation, river contamination, and protection of river habitat. In the 1980s, Boston solved similar issues by adding larger pipes, which were expensive and provided no surface benefits. The lawsuit prompted Tom Liptan, landscape architect and stormwater specialist for the City of Portland Bureau of Environmental Services, to look for alternative design solutions. He determined that green roofs, bio swales, and rain gardens offered the most practical and applicable solutions.

Liptan also recognized that structural load factors in urban and built environments often simply don't allow much increase in the substrate depth, which limits the form of a green roof garden. To answer that concern he designed on top of his garage what he called an "eco roof," defined as a nonirrigated roof with 6 inches (150 mm) or less of substrate comprised primarily of sedum and grass. The experiment succeeded by effectively mitigating

Tom Liptan demonstrating a stormwater flow measurement tool in Portland, Oregon.

Karla Reflects on the Things that Inspire Her

Filling the wall above the computer in my office are inspirational images that I have collected. Over the years, I have added and subtracted pictures based on what catches my eye, which reflects my own evolution in some small way. A photograph from my father's garden of a small

koi pool surrounded by purple iris and pink water lilies hangs below a postcard of two wood chairs in a corner of John Greenlee's nursery with lush grasses and magenta alliums in the foreground. These are landscapes crafted by people passionate about plants.

An old black-and-white image of Michelangelo's square, the Piazza del Campidoglio in Rome, is pinned next to a raked gravel and stone garden at Ryoanji Temple in Kyoto. These spaces are stark and seem so different, but in both, the dramatic composition plays out with

only the hardscape. The layout is simple yet complex with the dynamic strength coming from juxtaposing curved lines against straight, tantalizing the viewer with tricks of perspective.

Other images on the wall focus on water features. The way water dominates and structures the gardens at Granada in southern Spain and Villa Lante in central Italy inspires designers the world over. For me, the abalone shell-lined reflection pool created by Ganna Walska at Lotus Land in Santa Barbara, California, evokes ideas as

much as the swimming pool that Jack Chandler designed for the residence at Shafer Vineyards in Napa, California.

It is almost a cliché to say nature influences us, perhaps because of the power of landscape in its natural form. However, I continually stare at photographs of barrel cacti at Joshua Tree National Park in Southern California as well as pictures of lotus, protea, or sumac in the fall when their varying shades of pink are reminiscent of the horizontal bands in an Agnes Martin painting. Who isn't swayed by Iguazu Falls in South America, the Palouse in eastern Washington, Lake Placid in upstate New York, or Limantour Spit Beach, Point Reyes National Seashore, in Northern California?

Patterns of animals fascinate me like the pods of narwhals swimming just below the surface or a huge collection of eagles hanging out on a cliff in Homer, Alaska. The way those narwhals swim through the water may reappear as the layout of paving details on a roof patio. In my mind, I keep referencing the chance patterning of their positions as caught by the camera and there seems to be an intention behind the randomness. When I design a plan, what appears to be an arbitrary layout of the plant material is actually a composition created through the massing and layering of the plants.

What might look "natural" to the client is a predetermined, random pattern defined by the designer.

Finally, there's the inevitable influence of great buildings and architecture. My diverse collection of architectural references includes New York City's former Twin Towers, La Boca neighborhood in Buenos Aires, and the high-rise, modernist apartments in São Paulo. I'm also captivated by Louis Kahn's pencil sketches of Rome, Lebbeus Woods's intricate drawings of fantasy cities, Peter Zumthor's spa in Switzerland, and Herzog & de Meuron's Water Cube at Expo 2 in Beijing. In all of these, patterns and hierarchies of forms coalesce into seamless wholes. ■

BACKGROUND A collection of photos, drawings, and images on Karla Dakin's wall provides inspiration.

LEFT Pink lotus pond flower.

RIGHT Barrel cactus on a portion of the Getty Museum in Los Angeles.

TOP Green roof designed for biodiversity above the London Underground offices.

LEFT Freshly laid sedum mats at the Denver Justice Center.

BELOW Architect Cath Basilio collaborated with landscape designer Nigel Dunnett to create this biodiverse roof for the Sharrow School in Sheffield, England.

storm water, and his wife liked the results so much she suggested the addition of colorful plants and a fresh coat of paint for the garage. The visually pleasing result was a textbook case of form following function. Today, thanks in large part to Liptan's model, he's recognized internationally for his approach to stormwater mitigation, and the city of Portland now boasts over a thousand rain gardens and hundreds of green roofs.

Reducing the heat island effect in dense urban cores, extending the life of the waterproof membrane, and being energy efficient are other examples of function affecting design and implementation. The sedum roofs growing in a few inches of substrate constructed courtesy of the Ford Motor Company at their North American Headquarters in Irvine, California, the Denver Justice Center, and the Heinz 57 Center/Gimbels Building Restoration in Philadelphia all illustrate this point. In these instances, the vegetation was installed not as a viewshed for employees but as a way to address these practical issues.

Power to the People

While the physical world provides endless stimulation for garden design planning, the impetus to infuse urban landscapes with green rooftops has a whole other set of influences, and these circumstances are often at the root of why people create green rooftops in the first place. Sometimes it is environmental issues and the need for new regulations that incite a call to action.

Cities and industrial areas have a long history of neglecting the surrounding ecology and environment, and as awareness and concern about pollution

and quality of life grow, local policy makers and politicians around the globe are getting involved in reshaping urban landscapes and the attitudes of the people who inhabit them. Perhaps the most notable example is Chicago where former Mayor Richard Daley led the charge to turn the Windy City into the greenest city in America. His efforts resulted in the city planting or negotiating the construction of over 5.5 million square feet (about 511,000 sq m) of rooftop gardens, at the time more than all the other U.S. cities combined.

Attitudes are also changing in European cities. In London, Dusty Gedge, an environmental activist, has been instrumental in creating distinct policies for listing green roofs and walls as viable opportunities for improving quality of life and biodiversity. In Sheffield, Cath Basilio, an architect and professor at Sheffield Hallam University, and Nigel Dunnett, professor at the University of Sheffield, have collaborated on projects like the Sharrow School roof where the focus is on pictorial meadows filled with annuals and perennials, and biodiversity.

Incentives programs have also been instrumental in driving the desire to implement green rooftops. America's Leadership and Energy in Environmental Design (LEED), Green Globe from Canada, Australia's Green Star, and Comprehensive Assessment System for Built Environment Efficiency (CASBEE) in Japan continue to encourage the installation of green roofs. Many of these programs were formulated in direct response to growing concerns about the environment and the now-pressing need to change building and design practices.

The point is that inspiration for building green roof gardens and the designs that follow come from a variety

of sources. For Tom Liptan it was a lawsuit. For Richard Daley it was an environmental imperative. For a host of contemporary landscape designers and architects it is everything from cloud formations, to the curve of a building wall, to the graphic patterns in a piece of fabric, to the color in a favorite painting, to the simplicity of a cottonwood leaf. In the words of renowned painter Agnes Martin, "Inspiration is there all the time for everyone whose mind is not clouded over with thoughts, whether they realize it or not."

2
Shapes and Patterns

Garden accessories as puzzle pieces fill the floor
of 620 Jones, a rooftop bar in San Francisco,
designed by Lisa Lee Benjamin and Colleen Smith.

Designers desire to solve puzzles and are always assessing ways to combine practical considerations like budget and structural parameters with concepts that are more ethereal, such as the spirit of the site, the surroundings, the ecology of the region, and aesthetics. These sometimes-lofty ideals are often intuitive and are developed and brought into light through the creative process. The pieces then fit together to create a space, a feeling, or a conversation, and evoke something of value.

Designers work with clients to help determine what those values are. Is it a peaceful setting, a need for privacy, a place for a morning cup of coffee, or a shift in perception of the surrounding built environment?

To answer those questions we need only to look at the world around us: inspiring shapes and patterns are everywhere. It was colonies of shoreline plants that influenced the green roof on top of the Vancouver Convention Centre in British Columbia, and a random collection of gravels and seashells lying along the shore beside Heron's Head EcoCenter in San Francisco that provided the impetus for the green roof there.

Architecture also inspires designers, who can reference shapes in the buildings like the curve of a wall or some geometric construct. The design for the roof garden at the Museum of Contemporary Art in Denver (MCA) was sparked by a triangular skylight that architect David Adjaye incorporated into the children's education room. That skylight translated into a wedge-shaped bed that then broke apart and became trapezium-shaped beds floating above the roof deck.

At a design review for undergraduate environmental design, students at the University of Colorado created plans for a hypothetical public park. Their inspirations ranged from bold, curvilinear shapes in Islamic patterns, the repetition of landforms in architect Maya Linn's topographical installations, the veins in cottonwood leaves, and the formal orthogonal rooms, allées, and geometric gardens at Versailles. These seemingly disparate choices for inspiration all had a common theme: shapes and patterns. Instead of looking at site analysis as the first point of departure, these future landscape designers responded creatively to patterns that resonated for them. This ability to connect abstractions to a built environment is a critical part of the design process.

Art and the Creative Process

The art world is another primary source for sparking innovative uses of shapes and patterns because artists, like designers, must solve puzzles. We learn about forced perspective and edge conditions from James Turell's sky rooms (he encloses viewers to control their perception of light) and the simple complexity illustrated by where the edge of the room meets the sky.

Similar lessons exist in the crisp steel edge growing or disappearing in concert with the slightly uplifted grass planes of Robert Irwin's *Tilted Planes*, and in Cézanne's portraits. What is important to note is that the connection between the inspiration found by observing the works of these artists and the ideas that appear in an actual garden plan are neither linear nor necessarily clean cut.

When we ponder Cézanne's portrait, *Man with Crossed Arms,* our eyes are drawn from the lower left corner of flesh-colored furniture diagonally up to the left to the sitter's hands and then straight up to his face. These similarly colored elements create movement across the picture plane. This is a lesson in composition where similar colors lead your eye through the space of the picture plane.

Revisiting the same portrait on a different day or in a different mood will likely result in different revelations. We might notice how the dark paint outlines the hands, accentuating them without the artist actually having to detail the hands. This treatment of the edge condition and the way it calls attention comes up again in the crisp lines of Turell's and Irwin's works.

At the same time, all three artists play with perspective, almost forcing the viewer's eye while confusing it at the same time. Visitors to one of Turell's sky rooms often find it strangely impossible to tell where building ends and sky begins. That same confusion of perspective happens in Irwin's work: What is top? Where is the bottom? It is almost dizzying.

Obviously, the point isn't to make clients feel sick. Because designers manipulate space and these great artists provide insight on how to do that, we can employ their ideas when we think about how to make a small roof seem larger or a far-off view seem closer or disappear altogether.

For example, in a very small roof garden by Mossspace Landscape Design in London, weeping Atlas cedar creates a curtain that encloses the living room. From the couch, it is hard to tell how close or far away the trees are. They obscure the buildings behind and give the living room an airy expanse as if it goes on and on. The most amazing thing is that the space this garden occupies is a mere 3 feet (1 m) wide.

The abstract paintings of Arthur Dove or Robert Motherwell reveal secrets about composition, space, and proportion. Landscapes by Hiroshige and Emily Carr show possibilities about hierarchy and sequence. Images of Jan Vercruysse's *Labyrinths and Pleasure Gardens* inspire us to think about labyrinths and divided spaces in a completely new way. Donald Judd's boxes on display at the former Fort D. A. Russell in Marfa, Texas, are a lesson in austere elegance. His sculpture seems to have been made for the building and vice versa. The stark quality of the bunker with light coming in from two sides allows the viewer to focus on the way the boxes reflect the incoming light, mirror the architecture, and manipulate shadows. Site and object intertwine intricately.

Images of Agnes Martin's paintings remind us that we still have a lot to understand about the complex relationship between joy and geometry. The minimal way she works with color makes us ponder the possibility of recreating those subtle shifts in pinks with different shades of green. When Martin, who considered herself an abstract expressionist, describes her work, she speaks about her ideas coming from qualities such as divine inspiration, love, and the beauty of nature that surrounds us every day. However, the translation of inspiration is not direct; it is abstract as she transformed these qualities into mathematical equations that show up on the canvas in horizontal or vertical lines. It is almost as if she is creating abstract order out of ephemera, which begs the question, How do you recreate beauty?

Sedums create strong patterns on the roof of the Horno 3 Steel Museum in Monterrey, Mexico.

Love? Do you copy nature or do you create your own system?

Artists can teach us how to make compositional choices and their work illustrates how visual puzzles can be solved. Great paintings and sculptures have the ability to inspire us to make similar creative gestures in our own work. Landscape architect Claudia Harari achieved this type of artistic quality in her design for the Horno 3 Steel Museum in Monterrey, Mexico, where her choice of different plants set off a geometric pattern that plays with perspective somewhat like the Piazza del Campidoglio.

Color, Texture, and Movement

Almost everything in our world begins with the visual. What follows is our response to what we see in terms of patterns, shapes, colors, textures, and movement. The question is, How do we use shape and pattern to evoke responses? One answer is to create a sense of movement by employ-ing a sweep of plant material such as tall prairie grasses to create different contours. Additionally, massing species in similar or contrasting colors and textures and weaving them together can result in broad streaks of subtle or not-so-subtle color changes while offer-ing textural variety. This design gesture moves your eye across the garden.

Alternatively, consider filling roof-top containers with a mix of deep purple drumstick alliums, burgundy phormi-ums, and red, purple, and orange tulips. The resulting arrangement of these plants with their similar texture and leaf shapes creates a lushness and uplifting mood that can also serve to soften and green a barren white roof space. Massing species is particularly applicable to large rooftops seen from above where very simple but colorful geometric or organic patterns generate interesting views and provide something for people in neighboring office buildings to look at while at work.

When Angela Loder of the University of Toronto asked office dwellers in Chicago to compare the roof garden on City Hall with the simple sedum modular system green roof next door, the consensus was that the organic shapes, patterns, and drifts of prairie grasses on the City Hall roof garden were much more calming, interesting, and mood lifting.

Patterns emerge when we weave color, shape, and texture together like a quilt. Inspiration for these designs comes from many places such as the delicate vintage Japanese fabric Ian McDonald, artist and professor at San Francisco Art Institute, uses in the creation of his Is/was ties. The contrasting fabric presents a direct sense of movement, and the intention of the combination is to mix patterns and create mood.

TEXTURE

New York City–based landscape architect Ken Smith went to bold new heights by designing a roof garden out of nonliving material based on a camouflage pattern for New York's Museum of Modern Art (MoMA). The sea of undulating shapes fashioned from black and white gravel dotted with similarly shaped plastic rocks and miniature fake boxwood trees is a piece of art in its own right. When viewed from above,

TOP Rolling mounds of mowed and unmowed grass create texture and movement on this roof garden in Los Angeles.

LEFT The mismatched patterns on these ties designed by Ian McDonald induce new ways of thinking about patterns on rooftop gardens.

Four questions for

Claudia Harari,

co-founder of Harari Landscape Architecture in Monterrey, Mexico, about the role of shape and pattern at the Horno 3 Steel Museum in Monterrey.

---

1. How important was the plan view in the development of the Horno 3 Steel Museum?

It was extremely important to the design of both the intensive and extensive green roofs and their relationship with the entire landscape plan including composition, narrative, and the surrounding elements such as Fundidora Park and the mountains. In the case of the extensive roof, which is the central piece of the entire landscape narrative, having a circular steel disc with a pleated surface as the working plane was a challenge and an opportunity at the same time.

The architects wanted to fill up the entire disc into a flat garden, but we did not agree with this idea. We knew it had a greater potential, and we kept considering several possibilities until the construction of the impermeable membranes of

the system started. Then the inspiration and final design decision happened on site while standing on the surface of the structure, and we knew the extensive roof had to show to the visitors outside of the museum the richness and complexity of this structure. This green roof represents a transformation and use of the architectural structures into landscape living structures: a living piece of architecture, a piece of steel inhabited by sedums.

2. What inspired the shapes and patterns you selected? How did the architecture affect your design?

The entire design centers around the idea of recycled industrial materials and the narrative of the steel transformation process from the raw material in the ore mine to the final refined and clean steel product. The intensive roof, a mound that rises up from the ground plane just to the base of the furnace, represents the natural fields in the countryside where the ore mine is found. It is at the base and the beginning of the narrative and transformation process and is intentionally gentle and covered with wild grasses.

In contrast, the extensive green roof represents the final product of the process—the most refined, elaborated, and precious element. The amazing steel disc structure that constituted the structural base for this piece was influential in inspiring the shapes and patterns in the design. The architects intended for this origami-like pleated disk to be viewed from the interior of the gallery, never from the outside. Nevertheless, we decided visitors needed to see it from the heights of the museum as well. The well-defined pattern has become one of the icons of the museum, and because of that, it will be preserved for years.

3. How are the shapes and patterns defined?

The extensive roof is only 8 inches (200 mm) deep and each diamond, or petal, responds to specific sloping faces of the very complex steel structure. On site, we understood the hierarchy and rhythm of the structure and enhanced the main features and planes. We were given three layers of rays, or diamonds, the inner and outer layers being the smallest and flattest, with the middle layer being convex and larger. The shapes were traced with construction string and were created by a dense planting of sedums on the substrate: eight to ten pieces every 2 feet (600 mm). The shapes are precisely defined by the layout of the 15-inch (375-mm) wide maintenance access paths covered with gravel over a layer of filter mat to prevent the gravel from mixing into the substrate. There is no metal edging because of the different angles of slopes along the radius of the disc.

4. What specific plants and materials did you choose and why?

Due to the extreme climate in Monterrey, the location of the roof, and the low budget, the plant material chosen had to be extremely tolerant of drought, heat, and freeze, and able to survive with very little maintenance and in minimum substrate depth. To maintain the neat and clean look of a living tapestry, three different kinds of sedums were chosen that would differentiate with texture and color each of the three layers of the pattern: *Sedum rubrotinctum*, *S. griseum*, and *S. moranense*. These species grow well in Mexico and can be easily found or reproduced to supply the future needs of the roof maintenance. The substrate was specially designed from local materials. ■

it creates excitement and interest as the grays, blacks, and whites swirl below the city skyline.

Because most roof designs are living entities, structure and maintenance are critical for keeping the designs in place. In arid climates, gravel, rocks, and a few bold plants such as agaves and yuccas are ideal choices for constructing an enticing textural display. This technique can be very useful for green roof gardens when water is in short supply. A few tough plants can survive and multiply over time; and the textures of gravels and other materials can carry the roof through visually. This type of design puts plants where they best survive. As the aggregates spawn texture, they also establish specific ecologies and microclimates.

COLOR

We often have an idea of a green roof as all green in a literal sense but that's simply not true. Color can be the foundation of a garden when it appears in drifts of species or serves as an accent. It can add movement and stir emotion. The most traditional way to introduce color is with plant material, which will be discussed in-depth later on, but color can also be added in structural form like an enameled red chair, which brightens up a gravel courtyard or pops the privet hedge behind it. Welcome hues can also arrive in the form of art or sculpture. For environments with bleak winters, a bright orange pot can make all the difference.

Color on the roof also offers a myriad of opportunities for creativity that are very different from incorporating color on the ground. Because people

The artificial roof garden designed by Ken Smith for the New York City Museum of Modern Art was inspired by printed camouflage patterns.

often observe roof gardens from afar or above, splashes of bold color are dynamic as they draw the eye toward something it would usually pass over with the common grayscale of an urban environment.

A second and contradictory reason is that because the roof is not generally the first priority and may not have the significance of the ground landscape, it becomes a place where designers can try out crazy plant combinations and mixtures of interesting substrates. Think of it like dancing in the kitchen alone where you are more likely to be silly and uninhibited. Green roofs are so far removed, metaphorically and physically, from the ground plane that they offer the freedom of the frontier.

In a rural landscape we are bound by the surrounding environment of woods, mountains, or plains, but in urban roof gardens we can introduce nontraditional and bold accents as these gardens only have the city skyline to respect in terms of what is appropriate. Because we are not tied to some idealistic version of pastoral landscapes within our cities and metropolitan areas, there are greater opportunities for exploration.

Furthermore, urban environments often foster bold architecture—icons in which inhabitants orient themselves. This same drama and creativity can be carried over to green roofs. In a *New York Times* op-ed piece, Witold Rybczynski, professor of urbanism at the University of Pennsylvania, asks if the High Line in New York City or the Promenade Plantée in Paris could exist in the country. The answer is clearly *no*.

Even temporary roof installations strive to make strong imprints in the gray urban fabric like Work Architecture's *Public Farm 1*, a summer installation

Three questions about texture, color, and movement for

Rebecca Cole,

internationally renowned garden, interior, and floral designer.

1. How do color, texture, and movement come into play when you design a garden? Is one element more important than the others?

Color, texture, and movement—choose one? That's almost impossible. They are all so important. I start a design with a combination of gesture and form, calling on the architectural elements of the garden's surrounds to inform the look and feel of the plants. I love to juxtapose the hard cement pavers with a soft carpet of succulents or the shiny glass of a skyscraper with the natural wheat-like texture of miscanthus grass.

Nothing ruins a garden faster than a bad mix of color, and I prefer to limit the palette to a range of one or two complementary colors per garden. I always consider the surrounding colors of the city as the neutral to my urban garden. In a country garden, green is the neutral, in the city, gray, black, blue glass, white stone, and brick are the neutrals and I love to use gray, black, and bluish silver foliage to help meld the urban landscape with a green roof landscape.

Nevertheless, movement is the real ace in the hole for the urban landscape. The gusty wind is my conductor and plants are my orchestra. The placement of the plants is the composition, and the interaction of the folks who wind their way through the garden and the way the plants react and change is the music. The hard lines of the massive stationary architecture can dance with the right sweep of plantings. A grove of yellow groove bamboo bending in the wind, pennisetums en masse creating waves on a building's edge, or rudbeckias bobbing back and forth can stir the soul of the toughest urbanite.

2. What role does the surrounding urban landscape play in informing choices about these elements?

A roof garden must embrace the elements of the city that surrounds it because the city is the hardscape. If the building is made of steel, I make my containers of rusty or shiny metal. If a water tower shares the roof with my garden, I will match my deck with its wood. When the pavers are cement, I add a cementlike container and the plants seem to emerge from the building itself.

3. Can you share a little about your process for making up compositions for viewing in a garden? Do you consider both interior and exterior views? What components do you use in these compositions?

My first question for any client is, How will you be using this garden? I then take pictures from every angle, with every view from every window indoors and out because I want to consider every vignette and every background. I love to "frame" buildings, bridges, and water towers with trees and large shrubs. Everything must be considered in the design from the reflection of the sun off the glass on the adjacent buildings to how the black tar of the elevator shaft looks behind shocking pink roses. It is all part of the landscape of an urban garden and it should be embraced and enhanced, never hidden or dismissed. ■

A retreat designed by Rebecca Cole on a New York City rooftop.

TOP The grass palette creates movement atop the Los Angeles Museum of the Holocaust.

BOTTOM Feather grass and Easter lilies move gently in the wind on a roof in the Bermondsey district of London.

at MoMA PS1 in Long Island City, New York, that reinvented a leisure space that worked for the city by creating an urban farm. The green roof is a ramp comprised of cardboard tubes no longer than a yard in length. Some are filled with soil and planted with edibles while others remain open to the sky. The ramp affords shade in some spaces and forms a sparkling blue water play area when the structure meets the ground.

MOVEMENT

Finally, there is the idea of movement. Faced with a panorama of flat, static space, it's the designer's job to make the space sing and dance with a palette of plants and media. While working on the Los Angeles Museum of the Holocaust (LAMOTH) we discovered the building structure itself offered a framework that begged for movement. The movement and patterns that emerged from the design process generated a sense of freedom and nurturing that envelops visitors to the museum whether they are conscious of it or not.

Movement also happens when design elements lead your eye from one place to another like the curved lines on the Novartis campus in Basel, Switzerland. Implemented by Stephan Brenneisen, head of the Green Roof Competence Center at Zürich University, and his students, the project employed different substrates to form various habitats. The practical design used several offset organic flowing serpentine lines that divided the rectangle of the roof in perfect scale and successfully created movement.

This same type of movement can also occur with a specific arrangement

The Vancouver Public Library roof garden designed by Cornelia Oberlander can be viewed from many surrounding buildings, demonstrating the impact a roof garden has on the larger community.

of plants. A swath of taller grasses or similar toned species flowing into one another can lead your eye to the next place and make you feel as though something is happening even if there is no physical or direct movement like wind sweeping the grasses.

Micro versus Macro Views

Unlike ground level gardens that are observed and enjoyed by people inside the space, the views afforded by rooftop gardens need to be considered from three vantage points: above, inside the garden looking out, and the ground level.

VIEWS FROM ABOVE: CELEBRATING THE PLAN VIEW

Just about all of us have experienced flying into a city on a clear day and the minutes in the final approach when, from those tiny airplane portals, we are able to glimpse the total scope of an urban landscape. For a few magical moments we have that unique bird's-eye, or macro, view from which we can observe everything from the penthouse terraces on the high-rises to the expanses of green in the parks at ground level and all the iconic landmarks in between, such as the Chrysler Building and the Eiffel Tower. In such moments designers realize that city rooftops are blank canvasses of black, gray, or white gesso just waiting to be greened.

Plan views typically guide the design process of a ground level landscape despite the phenomenological perspective of the end user. You are in the garden and it beckons all five senses.

However, when you get up on the top floor of a building and start looking down, you realize the plan view from above offers a completely new design dimension. These macro vistas are the faraway views, similar to seeing mountains or the ocean in the distance. The distant view of a green roof or roof garden in a sea of concrete and built materials feels and looks like an oasis—something living against a static backdrop.

Creating a plan that remains visible from above forces us to think it through from a higher vision, angle, or perspective—an obsession designers are taught to focus on from the very beginnings of their design education. These macro plan views become as important as the view inside the garden. In an urban context, many people may have the opportunity to view the green from adjacent buildings or down the street. Even from as far away as several blocks, the simplest patterns of green contribute to defining the urban fabric.

From the upper floors of Xcel Energy's new headquarters building in Denver it is possible to see a series of green roofs and roof gardens: starting on the southwest and looking north, there's one, and across the street to the north and west are three more. It's as if a matrix or patchwork of green is being formed high above the street. This unplanned pattern of constructed nature throughout the urban core is increasingly visible. After decades of accepting street trees and median planters as the main source of color and greenery in city environments, urbanites are multiplying the percentage of green by establishing green on floors above ground level. Doing this changes people's perception of how they want to view urban landscapes in the future.

The view on the roof of Vancouver's Fairmont Waterfront Hotel is reminiscent of an English garden.

The macro view is a perfect place to think about shapes and patterns in a new way. Landscape designers generally think in terms of larger systems, with the primary context being the local geography and weather, and how those regional considerations dictate and lead design. We look from the large to the small scale much like anyone would look at something from the perspective of Google Earth. For example, if we were designing the roof for a building in San Francisco, after zeroing in on California, we would move closer to observe the larger geographical, urban, and civic contexts before getting in even closer to consider the existing plant life that surrounds the building. Designers know that none of these elements exists in isolation, that all these contexts are related. It is our job to begin with that overall viewpoint.

LOOKING OUT FROM THE GARDEN

Plants have long been used to soften the built environment, but so far, in dense urban cores the built environment is winning. It's time to reclaim some territory. From a planning and design perspective, designers can literally soften cityscape views with the addition of plant material, or, as it is referred to technically, *softscape*. When you are standing on a roof, the trees, shrubs, or grasses take on great importance—even more so than if you are on the ground—because they provide feelings of protection and shelter. Plant material is crucial to the view from within the garden because plants combine with the structure to frame the views beyond the roof.

For example, a row of cordylines or cabbage trees in planter boxes can

Cordylines decorate many rooftops in London.

TOP *Iris reticulata* reveals pattern and detail on a minute scale.

BOTTOM A colorful plant palette created for the roof garden at 620 Jones in San Francisco.

"Sky Trapezium," designed by Karla Dakin, hovers above the roof deck at Denver's Museum of Contemporary Art.

totally change how the wall of a neighboring building looks from your garden. Suddenly, the intersecting tufts of green leaves transform the sea of worn, crumbling brick. Depending on the building's orientation, a whimsical shadow play at sunset adds another layer of color and pattern to what you observe from inside the garden.

Taking advantage of the unused space on the roof of an apartment building or on a deck outside an office expands the possibility of more views or at least broader ones. Suddenly there are 360-degree vistas instead of just a narrow view to the south. Alternatively, it becomes possible to see below and down the street to the right where before the only view was to the building across the avenue. By expanding a built environment beyond the walls of the interior space into areas that can be physically occupied, like a roof or a deck, the building walls across the way that previously guided perspective and limited views metaphorically fall away.

In addition, for those individuals across the street, down the street, or in the street, live material has the added advantage of bridging the gap between horizontal spatial levels by breaking up the gray with stripes of green. For someone strolling along the sidewalk, looking up to a lush rolling carpet of wisteria hanging over a precipice, or across

the alley at dwarf palms planted along a parapet, there is something soothing about seeing live material that offsets the cold elements of architecture. The designer is enhancing a view of existing streetscapes, adding splashes of color and interest, complementing the overall composition of the urban environment.

VIEWS INSIDE THE GARDEN

Similar to a ground level garden, the most intimate, or micro, view in a roof garden becomes very important to those utilizing the space. The opportunity to observe vegetation close up reveals contrasting delicacies of texture, color, and size as well as the broader elements that change with the seasons such as yellow flowers in the spring and burgundy seed heads in the fall. The art exists in playing with these micro details and arranging the different varieties, textures, or shapes so that they cannot only be viewed as patterns from above but also can be discerned by those in the garden. This detail often lies within the planter beds and the edges of the roof gardens where such close views are accessible. Waves of bronze oxalis engulfing the tips of dark green asparagus ferns, the coppery paper trunk of arbutus trees, and the similarly colored spikes of *Cordyline* 'Dark Star' form a

micro world that draws us in just as it would on the ground.

So often when we stand on a rooftop we are overwhelmed by the larger views and that sense of wow that comes from taking in the vast cityscape. By placing plant material in such a way that it brings things back to a more human and personal level, we formulate spaces that are more intimate. The roof garden at Denver's Museum of Contemporary Art intentionally features three lower beds at belly view so visitors enjoying their lunches also come face-to-face with cobra lilies and alpine daphnes in the middle of the city.

In roof gardens, every bed raised or flush with the roof surface becomes an opportunity to showcase a micro view. These smaller moments are more precious when seen several floors above street level where they are unexpected. But the conversation doesn't need to be confined to plant material; the viewer also benefits from being close to water features, art objects, or furniture.

3

Creating Living Spaces

'Darlow's Enigma' rose and a desert willow soften the edges of a shaded seating area on the rooftop of Denver's Museum of Contemporary Art.

his chapter focuses on the role of roof gardens as living areas: places where people relax, dine, entertain, and play. Technically speaking, green rooftop gardens are installations with soil depths greater than 6 inches (150 mm), but rather than concentrating on issues such as heat island mitigation or stormwater filtration systems, this chapter emphasizes the interaction factor and what happens when socializing comes into play. Under these circumstances, roof gardens become amenity spaces and might even be considered a luxury, but referring to them as luxurious is really a misnomer because creating beautiful, functional exterior spaces amid the urban grind is vital to the health of both a city and its residents.

Transforming previously uninhabitable rooftops into usable green niches adds value to our lives in several ways: physically by adding square footage to our personal footprints; financially by increasing real estate values; and along with the psychological value of watching our children and pets playing safely outside within the confines of the city, they provide respites for our friends and ourselves.

Except for the very wealthy, most city dwellers reside in apartments or even single-family dwellings that are on the small side. Utilizing a roof space on top of an apartment could very well double the usable square footage. Including a roof garden can quite literally add another room or two, and if that space is a deck outside the apartment, that extra 6 by 12 feet (1.8 by 3.6 m) means the occupants can sit outside to

Planted garage rooftop in Pratteln, Switzerland.

Karla Remembers Her First Rooftop Garden

During the 1980s, I lived in New York City. My home was a fifth-floor walk-up above a Mexican restaurant in the yet-to-be trendy East Village. Other than being affordable, there wasn't much to recommend the cramped one-bedroom apartment except that it opened to a small

8- by 12-foot (2.4- by 3.6-m) deck and that minuscule space became my saving grace.

Surrounded on four sides by apartment high-rises several stories taller than my own building, the deck was further hampered by a 7-foot (2-m) tall chain-link fence that totally enclosed it. Undaunted, I covered the fence with white canvas, set up a hammock in the far end, and placed director's chairs just outside the half glass door. From the first sign of spring until late into the fall, my friends and I flocked to that tiny outdoor patch for fresh air and sunshine.

It was obvious to me then, and it continues to be so now, that urban life is spent mostly indoors. Individuals residing in built environments like New York City crave and need contact with the outdoors, and the desire to create outdoor living spaces is almost instinctual. When people are surrounded by

concrete, having a bit of nature can make them happy or calm as evidenced by the doctoral work of Angela Loder of Toronto whose studies looked at the health benefits of green roofs. Roof gardens can provide humans with this elemental connection back to nature.

The imperative that designers feel to create green roof environments where city dwellers can have a closer relationship with nature is a natural extension of this idea. The positive mental and physical health benefits of green roofs for individuals and the public-at-large are just beginning to be realized, but there's little question that anything done to balance the harshness of concrete can only improve the lives of those who get to experience it. As designers we need to strive to integrate people back into nature, emphasizing that we can be a part of nature rather than separate from it. ■

The High Line in New York City provides interest for visitors even in November.

read, eat, and watch the street life below. In Switzerland, garage rooftops from formal rose gardens to productive vegetable gardens are a way of life.

That additional space also adds value to the property as the real estate description changes from "800-square-foot [74-sq-m], one-bedroom apartment" to "800-square-foot, one-bedroom with a roof garden including expansive views of the city." A place with a deck rents or sells for more than one without a deck. On a roof garden, you can experience green and not have to deal with the crush of the city below and the constant assault of horns and sirens in your ears. This somewhat daring gesture of turning black to green makes these spaces seem even more precious.

While roof gardens provide people the opportunity to exchange a predominantly inside lifestyle for exposure to elements like fresh air and sunshine, these small lush green ecosystems can also bring surprising guests like birds and butterflies. Thanks to the green roof movement, nature, often alien in the built environment, is now making an entrance in a variety of forms and is transforming outdoor spaces. Former barren slabs of concrete have become havens for butterflies and birds. One example is the Anna's hummingbird that frequents the roof garden at 620 Jones, a bar in San Francisco, and hangs out in the tops of newly planted *Arbutus* 'Marina'.

Relaxing, Dining, and Entertaining

Like ground landscapes, roof gardens come in different classifications from the more public arenas like parks and plazas to the private roof gardens located on top of or attached to residences or offices reserved for those who live and/or work there. In between the two are semipublic spaces such as those found in hotels, restaurants, and nightclubs.

PUBLIC SPACES

City dwellers love to flock to public spaces and public parks found on rooftops. Outstanding examples of these can be found in New York, Paris, Chicago, Los Angeles, and Denver. Designs such as the five profiled here invite the public to interact and utilize the roof as they would a ground level park. Even though they are covering a building, transit center, or parking structure, they offer a garden experience. They also bring much needed greenery to an otherwise concrete environment.

High Line Park in New York City
A stellar example of a popular public space is the High Line Park designed by New York City landscape architect James Corner and his firm, Field Operations. Located on Manhattan's lower West Side, a stone's throw from the Hudson River and out of the way for most visitors except for art aficionados making the pilgrimage to Chelsea galleries, the High Line was originally constructed in the 1930s to lift dangerous freight trains off city streets. Many years later when the tracks were under threat of demolition, an international competition was staged to redesign the space, and the project was awarded to Field Operations.

Although a natural ecology had been established on the abandoned railway, the design team wanted to step it up a notch and incorporate people into the equation. Therefore, everything was scraped off, cleaned up, and replaced with a green promenade replete with the original rails patterned more as a metaphor of the railroad history than as operational tracks. There are benches, built-in lounge chairs, and an amphitheater overlooking the streets.

Locals and visitors from afar continuously pack the park. Undeterred by six flights of stairs, people line up to access the High Line as if they were trying to enter a sold-out concert. There is the feel that this park is the ultimate ride at an amusement park, and it delivers with long views of the city and the thrill of walking through green while in the air, so to speak. In one spot, visitors enjoy the juxtaposition of grasses and alliums in the foreground, and architect Frank Gehry's gray-pearl headquarters of InterActiveCorp's high-rise in the background. There is the voyeuristic opportunity to peer in the windows of adjacent buildings, search out roof gardens across the street, and catch glimpses of the Hudson River when crossing a side street along the north-south axis of the park.

The mere existence of the High Line validates the fact that city dwellers crave the outdoor experience that is often best supplied by a rooftop-style environment. The High Line has become not only a major tourist destination, but more importantly is a place where local residents feel they can get away from it all.

Promenade Plantée in Paris

Another striking example of a public space resides in Paris's 12th arrondissement, where the Promenade Plantée, or

TOP Roses line the Promenade Plantée in Paris.

BOTTOM The Promenade Plantée sits atop an old viaduct.

Coulée Verte ("green flow"), designed by landscape architect Jacques Vergely and architect Philippe Mathieux, was created on an abandoned 19th-century railway viaduct, the terminus of a suburban train line that serviced Vincennes and eastward. The aboveground park runs from the Opéra Bastille to the Jardin de Reuilly and is a very popular locale for people to walk or jog. Visitors to the public site enjoy a lush corridor filled with wisteria and roses, and dotted with secluded benches for stolen kisses.

This elevated park occupies the next frontier beyond *brownfield* sites, a term coined by Europeans to describe abandoned or underused industrial and commercial facilities available for re-use. Accessible by stairs and elevators from the street, and a ramp between buildings, the promenade is home to a series of visual events taking place inside and outside the narrow confines of the park. The park overlooks sculptures on the walls of the police station that emerge from the façade like a dramatic bas-relief. Plantings include a tunnel of bamboo, and the park transitions to the ground by slicing through buildings onto a deck that brings visitors to street level.

Millennium Park in Chicago

The nice thing about roof parks is that they can occupy any area with adequate square footage and easy public access. Leave it to Chicago to turn the tops of parking garages and a railroad yard into a stunning public space. Millennium Park offers the Jay Pritzker Pavilion, a band shell designed by Frank Gehry; "Cloud Gate," a sculpture by Anish Kapoor; Jaume Plensa's Crown Fountain, a water feature of tall, flat, paneled walls lined by changing faces of Chicagoans with

Millennium Park's Lurie Garden in Chicago, designed by Piet Oudolf.

water running down their faces; the Lurie Garden of ornamental grasses designed by Piet Oudolf; and a bridge to the new wing of the Chicago Art Institute. Moreover, if that isn't enough, it encompasses views of Lake Michigan. In terms of attracting tourists to the city, Millennium Park is second only to the Navy Pier.

Los Angeles Museum of the Holocaust

Another successful public park green roof is the Los Angeles Museum of the Holocaust (LAMOTH), designed by Lisa Lee Benjamin and Karla Dakin. Built as part of the western edge of Pan Pacific Park in the mid-Wilshire area of Los Angeles, the swooping museum roof reaches down to touch the ground in two places, allowing park visitors to circle areas of the roof as part of their morning jog or stroll. The green roof is open the same hours as the park.

REI Parking Garage in Denver

An older roof garden that most people do not even realize is a roof garden at all is located on top of the parking garage of the REI flagship store in Denver. Designed to emulate a mountain setting, the rooftop resembles mountains come to rest in the flat prairie filled with aspen trees. Rounded granite boulders nestle in a stream that meanders through the parklike setting. A café with a deck connects the store to the roof garden while providing a seamless transition to additional parking beyond.

SEMIPRIVATE ROOF GARDENS

Despite the recent allure of rooftop restaurants, clubs, and swimming pools, this concept is far from new as evidenced by a 1909 *New York Times*

Asparagus fern in concrete planters at 620 Jones in San Francisco.

article that extolled the virtues of aerial gardens. In the piece, the author waxed poetic about the after-work delight of taking an elevator to the roof of a favorite club, plunging into a swimming pool, and then quietly eating dinner under the stars. He concluded his plug for rooftop amenities by calling them a luxury and comfort that don't require a tiring journey to enjoy.

Following this notion that everything old is new again, the number of developers building new hotels, clubs, and restaurants keen on attracting customers to the rooftop scene is on the rise, and these semiprivate roof gardens, like those popping up on hotels around the world, emphasize amenities. Even in lower-density cities such as Denver with its relatively overcrowded restaurant market, attractive rooftop drinking and dining areas are a huge draw for customers. If square footage on the sidewalk is insufficient to provide dining space, and if the load factors on the roof are up to the task, the roof is a clear bonus.

Simply stated, views are the big draw, and getting people upstairs and outside increases marketability, profitability, and opportunity. A case in point is the willingness of New Yorkers to pay as much as $18 for a drink, validating the roof setting as being worth the inflated prices. Club owner Peter Glikshtern capitalized on this when, along with architect Peter Strzebniok of Nottoscale Architects, he transformed a dilapidated roof garden over a parking garage into 620 Jones, a hip San Francisco bar. Intent on taking the design to new heights, and with the help of designers Lisa Lee Benjamin and Colleen Smith, the team came up with a floor plan and a bold plant palette brimming with the strong foliage of pukas, cordylines, astelias, leucadendrons, and asparagus ferns. All the plants look good day and night, and are inviting and alluring even in the fog of summer. The bar's slogan, "Take It Outside," underscores the fact that wanting to see sky and be outside is a strong impetus for potential customers.

Rooftop Amenities

Dining outside takes on a new perspective in London on the roof of the Boundary Hotel where the setting affords 360-degree views from Canary Wharf, to Gherkin and Barbican, and back again to the rooftops and spires of East London. The roof area includes a large bar with seating arranged around an open fireplace, and a 48-seat restaurant and garden designed by Nicola Lesbirel. The main attraction is the view and the cozy blankets provided when the temperatures drop. The roof also has a small production area for herbs and greens that supplement the restaurant. There is simply nothing comparable at ground level.

Not surprisingly, hotels around the world are increasingly transforming their rooftops into amenity spaces because the high-up location has the advantage of cool breezes and those unique vistas. After a hot and steamy day of sightseeing in Singapore, guests at the Marina Bay Sands resort can change into their swimsuits and lounge on the SkyPark around a huge pool overlooking the spectacular city skyline. Fifty-five stories high, the SkyPark reclines atop three striking towers longer in dimension than the Eiffel Tower laid flat. Internationally renowned architect Moshe Safdie designed the towers to look like a house of cards. The infinity pool spans this

shiplike structure and measures three times the length of an Olympic pool. With the edge of the pool so high in the sky, swimmers might experience the dizzying feeling of falling, but the design provides a catchment area below the edge, saving even the most daring from plummeting.

At the Molino Stucky Hilton in Venice, guests can partake in a sumptuous breakfast on the Skyline Rooftop Bar while watching gondolas float by in the canals below. Tables are arranged on either side of the roof along the parapet walls with the main circulation down the center. Like a falcon perched on a cornice overlooking the city skylines near and far, the bar's clients have a view that is simply unavailable at ground level.

From the street, the Heritance Kandalama hotel outside of Colombo, Sri Lanka, emerges as a mountain covered in native plants of the surrounding jungle. Customers sipping cool drinks at the rooftop bar don't even have to leave the hotel to sit in the jungle and experience the wildness of the native flora.

Roof gardens have also become destinations for locals and others not staying at the hotel. The Standard Hotel in Los Angeles and the Nines Hotel in Portland, Oregon, boast popular upper-level nightclubs where on any given night the clientele is mostly area residents. Along with the on-going success of creating outdoor lounging and dining experiences on the roof—happy hours worldwide have become big marketing tools—there has been a push since 2007 to add exterior spaces to the footprints of commercial buildings.

The Plunge bar and restaurant at Hotel Gansevoort in New York City is open 365 days a year and draws endless crowds drinking exorbitantly priced cocktails, posing, and gazing at the stunning views of the Hudson River and Midtown Manhattan. Salon de Ning, the stylish bar and lounge on the roof of the Peninsula Hotel in Midtown Manhattan, offers sweeping views of Fifth Avenue. As Dan Worden, California landscape designer of the W Hotel rooftops, says, "People enjoy being outdoors and there is something sexier about flirting with someone across an open bar on a rooftop than looking at a mirrored wall of liquor indoors."

Feel-Good Benefits

If you accept the virtues of fresh air as a long accepted medical fact, then you know getting outside and being physically active is far superior to being stuck in a gym looking at a television screen. Forward-thinking employers often convert rooftops to play areas that might include a swimming pool or basketball court and make these amenities available to their employees. In the early 2000s, a Denver developer created a series of semiprivate roof gardens that included basketball courts, putting greens, and tennis and bocce ball courts.

In these cases, the garden or plant material plays second fiddle to the sports. In one instance, live material is relegated to planters around the parapet of the roof. In another, turf areas and changing annual beds are mixed in with the putting green. On a third roof, there is no plant life at all, only the green of a tennis court. While the emphasis is on exercise, the addition of mature Ponderosa pines provides welcome shade, and tables scattered around the edges offer seating for those enjoying lunch outside.

Institutions like hospitals and schools create roof gardens with the needs of children in mind. Vegetable gardens located on the top floor of a

TOP Comfortable seating and incredible city views are part of the attraction at Departure Restaurant on the top floor of the Nines Hotel in Portland, Oregon.

BOTTOM The rooftop Tinguely Water Park in Basel, Switzerland.

TOP Wire vine, fan palm, and drumstick allium add interest to this rooftop designed by Mossspace in London.

BOTTOM A homeowner in Brooklyn enjoys a quiet moment on a roof garden designed by Amy Falder.

high-rise provide educational opportunities to children who rarely see countryside farms. Increasingly, cities are taking up the charge to make more universal play areas for children on rooftops. A water park created by artist Jean Tinguely draws thousands of visitors every year. Located on top of a parking garage in Basel, Switzerland, it is filled with moving sculptures that spout water.

PRIVATE SPACES

Nothing is quite as wonderful as entertaining friends and family outside on a warm summer evening several flights above the grimy city streets. It is the lure of the suburbs come back to roost in the city. When summer arrives, many city dwellers drag their furniture up to the roof to escape the stifling heat of an apartment without air conditioning. Add a grill and string some holiday lights along the parapet and you have the beginnings of a great outdoor room. These outdoor rooms are the above-ground equivalent of a suburban backyard, offering sanctuary, privacy, and a bit of greenery.

It's hard to appreciate private roof spaces from the street where all that is visible are wisps of vegetation, and the solitude and beauty found above are illusive. On a London rooftop terrace designed by Mossspace, wire vine, phormium, and miscanthus grass make up the base of the urban space. The planting is dotted with drumstick allium in early summer and is a perfect place to unwind on one of two reclining white lounge chairs that bring out the color in the garden year-round.

In Brooklyn, a bedroom opens up off a three-story brownstone where a

green ground cover of pachysandra and vinca surround two chairs and a small teak table. Designed by Amy Falder of New York Green Roofs, a design/build company, the small rooftop terrace allows the homeowners to enjoy peaceful cups of coffee and the morning birds among the treetops of the neighborhood.

Shelter from the Elements and Privacy Screening

Not unlike an open prairie, green rooftops and rooftop gardens are exposed and therefore are subject to many harsh elements. Depending on the geographical locale and orientation of the site, the effects of intense sun and heat, cold breezes, and strong winds all need to be addressed to turn these raw, exposed surfaces into welcoming places where people can participate in an array of activities. As designers, we can use the tools available to us to enhance these special environments. Once we identify the specific microclimates, we can make the necessary adjustments for enjoying a cup of tea or a book with just the right combination of sun and breeze.

SHADE AND WIND PROTECTION

Let's face it, there is nothing like a tree for making shade and reducing the temperature on a hot sunny day. Oak trees are planted on the High Line in New York City, tall Ponderosa pines and mature crabapples thrive on Denver rooftops, and espaliered trees, citrus, and kumquats bear

A San Francisco roof garden designed by Beth Mullins uses recycled elements to add artful gestures to a plain fence that provides wind protection and screening from the neighbors.

Vines growing up steel trellises at Stücki Shopping Center in Basel, Switzerland, provide green screening.

Galvanized roof jacks and used beehive panels provide screening in designer Emmanuel Donval's garden.

fruit atop the Petit Ermitage hotel in Los Angeles. Aspens and spruces grow on the roof of the Church of Jesus Christ of Latter-Day Saints Conference Center in Salt Lake City.

Beyond the practical considerations, these trees evoke an emotional response. Most people have fond childhood memories of climbing stately oaks and willows in their backyards or seeking a shady place to read a book in a nearby park. In the classic novel *A Tree Grows in Brooklyn*, the sight of a tree sprouting through the cement in a poor section of Williamsburg, Brooklyn, provides a source of strength for the main character. It's because of such emotions and memories that finding ways to grow trees up on the roof has so much significance.

Planters with a depth of 2 feet (60 cm) or greater are very practical on rooftops as they can sustain a wide variety of trees ranging from evergreens to deciduous. Special considerations must be given to how certain trees mature, so if their roots become bound and constricted, they maintain their health and exist like bonsai trees. It is vital to provide stabilization against high winds and ensure, especially in cold climates when irrigation systems are shut down for the winter months, that all the trees are getting watered. Planters on a roof tend to dry out faster than ground level gardens.

Next in popularity for providing shade in rooftop gardens are nonliving alternates like umbrellas and shade sails, which have the advantage of not requiring water or any kind of consistent maintenance. On the down side, umbrellas cover only a limited area and, if not anchored properly, can and will blow away. Shade sails have a much broader reach, as they resolve direct sun issues by softening the light and providing large swathes of shade.

Mitigating wind on a flat, open rooftop is no easy task. Large planters with trees are one way to protect against the wind in enclosed dining areas. Trellises can also provide protection from the wind but perhaps are better at screening, and glass walls are often added to parapet edges.

Various vertical garden options provide unique shading possibilities and create interest in a roof space. On the simplistic end of the spectrum are cable systems designed to support lush green vines, as seen on the wall on the face of a shopping arcade in Basel, Switzerland. The plants are happy as they are growing in a suitable amount of media, and the clients are happy as the vines grow quickly.

More complex vertical garden designs that provide shade and wind protection are the redwood-framed succulent gardens created by San Francisco landscape designer Colleen Smith, who mixed burgundy heuchera, baby tears, and silver sempervivums to fill a vertical space with intricate flowing patterns and textures. Alternatively, there's a brilliant wall of mounted silver roof jacks stuffed with blood-red sempervivums, lime-green sedums, and other succulents. Designed by landscape architect Emmanuel Donval, this wall could easily create a backdrop or unique screen to some unsightly rooftop view. Thinking outside the box in yet another way, San Francisco designers Beth Mullins and Shirley Watts designed protective barriers sheathed in interesting old billboards. These artful barriers block prevailing winds, immediately making the space warmer.

Three questions for

Beth Mullins,

artist, garden designer, and owner of Growsgreen Landscape Design in San Francisco, about screening on rooftop gardens.

1. What is the most unusual idea you have used for screening a rooftop garden?

I love using multistem, nonfruiting olive trees. They can handle wind and sun, and add an instant canopy to the garden. They don't mind being in a container either. In one particular roof garden I hung letters, using the text to add a nice element to the wall space, much like hanging a piece of art (see photo on page 55).

2. Can you give some examples of materials you've used that people often overlook?

I like to use objects that are not available commercially. I try to boycott chain stores and shop local. If I can use something from the flea market, a found item, or an object made by a local artist or welder, I prefer it. It already has a patina, a feeling of travel, and it often adds unique structure and focus to the garden.

3. Have you used the same screening materials on the roof as you use on the ground? If yes, what are the special considerations for using that material in a roof environment?

You can use a lot of the same materials on the roof as on the ground. On one rooftop garden we used Ipe slatted wood screening but instead of fastening the slats to posts as you would in the ground, we fastened the slats to built-in planters and benches. You might need to consider wind if a structure or privacy screen were impermeable to air since it would act like a sail. ■

Another solution is to construct solid walls, although fastening systems and load factors become much more of an issue on the rooftop. Where do you attach the wall on the roof? Are there adjacent walls to which you can attach an extra vertical, solid surface? The vertical structural supports must be engineered to prevent leakage and hold up to higher winds.

Grape vines create screening for an apartment in Basel, Switzerland.

SCREENING FROM THE NEIGHBORS

Wood trellises and climbing vines are two very simple, practical, and effective screening methods. In an alley in San Francisco, a climbing vine and a cedar trellis were used to afford privacy and wind protection for a small roof deck.

When there is ample planning time, screening can also be provided from plantings on the ground like in the one-story studio in San Francisco designed by artist Kevin Smith and Flora Grubb, owner of Flora Grubb Gardens and known for ingenuity with climate appropriate plants. A concrete planter box installed in the front along the street serves a dual purpose. First, it provides beauty and screening for the studio with silver astelias and chartreuse pittosporum. Second, it holds vigorous azara trees that grow quickly and fulfill their purpose of screening the rooftop garden.

Trellises can also be placed in planters if they are effectively attached to the planter. Whether the planter is rectangular or circular, a metal screen trellis system can add verticality and screening. Attaching screens to structural parapet walls is another option with the addition of a planter in front. If building walls surround the area, you can attach cable systems to the wall and plant underneath.

The fishbowl aspect of rooftop gardens mandates some kind of screening at least to create an illusion of privacy. Given time, shrubs and trees in planter boxes will grow large enough to serve this purpose. Grouping several of them together can result in a wall of leaves and greenery that feels quite comforting.

Vines also work well in this instance because in a cold climate where the plants go dormant, vines give you shade in the summer and allow the sun to shine through in the winter. Some vines such as wisteria, clematis, and passion vine also come with beautiful flowers, and other vines like honeysuckle and jasmine bloom fragrantly at night. Even vegetables like tomatoes and cucumbers can be trained to grow beautifully on trellises. There is something magical, if a little unnatural, about seeing a 7-pound (3-kg) brilliant orange 'Rouge Vif d'Etampes' pumpkin hanging off a trellis on a rooftop.

If there is not enough room for plant material, even a 1-foot (30-cm) depth for vines with screens of wood, glass, plastic, or metal are beautiful decorative elements that can screen adjacent neighbors. Designers can vary the transparency or translucency depending on what material is used and how it is used. Prefabricated screens are available as well as custom applications. Screens can be designed as cutouts in metal and weavings of material, whether fabric, copper, steel, or plant-based like hemp or wood. Glass screens can be frosted and etched.

Hardscape

The amount of weight a roof can hold directly affects the choice of hardscape material. Pavers made of stone, concrete, or certain recycled materials may be heavier than wood tiles, but they are less expensive. Much of the new technology addresses lightweight tiling systems. Aggregates like decomposed granite, gravel, or river stone are also suitable as hardscape, but their weight needs to be a major consideration, and unless they sit on a support system that lifts them off the membrane, they should not be walked on.

If there is one hard-and-fast rule on green rooftops, it's that the waterproof membrane is not to be used as a surface to walk or sit on. Actually, these actions risk damaging the membrane and might void the warranty.

An integral part of the layout plan, the hardscape on top of the roof encompasses materials like paving, aggregates, decking, and edging, all normally considered permanent fixtures. Many new systems are available in wood, stone, concrete, and composites.

Before the advent of modular roof deck systems, people ripped down sleepers, scraps of wood or other material used as shims, to match the grade on roof membranes, adding deck frames and joists directly on top. On a Denver roof, bricks and pieces of 2- by 6-inch [5- by 15-cm] shims were set directly on the membrane underneath the deck frame to build a framing system for roof decking. This act not only destroyed the roof membrane but also made it nearly impossible to access anything below the deck when servicing drains or the membrane.

One major change in the early 2000s was the advent of the pedestal paver system adapted from European green roof technology. Lightweight, extremely strong, adaptable pedestals, or deck jacks, hold up pavers or tiles in wood, concrete, and stone. The pedestals are made to sit on waterproof membranes without destroying them. The pavers then rest on the pedestals and are more lightweight but just as strong as stone or concrete pavers typically put in at ground level, or even traditional wood decking.

Other products combine natural stone like granite, quartzite, or slate with a composite back that can be installed on a traditional framing system or on deck jacks, and support up to 4000 pounds per square foot [19,530 kg per sq m]. New to the market are concrete pavers that have reflectance and emissivity values to reduce energy consumption in the building below and enhance performance of the green roof concepts like heat island mitigation. They work in concert with the plant material to provide environmental benefits.

All of these systems are modular in nature and thus relatively easy to install, provide positive drainage and easy access, and simplify repairs to the membrane below. They come in different colors and can form a ballast system that secures single-ply membranes. These systems are fireproof, and protect from wind and UV damage as well as serve as walkways. Solar roof tiles are currently on the market, and in the near future a paver complete with a solar cell built into it should be available.

Decking is often lighter than stone or concrete and is optimal for rooftops that can only bear lighter loads. A wide variety of woods including recycled

and sustainably harvested varieties are popular as are other examples such as Ipe or Brazilian redwood (these are sustainably harvested products as well) that hold up particularly well to the harsher elements found on rooftops. The key considerations here are access to the membrane and drains below, and long-term maintenance. Many natural woods, even the hardwoods coming out of Brazil, must be resealed as part of a regular maintenance program.

Like ground level gardens, rooftop gardens may incorporate hardscape in many interesting ways to delineate sitting and dining areas or to call out paths. Nevertheless, on the roof, those all-important macro, or plan, views come back into play as paving patterns are easily seen from above, and details like the shapes, patterns, and textures become important to the overall scheme.

At the Museum of Contemporary Art (MCA) in Denver, the roof garden deck designed by Karla Dakin is made of the same Brazilian redwood as the rest of the roof decking in the garden, but the pattern of the decking varies, running on angles in modules to reiterate the angled beds. The modules were designed to be small enough so they could be lifted should there be a need to access the membrane and drains underneath. This feature came in handy when the water line to the water feature broke one winter and had to be replaced.

Accessories

Pots, furniture, water features, art, lighting, heating—so many accessories to choose from, it's hard to decide where to start. A good place to begin is with the budget and making sure these

Overhead view of an outdoor living area and green roof in Denver, Colorado.

Metal and lightweight pots at Flora Grubb Gardens in San Francisco make a wonderful sculptural addition to any green roof.

key features are not overlooked. The tendency is to put these details last on the list, but oversight in the accessory department can mean death to a roof garden. The color accent introduced with pots, the comfort of a chair for enjoying the view, or planters that effectively screen the neighbor in the next apartment are all essential.

Chris Brunner of New York Green Roofs cuts a hole in a foam form to secure containers, which will hold trees in place in Brooklyn.

POTS AND PLANTERS

Pots, dirt, and plants are all easy to transport up to a roof, fit through most doorways, and don't require the aid of an expensive crane. Today, the creativity behind the production of pots has turned a corner. In their wide range of color, height, shape, texture, and form, vessels of ceramic, metal, or plastic really brighten up the gray urban environment. There are also elegant, simple planters made of steel, aluminum, and zinc in an array of powder-coated colors that are ideal for roof garden situations.

Many considerations beyond style and color go into purchasing pots, and the art of choosing pots and placing them can be a compositional exercise worthy of a sculptor. Varying the sizes and shapes adds layers and differing possibilities for plants. Pansies and flowering plants are fine for small pots or as filler, but for small trees or shrubs the size of the pots goes up exponentially. In addition, pots have the advantage of being moveable so you can create different compositions annually or seasonally.

Unlike on ground level landscapes where you can put plant vessels anywhere, the options for placing pots and building containers on a roof are limited by the roof's structure and load capacity. Generally, plant containers belong on areas that can be point loaded to support soil depths that can reach 18 to 24 inches (450–600 mm). Lightweight soils weigh around 8 pounds per square inch (560 g per sq cm) when saturated and can be used in a roof container. Anchoring systems that do not penetrate the waterproof membrane are especially important when considering containers with trees. Larger containers planted with larger trees tend not to blow over, but the trees may need to be staked so they do not blow over themselves.

Beyond form, the function of pots ranges from accent to screening. Nursery woman Flora Grubb has become an expert at dressing small outdoor spaces and rooftops. After living in San Francisco for over ten years, she began to notice that bamboo did not fare well in the windy environment of a rooftop. Despite bamboo's haggard appearance after only a few seasons, its popularity remained strong as a cheap and easy solution for rooftop gardens for screening and accenting otherwise barren spaces. By redirecting her clients toward climate appropriate plants like agaves and aloes and colorful, unusual foliage combinations such as the neon green and red of *Oxalis* 'Sunset Velvet' with the lime-green of *Aeonium undulatum* and internal burgundy leaves of *Sempervivum* 'Rita Jane' which dazzle no matter the season, Flora began shifting public opinion about plant selection. With her unique style of layering pots enhanced by bold plant textures, her compositions created scenery as well as privacy from neighbors.

When weight is a factor, in lieu of heavy ceramic or concrete pots, plastic and aluminum varieties are great choices for getting the depth of soil

required on a roof to plant larger trees and shrubs. Fabric planters are another alternative to solid, hard materials. Made of felt, they are more portable than planters are and come in sizes large enough to accommodate small trees and shrubs.

Compared to pots, whose arrangement in a garden is highly flexible, planters that can accommodate large trees and shrubs demand considerable forethought. For one thing, they are permanent fixtures that may require the use of more elaborate and expensive installation aids like cranes. Additionally, large trees and shrubs need to be accommodated for their eventual mature growth, so planning ahead and selecting a planter where they have room to spread is worth the effort. Borrowing from the bonsai tradition, trees can also have their roots constricted to slow their growth. Not paying attention to this could result in switching out for a larger pot or planter later on when the crane is gone and the elevator is clean.

Regardless of the container, trees and other perennials planted on rooftops are exposed to more desiccation brought on by higher wind exposure, and are subject to fluctuations in temperature that can cause heaving and shrinking of soil. It is worth repeating that irrigation to pots, especially in cold climates, is a critical variable that must be maintained throughout the winter to ensure the health of the plant material.

FURNITURE

There really aren't any major differences between furniture selections available for ground level and rooftop gardens. Many chairs are simply beautiful to look

at, but whether they will stand up to the often-harsh sun and wind conditions of the roof is a question worth asking. The same bright fabrics that last for years in a backyard will fade more quickly in the intense sun that characterizes roof terraces, so selecting weatherproof fabrics or those marked UV resistant is the way to go. Similarly, the medium-weight holder that keeps most umbrellas tethered to the earth at ground level is likely to blow over on a rooftop, where strong winds build up. More substantial anchoring is necessary on a roof terrace than on a ground terrace.

No one wants furniture that takes flight either, and items like stone tables—be sure to consider weight loads—and built-ins are increasingly popular. Built-in benches not only stay put, but they also are space efficient, a key consideration when selecting furnishings for places with limited square footage. Benches can do double duty as storage for pillows and cushions.

WATER AND FIRE

The most enduring water feature found on rooftops is a swimming pool, which today tends to function less as a place to swim than as a visually alluring centerpiece. At the Unique Hotel in São Paulo, it is worth the circuitous journey through the hotel architecture to sit by the red swimming pool sipping a nightcap and enjoying the view of the city skyline. Several of the hotels designed by Grupo Habita in Mexico also have daring pools with infinity edges that allow you to swim to the edge of the horizon, looking at the view of the city beyond.

In arid climates, it is possible to create smaller water features that use

A small water feature adds tranquility to a New York City rooftop, designed by Rebecca Cole.

water more responsibly without losing the visual and sound benefits of water, always-attractive qualities, even while, metaphorically, they seem to ameliorate the heat. A small portable, plug-in water feature, for example, will provide the cooling, soothing effect of water while distracting from the street noises below.

The initial response to fire on a rooftop would likely be that it is undesirable due to concerns of safety and logistics. Contemporary options are very different from wood fires blowing embers in the night sky. Many fire elements are now self-contained, fueled by piped gas or white gas which can be burned in a shallow basin and lit per use. The same precautions should be taken on the rooftop as in ground level amenity spaces, including having a fire extinguisher on hand and a safe exit plan in place. Roof gardens also have that unmistakable advantage of getting you above the pollution and closer to the stars. Sitting around a fire on a warm evening staring at the sky on your roof makes going camping seem like a lot of unnecessary effort.

LIGHTING

Lighting is another critical accessory. This can be as simple as twinkling holiday lights strung along the parapet edge to more complex in-ground accent lighting. Depending on the roof access, including a system to light the way safely is an important consideration.

Lighting can also add ambiance to public as well as private roof gardens as these spaces are often used after dark, when the heat of the day has passed and people want to enjoy night air and the city skyline. At Richard Branson's Roof

A detailed fireplace on the roof of the Petit Ermitage hotel in Los Angeles provides an intimate gathering space year-round, designed by Mayita Dinos.

Steel sculpture on a ground floor rooftop in London.

Gardens in Kensington, the restaurant on the top floor has a deck overlooking London as well as the roof garden below. It is a forest oasis and even has flamingos. The night lighting adds to the fantasy of the space with a subtle changing array of colors from blues to greens to yellows and reds. From the restaurant above the lighting enhances a sense of floating in the air while looking out to the city lights beyond.

Many lighting options that work well also consider the elements. For example, plantings can be accented with lightweight pendulous fixtures hung from trellises or trees, or wall sconces can be attached to the building. Another more practical example is path lighting, which can be defined as lighting to direct people from one place to another. Solar lighting and lanterns are energy-saving alternatives. If wind is a major factor, consider sturdy fixtures that will stand up to a forceful breeze, and in all cases, check on codes for light usage and types.

San Francisco landscape architect Andrea Cochran's design for Maria McVarish's loft apartment in the city's Hayes District demonstrates a creative use of lighting with sconces on a dividing wall and soft overhead lighting in shade structures above a deck with chaise lounges. A rill of soft yellow light runs through the floor and soft uplighting bathes the parapet walls. This subtle lighting gives a sense of depth to the garden.

At ABH, the rooftop bar and lounge at the Thompson Hotel in Beverly Hills, there is candlelight on the bar counter and the light washes up the bar wall. Along with tube lights suspended from trellis rafters, and accent lights in the parapet planters, the overall lighting scheme enhances the romantic atmosphere on a warm night overlooking the city.

ART

Last, but by no means least, is the presence of art, especially sculpture on the roof. Well-placed sculpture adds immense value and beauty to a roof garden as well as providing a striking focal point when visible from inside an office or apartment. At the Lichtenstein Foundation in New York, New York Green Roofs installed a sedum mat and a cedar deck punctuated by rounded skylights as a backdrop for the abstract, pop art sculptures of Roy Lichtenstein.

The Metropolitan Museum of Art in New York City has the perfect roof garden for art, if you can find it. The entrance is buried in the back of the museum with very few signs to guide you, but your efforts will be rewarded. The setting is plain, the planting minimal—planters along the parapet walls and an entry trellis—but the south and west views over Central Park are worth the visit alone. There is a bar/café where visitors can sip iced tea while taking in one of the installations that change every summer.

4

Wildlife
Friendly
Spaces

Art and wildlife meet in this whimsical squirrel
painted by street artist Roa in the Shoreditch area
of London.

Lisa's Lessons from a Landfill

In February 2010, Tom Liptan, Stephan Brenneisen, and I visited Portland's now-defunct St. John's Landfill in response to requests from several advocacy groups and the Port of Portland to determine if habitat for the rare streaked horned lark could be mimicked on the  city's industrial roofs. The Port had recently discovered a lark habitat at the site and therefore could not develop the land due to the presence of the rare bird.

Ironically, by tilling the ground to prevent secondary succession of river willows, the Port inadvertently created a welcoming habitat for the lark on the freshly tilled sandy soil, but the Port needed to keep the property open as it still had significant economic and development potential. Successfully relocating the lark on a rooftop in the same location could potentially be a win-win for everyone. By trading off habitat on the ground for similar habitat on rooftops, the development could move forward while incorporating the economic benefits into habitat restoration. First, however, the Port needed to accommodate the bird and determine if the lark would comply. Nothing was guaranteed when the Port called in the green roof experts to address the questions.

The idea that not only could something good emerge from an unsightly landfill but also that it could serve as a model for green roof design was incredible. More amazing was that the lark was not the only inhabitant: the rolling hills of clay-capped waste were filled with wildlife. In addition to the rare lark, we spotted two foxes, two coyotes, a bald eagle, three blue herons, a red-tailed hawk, numerous bird species, and a small herd of deer. What had formerly been a wasteland was now a rich habitat, further proof that often our seemingly destructive activities create wildlife habitat unintentionally. ■

One of the most cutting-edge directions of green roofs involves creating habitats for biodiversity. Most designers are familiar with gardening for wildlife on the ground in suburban and rural gardens, but many haven't thought about inviting insects and wildlife into the urban roofs context.

Closer examination of urban environments reveals an entourage of insects and native bees already living there along with a multitude of tenacious and persistent plants, which work their way into sidewalk cracks, brick walls, and chimney tops. There are peregrine falcons roosting on skyline parapets, flushes of summer butterflies on flowers in sidewalk beds, and bird songs in the early mornings. Nature is in the city, and we can create more footholds, nooks, and niches for wildlife and instigate more habitats on green roofs with intentional design.

With the growing acceptance of rooftops as the new landscape frontier, designers have a unique opportunity to bring nature back into the city, but establishing natural habitats in urban environments is no slam-dunk affair. Creating a functioning living system of plants and soil from scratch requires considerable research and reinvention. The exciting thing is we have the option to design systems that function ecologically and encourage biodiversity with the added bonus of specifying the types of habitats we wish to foster and for whom.

In his book *Last Child in the Woods*, Richard Louv substantiated the position for more green roofs. After examining the connection between nature and humans, he concluded that urban dwellers are nature starved and that many city kids now experience what he describes as nature-deficit disorder. His studies revealed that urban children and adults spend more time engaged with technology than getting their hands dirty exploring a creek bed. Louv also described the decline of natural world exploration in urban school curriculums, claiming that students are taught more about genetic engineering than entomology.

Traditionally, the history of landscape design has been more about conquering or taming nature than about embracing it. However, we need more animals and green space in our cities to be healthy and happy. Green roof designers have a unique opportunity to lead the way in making this happen.

One way to accomplish this goal is to learn methods for allowing nature to seed itself and thrive in urban areas, all the while encouraging the intertwining of humans and nature. This new age of active coexistence could be framed as an *age of integration*, a term we have been using in our work to describe the premise that we are nature, and figuring out how to design from there rather than from the notion that we are separate. Shifting this basic perspective allows for new and lasting design solutions to be developed.

Urban Nature

The accidental thriving of biodiversity is counterintuitive to our current belief system that humans are destroying the planet. While there is no doubt that we create messes, the silver lining in this rather large gray cloud is that these

ABOVE St. John's Landfill, an accidental wildlife habitat, in Portland, Oregon.

BELOW A painted lady butterfly resting on a purple wall flower. Heat-, drought-, and wind-tolerance make wall flowers great plants for a green roof, while their nectar makes them attractive to all kinds of butterflies.

Four questions about the role of biodiversity for

Stephan Brenneisen,

biodiversity and ecology research scientist
in Switzerland.

---

1. What role does biodiversity play in urban areas? Why is it important?

The most important aspect of having and promoting biodiversity in urban areas is environmental education, which includes learning about ecosystems, diversity, and behaviors of certain species, such as that certain spiders migrate by air versus by transport of substrates. This knowledge is important because in some rare cases cities have an opportunity to conserve an endangered species.

2. How do you encourage biodiversity in green roof design?

If a design is made according to the needs of the plants and animals of the region, it will attract a wide range of biodiversity to the roof. The main factor is varying depth of substrates. To add more species, vary the types of substrate. For example, add sand and collections of logs to provide habitat for different species. To create even more impact, enter the realm of environmental education by providing signage for visitors and by organizing the habitats and substrates in patterns or aesthetically pleasing arrangements.

3. When replacing habitat, what expectations should the client have?

There is no guarantee that designing habitat on a roof as a replacement for ground level habitat will yield the same amount of biodiversity. Much of this is due to lack of water or other known factors. The better the new habitat mimics the original habitat, the more biodiversity it will attract.

4. What information about biodiversity do you take from the ground to the roof?

Very specific parameters are important for different plants and animals. Certain animals live in micropores, or small caves, which suggests using larger stones in a substrate to create more of these spaces. Another example is the native orchids we found that prefer standing water and are able to survive on a rooftop, just as they do in their native habitats, as they are not competing with grass populations. ■

The biodiverse green roof at the headquarters of the design firm Gemperle AG in Sins, Switzerland.

BOTTOM Solidago thrives above a drainage pipe in London.

mistakes are leading to discoveries that direct our actions and provide solutions for green roof design. Sometimes the wrong thing can lead to the right action, and there are unprecedented opportunities to do regenerative healing with habitats. Mimicking a railside wasteland could enhance the carrying capacity for a multitude of insects. This counterintuitive approach asks us to view habitat in a new and critical fashion, a paradigm shift in how we look at the industrialized world.

St. John's Landfill exemplifies that nature will creep back in despite our best efforts to destroy it. As we are discovering, wastelands like St. John's along with roadside cutouts, train tracks, and leftover areas yield some of the most bountiful populations and diversity of insects. In the end, these wastelands are sources for green roof design ideas.

As valuable sites of biodiversity, these wastelands have been inspiration for green roof design by European designers and researchers such as Stephan Brenneisen, green roof and biodiversity expert Dusty Gedge, and garden designer and builder John Little of the Grass Roof Company in Essex, England. Their work reveals that we have the ability to create landscape with co-habitation in mind, just like all other animals on the planet. These designers mimic the habitats of insects, paying close attention to the ways insects create, excavate, war with each other, partner with each other, and rely on each other for survival—many behaviors that are similar to ours.

Defining Biodiversity

Biodiversity is defined as the amount of variation within an ecosystem,

LEFT Strategically placed logs create microclimates and opportunities for biodiversity at the IKEA store in St. Gallen, Switzerland.

RIGHT Estuary crab found on a green roof in South Carolina.

BELOW A roof designed to mimic the surrounding estuary in Asheville, North Carolina, by Emilio and Kate Ancaya of Living Roofs.

watershed, biome, climatic region, continent, or planet. When we define biodiversity in an urban environment, we often just pick the pretty inhabitants or the ones we determine to be beneficial such as butterflies, bees, and birds, but true biodiversity in an urban context can include rats, pigeons, cockroaches, spiders, ants, and beetles. All of these creatures do serve a purpose. For instance, spiders are responsible for eating other nuisances such as fruit flies, mosquitoes, hornets, and flies; the latter can be vectors for disease as they feast on our refuse. We need to reframe and give a hard look at what we want to invite in and examine design techniques for encouraging more than just the pretty wildlife.

Urban rooftops are the perfect place to start facilitating wildlife habitats, especially those designed with no human interaction. Without foot traffic to disturb their nesting sites, animals and insects can thrive. Whether facilitating on commercial or residential projects, the design guidelines are similar. Biodiversity can generally be encouraged in either situation by varying substrates and plant communities, which contain food and nectar sources, giving particular animals, birds, or insects as many options as possible. Factors influencing the overall design involve human interface and what is desired aesthetically, where the building or residence is located, and/or if there is interest in attracting a particular species.

At Heron's Head EcoCenter in San Francisco, one goal was to match the native ecology of the Bay and provide habitat for the prolific numbers of bird species that frequented the site. Care was taken to design with the landforms of the Bay in mind, resulting in habitats

with collections of logs on their sides, larger rocks and branch pieces, and varying plant material with differing bloom times to provide nectar sources yearlong. The intention was to provide adequate nooks and crannies for small invertebrates that were an offering for them to colonize but not a guarantee. If a blue heron visits the small water pools on the roof, then true success can be claimed.

As part of a healthy ecosystem, spiders, beetles, butterflies, and bees provide valuable services for the planet and should be encouraged to thrive in all environmental settings including urban ones. These small creatures are responsible for pollination, decomposition, and predation as well as a valuable food source for the larger animals.

Stephan Brenneisen was the first to start asking questions about creating habitat while researching possible outcomes. He recognized that increasing biodiversity on green roofs was an effective tool to preserve and restore threatened biodiversity on ground environments.

BIODIVERSITY OPTIONS

Aside from plants, there are many biodiversity possibilities for roof gardens. For obvious reasons, access among them, large mammals, with the exception of humans and their pets, won't work, although in different locales some people add rabbits, chickens, and doves for food and hobbies. In a demonstration of how domestic wildlife can be incorporated, the New York City design firm Goode Green created a garden off an apartment complete with a lawn and chickens to provide eggs for Sunday morning omelets.

Occasionally, a surprise visitor shows up in rural areas, such as the bull elk grazing atop a roof in Vail or crabs on a coastal roof garden in South Carolina. The point is that sometimes we bring these animals in intentionally, but sometimes they just show up on their own. Even when we plan for them, they may not choose to make their home on the roof. These unexpected happenings make things interesting and keep our designs fresh.

When the surface mimics the sand bars and riverside habitats they are accustomed to, ground nesting birds such as the little ring plover, lapwings, and skylarks have been known to nest on green roofs. Mimicking their habitat doesn't guarantee that nesting birds will appear, but emulating gravel bars and shore plants increases the chances that they will. Some examples of mimic habitats include larger gravels and aggregates interspersed with grasses.

A home office commissioned by Nigel Dunnett, director of the Green Roof Centre at the University of Sheffield in England, and designed by Green Roof Shelters for the Chelsea Flower Show used multiple wildlife habitat techniques. The design featured roof and habitat panels created by green roof designer John Little and Lisa Lee Benjamin. Inspired by the work of artist Agnes Martin, the roof was planted with subtle lines comprised of carefully selected meadow plants and raised grassy areas designed specifically for beetles. Pipes of varying heights were arranged as watering holes, and two boxes of sand, each 6 inches (150 mm) deep, were inserted into the roof for ground nesting bees. Habitat panels on the sides of the structure were filled with a variety of materials such as sheep's wool, ivy roots, stone

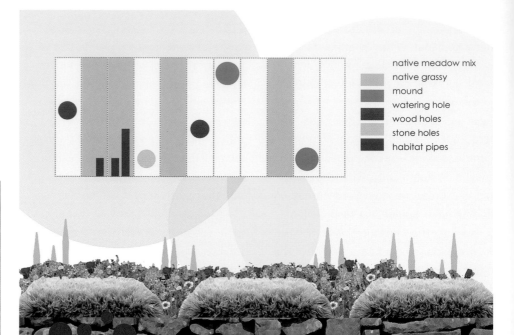

native meadow mix
native grassy
mound
watering hole
wood holes
stone holes
habitat pipes

A finished shipping container by Green Roof Shelters was the centerpiece in Nigel Dunnett's New Wild garden, which won a Silver-gilt Flora in the 2011 Chelsea Flower Show.

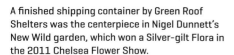

and wood blocks, and at the top of the wall, a blue tit nesting box. It is important to note that not all visitors to the roof or garden areas will nest on the ground or in bird boxes. Blue tits, chickadees, finches, and songbirds can be encouraged to vegetated roofs because landing on plant matter beats touching down on hot asphalt.

And don't forget the invertebrates. Butterflies, ants, beetles, spiders, and bees perform the bulk of pollination and add to our planetary food chain and decomposition services.

ATTRACTING INSECTS AND INVERTEBRATES

Pioneers in the green roof industry are moving beyond sedum mats by creating habitats, and basing that information on entomological studies with agricultural crops. Some designers like Lisa Lee Benjamin mirror ancient theories of hedgerow design to encourage a balance of diversity while discouraging pest population outbreaks. Within modern hedgerow design, particular plants provide shelter, safety, and nectar, or so-called ecological value, for beneficial insects. For example, a clipped border of goldenrod (*Solidago* spp.) will be brimming with six to eight species of native bees and pollinating beetles as well as several species of skippers and butterflies. Other designers plant corridors in modern ways along parapet walls, multiplying the veins of green through a city in a strategic pattern, just as traditional hedgerows finger through the English countryside.

Another way to encourage biodiversity is by specifying native or climate appropriate plants as potential food or nectar sources. This can be as simple as planting a few plugs of coastal buckwheat that provide a critical nectar source for the endangered green hairstreak butterfly or allowing pellitory, an European street weed, to sneak into the back of a green roof garden to serve as a host for a flutter of West Coast lady butterflies in the spring. Pollinators and nectar-feeding insects have a much easier time when their nectar sources are in mass or grouped together, making drifts and lines of perennials a good design solution. A striking illustration of this is Xcel Energy's building in Denver, which features massing of lavender (*Lavandula*), grasses, and black-eyed Susan (*Rudbeckia hirta*).

It is also possible to attract beneficial insects with nonvegetated gravel, wood pieces, sand banks, and dry biomass that provide shelter. Like humans, insects need a place that is safe and protected. Stacking wood in creative ways either linearly or in patterns that utilize the lines of the roof is one way to encourage microclimates and create interest on the roof.

Another way of increasing biodiversity and design potential is by undulating topography and changing substrate types. In commercial applications such as the roof atop an IKEA building in Switzerland, a grid pattern was laid out, and solar panels and logs were used to establish visual interest. Although viewers do not find the roof showstopping, they do agree it is more fun to explore the varying landscapes than to look at a sea of sedums.

Biodiversity expert J. Scott MacIvor at York University in Toronto, and Jeremy Lundholm, associate professor at St. Mary's University in Halifax, published a study in 2010 on the amount of invertebrate biodiversity found on

OPPOSITE, LEFT A common blue butterfly nectaring on a yellow lotus flower growing on the Seewasserwerk Moos roof in Wollishofen, a suburb of Zürich, Switzerland.

OPPOSITE, RIGHT Habitat design by John Little and Lisa Lee Benjamin informs the shipping container's roof for the New Wild Garden.

BELOW Black-eyed Susans and feather reed grass on the Xcel roof in Denver.

The caterpillar of the anise swallowtail on the stem of a wild fennel.

BELOW Lavender flowers attract pollinators on a green roof in Denver, Colorado.

the ground versus a rooftop. They were curious about the amount of biodiversity and if specific invertebrate habitats make a significant difference for the ecological value. Their research was particularly applicable for projects with varied substrate depth, composition, and differing microclimates, and less germane for predominately sedum roofs.

The conclusion of this study suggests that green roofs do indeed add biodiversity and provide ecological value equal to that of ground gardens. From there it's easy to hypothesize that the more roof gardens designed and constructed, the more urban biodiversity increases. Having visible signs of wildlife translates into tangible value as people feel the counter effects of nature-deficit disorder.

The larger ecological picture encompasses invertebrate advocacy groups like Xerces Society, Bug Life, the London Biodiversity Partnership, and the Pollinator Partnership, which are influential pioneers in emerging biodiversity policies. Currently, Basel, Switzerland, and London are leading the way. Basel now requires every new residential and commercial flat roof to be vegetated and to follow biodiversity guidelines, while London Biodiversity Partnership created and enforces an overall biodiversity policy for the city as well as one that specifically relates to green roofs.

Food and Nectar Sources

Food and nectar sources are also referred to as host plants because they provide certain benefits like nourishment and nesting sites. Host plants cater to invertebrates with diverse life cycles that require different parts of a plant to survive. For example, the anise swallowtail lays eggs on the prolific street weed fennel, which thrives in vacant lots and hillsides. The eggs hatch into caterpillars, which in turn feed on the entire fennel plant. In two to three weeks, the caterpillar transforms into a tiger-striped yellow and black glory.

Opportunities for bold, inventive design abound here. Try planting hedges of lavender (*Lavandula*) or swaths of ceanothus across a roof garden. Pollen collectors and nectar feeders prefer stands of one species because it is much more efficient for them. This massing technique is also a plus for creating elegant aesthetics of geometric shapes, streamline hedges, and large, drift plantings. Host plants for the coastal and Mediterranean areas in the categories of perennials, vines, and shrubs with sweet nectar—the primary interest of hummingbirds, butterflies, moths, beetles, honeybees, wild bees, and wasps—include sage, rosemary, lavender, and honeysuckle. In boreal mountain regions, solidagos, echinaceas, and penstemons will create the same effect.

In the spirit of "If you plant it, they will come," you will establish a happy habitat by providing a variety of food and nectar sources beneficial to insects in your area. The host plants and nectar sources are critical to a given population's survival. However, if you want to dig deeper, take the time to research existing insect populations around your site. Consider a multitude of factors and design the roof habitat holistically to get your desired results.

Designing host plants onto a green roof to increase invertebrate biodiversity in dense urban areas also provides basic

Honeybees on a ruby echinacea flower.

BELOW Active beehives on the Vancouver Fairmont Waterfront Hotel roof garden. In the background is the green roof of the Vancouver Convention Centre.

services for migratory birds and other animals. For example, the footprint of coastal urban centers like San Francisco reveals a gap in food sources and resting areas for the long journeys of migratory birds. The Pacific Coast Flyway runs right through San Francisco, a city of close to 6 square miles (15 sq km) that is devoid of targeted bird habitat except for a few sporadic trees. However, pivotal native coastal plant species exist, like the coast live oak tree that houses over 5000 species of invertebrates. These trees planted on the ground level, in addition to nectar-rich native perennial species planted on rooftops, are ideal for urban design and will be the roadside buffets and hotels that the weary bird travelers need.

We can take this idea of linking habitats to a larger context by providing food on rooftops along flyways and existing habitat corridors that will influence survival and performance of both the migratory birds and the insects that feed them. Doing this responsibly requires researching host plants, both native and nonnative, and planting them within reasonable distances for the animals and insects to feed on them. San Francisco's Nature in the City and Mission Green Belt, two groups working to bring nature back into the urban environment, are finding that simply placing a small number of host plants in sidewalks, gardens, or on green roofs along a habitat corridor can help rare butterfly species like green hairstreaks or mission blues gain a foothold to increase their populations.

Efforts to link habitat can also be found on the roof of the California Academy of Sciences (CAS) where design team member Paul Kephart of Rana Creek proposed plants with biodiversity in mind. The roof now hosts many insects, according to studies led by John Hafernik, an entomologist and CAS president. A primary goal was to draw in an endangered Bay checkerspot butterfly, historically native to Golden Gate Park. However, the closest linking habitat for the butterfly is several miles away on San Bruno Mountain and it will be difficult for the butterflies to find the roof as their typical range of travel is less than a mile. As a result, no checkerspot butterflies visit this roof, but other species for which the new habitat was not so much of a leap are present.

THE POWER OF POLLINATION

Perhaps the single most important reason for biodiversity as it pertains to the survival of the human species is pollination. Without pollination, there would not be enough food to sustain us and diversity on this planet would diminish significantly. Once again, it's green rooftops to the rescue.

One of the most important pollinators is the honeybee. Apiaries are a billion dollar business that directly affects our fruit and vegetable supply. If increasing bee populations isn't enough incentive, concerns over colony collapse disorder that results in the inexplicable death and exodus of honeybee colonies need to be taken seriously. Recently, we are seeing a resurgence in beekeeping and an increase in apiaries on roofs. A Hong Kong advertisement sponsored by Nokia follows a young product designer/beekeeper from rooftop to rooftop as he interacts with Hong Kong and his bees. Viewers are learning about the vital importance of bees in an urban environment and how cities threaten bee populations.

From the green roof of Chicago's City Hall to the roof of a BMW car dealership in a suburb of Vancouver, British Columbia, beehives are proliferating in unexpected places. Restaurateurs in the Mission District of San Francisco have put apiaries on top of popular establishments like Bi-Rite Market, and Flour + Water restaurant. Meg Paska of Brooklyn Honey operates a dozen hives on Brooklyn rooftops, and the local urban honey shows up in high-end bodegas and at farmer's markets.

For people who get nervous about being stung or having a severe allergic reaction to bees, the roof supplies an excellent solution by housing bees away from the general populace. By creating flowering attractions up high, bees can forage from roof to roof with little need to come to street level. While some cities prohibit beekeeping in residential areas or do not address it, there is a renewed interest in urban centers like Spokane and Vancouver, where community groups have promoted and passed beekeeping ordinances.

NOT ALL BEES ARE CREATED EQUAL

Alternatives to honeybees exist, and research is being conducted on native bees to add diversity into urban and agricultural areas and ensure pollinators are always present even if one species is wiped out. For instance, 250 ground nesting blue orchard bees can pollinate an acre (0.4 ha) of apples as compared with 20,000 honeybees. These wild bees don't produce honey but are still beneficial. Like most native bees, blue orchard is a solitary species that nests in a piece of wood or a warm and dry sand bank. Green roofs without a lot of foot traffic

A scabiosa flower provides nectar and pollen for a wild bee.

Three questions for

J. Scott MacIvor,

researcher at York University in Toronto, about wild bees on rooftops.

---

1. What role does pollination play for the planet?

Pollination is an essential ecosystem function required to sustain flowering plant species diversity, productivity, and food web stability. Bees, flies, beetles, butterflies, moths, birds, bats, and other pollinators transfer pollen grains between flowers, a necessary step in the production of many fruits, vegetables, fibers, feed crops, seeds, and nuts. As well, pollination by honeybees and stingless bees produces honey that humans can consume and sell. Pollinators are also integral components of aesthetic and ecologically functional designs of urban green spaces. Many pollinators are adapted to spatially separated foraging and nesting spaces, and able to move between fragmented urban green spaces—including green roofs.

2. What ecosystem services do invertebrates provide?

Invertebrates, which comprise the bulk of macro species diversity in all habitats, directly affect human quality of life (and that of many other species) in a variety of ways, including the following:

- Pollination and plant productivity by bees, flies, beetles, butterflies, moths, and more. This activity is essential for many ecological and economic processes.

- Control of agricultural pest invertebrates and plants, disease vectors, and nuisance insects by solitary wasps, spiders, beetles, dragonflies, centipedes, and more.

- Nutrient cycling by detritivores like springtails, beetles, and millipedes. In addition to improving soil structure and aeration, nutrient cycling liberates nutrients from decomposing material so that plants can then access the nutrients.

·   Forming the lower pillars of the food web and feeding all kinds of desirable species like birds, especially in city green spaces.

3. How do we create habitats for native pollinators?

Native bees require just three essential, yet designable, elements for survival: flowers for forage, a suitable place to make a nest, and material to build it. Encouraging the availability of nectar and pollen sources is the first step. This requires careful plant palette planning so that flowering occurs over the entire season by different species and so that native species and plants with noncomplex flowers are used. Although native plants are more valuable sources of nectar for native pollinators, many pollinators are able to collect pollen and nectar from a variety of flowering plants.

Since many pollinating bees nest in the ground, suitable habitat for them includes bare or lightly vegetated, small aggregate, well-draining clay or loamy soil—the deeper the better. Because shallow soils may dry out completely or freeze over in temperate regions, extensive green roofs or soil-over-impervious-pavers are less likely to be colonized. However, these spaces can provide ample foraging opportunity if a suitable plant palette is used.

Many other pollinator species are more easily able to nest on green roofs, because they prefer small, dark and dry holes such as those created by cut-and-left stems of many woody plants with soft pith (these can be bundled together and left on-site), the brickwork and awnings of buildings, and beetle-bored holes in living and dead wood. Even drilling holes 6 inches (150 mm) into pieces of untreated wood will work great—but these become unusable after a few years from the build-up of nesting material and detritus. Coupling habitat creation on a roof, or at ground level, with pollinator stewardship in your neighborhood or community will further enhance the foraging and nesting value of a space. ∎

Rolled burlap and spring green plum shoots are perfect habitat materials for beetles and spiders.

and consequent substrate compaction are a perfect habitat for ground nesting bees. In the San Francisco Bay area alone, there are over 300 species of native bees out of 1600 species found statewide.

Two varieties of ground nesting bees that do exceptionally well on roofs are sweat bees and bumblebees. The sweat bees thrive because they are small and require only 3 inches (75 mm) or so of soil to live in. Bumblebees do well because they are bigger and more resilient. They can easily access roofs and are not bothered by the high winds and harsher environments found several stories up.

Cavity nesting bees also inhabit green roofs and are well adapted to the urban environment, residing in the cracks and crevices of wood and masonry. Provided with enough nectar sources, these bees will happily make homes in man-made bee hotels, woodpiles, or niches in building surfaces. Sainsbury's, a grocery store chain in London, launched a campaign in 2010 to install native bee boxes on rooftops as a way of promoting biodiversity in the urban core.

In 2010, J. Scott MacIvor began a study using nest boxes for native bees on green roofs that in the coming years will reveal the numbers of cavity nesting bees. Along with other researchers like Gordon Frankie, an entomologist at the University of California at Berkeley specializing in native pollinators, MacIvor is making tremendous headway in recording and defining what biodiversity can mean for the future of pollination on green rooftops.

Urban Hedgerow wall habitat designed and made by Lisa Lee Benjamin and artist-builder Kevin Smith.

Shelter and Habitat Design

As previously discussed, climates are harsher on a green roof than on the ground. However, with creative design it's possible to invent comfortable environments where animals can survive.

Often the best materials for making microclimates are native soils, subsoils, and gravels found on site. You can pile up and organize these materials in interesting ways, remembering that small differences or stone placements can make the perfect home for a spider or beetle.

Another way to create shelter is with leftover building materials such as broken-up concrete, bricks, sawn logs, and two-by-four lumber that can be reused as bee blocks and mounted. It's also worth poking around the neighborhood and local area parks to see what you can find. Materials such as old burlap and fresh spring green plum suckers are useful for creating beautiful hanging pieces or mosaics.

Inspired by her collaboration with British green roof designer and builder John Little, Lisa Lee Benjamin started a global campaign in 2009 titled Urban Hedgerow. Her mission was to address the need for invertebrate habitat utilizing the creativity of artists to design bug hotels as well as create and link wildlife corridors that vein through cities. These urban hedgerows include backyards, public parks, sidewalk gardens, green roofs, and vertical gardens. Lisa has organized pop-up art installations in several major cities and created permanent pieces like the bug hotel she designed with artist Kevin Smith. Using repurposed construction materials including metal pipes, rope, and natural materials such as pine boughs, sticks, and bamboo, they organized the items into a hanging wall panel to provide habitat for cavity nesting bees, beetles, and spiders.

In Switzerland, Stephan Brenneisen has also been looking at habitats artistically by painting with gravels and creating habitat sculptures on roofs. One of the most striking habitat sculptures happened by accident when the sticks arrived too long to make the intended habitat piles. Artists Monica Ursina Jaeger and Michael Zogg were on site and they placed the sticks inwards toward the center, crafting a spectacular circle by stacking the wood up as they went round and round. Even if insects and spiders don't care how the wood is stacked or whether the gravel is in a checker or swirl pattern, people can appreciate the artfulness.

Birds also need shelter but have an easier go of it because they can fly where they choose. Historic examples of bird habitats built for centuries on rooftops are the ornate dovecotes and the birdhouses for specific species that can be added easily to any roof garden. Londoners have had excellent success with building up blue tit populations by putting nest boxes on green roofs and into roof gardens.

The point is, biodiversity and creating wildlife-friendly green roofs can be readily implemented with some research and thoughtfulness. The importance of designing nature into our spaces and moving into this new age of integration is necessary for everyone's well being and survival.

Stick Sculpture, Exhibition Hall 1. Basel, Switzerland.

5

Plant-Driven Environments

Flourishing perennials cover this unique mountain roof in Steamboat Springs, Colorado.

Karla Seeks Out Science

Living in New York City gave me the opportunity to begin my relationship with plants by experimenting with planter boxes on the fire escape off my Chelsea apartment. This period occurred long before I had any knowledge of the science behind green roofs. All my efforts were intuitive:

dirt, sunlight, and water. Unfortunately, my intuition went out the window when I fled the swelter of Manhattan summers, leaving the potted plants on the fire escape without irrigation, and returning to find them crispy critters.

Fast forward to 2007 when I created an art installation, aka green roof, on top of the Museum of Contemporary Art (MCA) in Denver. In the beginning, my intuition overruled science, as I wanted to experiment beyond the realm of sedums that typically populated the green roofs I had seen published elsewhere. I wanted to push the plant design envelope with a selection that emulated the prairie and alpine ecosystems that I loved. Additionally, I wanted plants with rounded shapes and/or ball-like blossoms, harkening back to the ball shapes that appeared repeatedly in my etchings from my years

in Manhattan. My artistic vision was more resolute than some ecological imperative wedded to natives.

Fortunately, I was smart enough to seek out science, too. I turned to the experts at Denver Botanic Gardens, where they too were designing their first green roof, and sought the assistance of Panyoti Kelaidis, the horticultural guru there. He redirected me to Mark Fusco, whom I hired on the spot. Thinking myself plant savvy, I was in for a grand surprise when Mark gave me a list that took me three days to research on the Internet. The plants on the museum roof needed to thrive in wild fluctuations of temperature, from increases or decreases of up to 50 degrees Fahrenheit (a change of 28° Celsius) in a matter of hours, dry winds throughout the year, and 14 to 16 inches (350–400 mm) of precipitation. ■

A desert willow with a long bloom season is a good ornamental tree for a planter on a roof and a desirable source of nectar for a foraging native carpenter bee.

Plant selection is a critical element to green roof garden design and, in fact, can make or break a design. A second consideration is how a plant interacts with the ecosystem and other plants in the garden. Plants belong to communities and flourish when surrounded by other members of their group. In this chapter, we will look at how microclimates, substrates, plant communities, and plant materials influence plant selection. It is not enough simply to choose a plant by intuition, as the following story by Karla demonstrates. You must know your science, and then you can ask what functions you want your roof to perform visually and ecologically, and design your plant communities accordingly.

Microclimates

In a broader sense, microclimates are localized zones created by atmospheric variances. These occur naturally where the typography changes or large plants, rocks, or fallen trees shorten the sun's exposure, prevent rainfall as in a rain shadow or cause rainfall to hesitate, slow down, or pool. These microclimates offer opportunities for plants not normally found in the broader area to flourish.

On green roofs, microclimates are created by different factors such as the predetermined location of walls, vents, photovoltaic panels, air conditioning units, or walls of adjacent buildings. These items by their vertical nature interrupt the roof plan and create climatic conditions that are different

A diverse and naturalized green roof on Restaurant Seegarten in Grün 80 park, in Münchenstein, Switzerland.

from those on the normal typography of a roof.

Beyond set conditions, it is possible to establish microclimates by varying the topography of the substrate through loading more media on the structural beams or close to the structurally reinforced exterior walls of a building. By placing objects like logs, larger plants, or pots to break up the ground plane on the roof, a bit of shade or shelter is established that allows different plants to flourish or animals to inhabit.

The green roof on top of the EPA (Environmental Protection Agency) in Denver has photovoltaic panels that generate shade conditions on an otherwise sunny, south-facing exposure. In these conditions sun-loving sedums thrived in the shade of the panels while their nearby cousins suffered in full sun even after the irrigation system was amended. In a different situation the tall beds of the Museum of Contemporary Art (MCA) produced a shade bed below where *Paxistima canbyi*, *Rosa* 'Darlow's Enigma', and *Chilopsis linearis* flourish.

Microclimates can also be established with plants, such as by placing tall grasses on the south side of lower perennials requiring more shade. Green roof expert Stephan Brenneisen used logs secured in place to provide a little bit of shade and more moisture for ligularia and mosses, plants that typically prefer more shade (see accompanying photo). These simple gestures can make a world of difference as to what grows.

Substrates

A substrate, as defined in the green roof world, is the soil or medium in which things grow. It is the foundation of green roof garden design and above all else determines the success or failure of the plant material on any given project. Although sedums are the primary plants grown on extensive green roofs, a much bigger world of plant choices is available which can be used to elevate the level of design. By varying and experimenting with substrates, it is possible to create a diverse and interesting plant palette even in shallow depths.

In our exploration of designing foundations with substrates, we will see how plants communities develop and how their performance is enhanced or decreased by the substrate in which they sit. Since 1995, Stephen Brenneisen has extensively tested this concept of varying plant performance based on substrate composition on green roofs. His original test was done with three substrates—garden soil, lava pumice, and sandy gravel—and three depths—2 inches (50 mm), 3 inches (75 mm), and 5 inches (125 mm). He concluded that substrates with large water-holding capacity produce the most biomass.

Principles like this one can be utilized to influence and direct plant growth and, in turn, design strategy. Playing with and varying substrates and depths encourages different plant communities to show up and evolve, some of which will flourish and others of which will be stunted. Some of these function well as ecosystems and others do not. By employing these principles, it becomes possible to implement design foundations where plant communities can spontaneously emerge versus being forced by our hand or vision.

Brenneisen has since tested reclaimed brick material, garden soils, engineered soils, gravels, and chopped China reed (*Miscanthus sinensis*), a

Microclimates created by logs laid together on a roof in St. Gallen, Switzerland.

Lisa Weighs Substrates

While on a roof with colleague John Little in Essex, I had a small epiphany about substrates, which led to a much bigger epiphany about design, structure, and basic foundations. In my practice as a designer, I am often waiting for that one perfect, sunny, late afternoon when the

mature seed heads of tall grasses are held just right by the perfectly scaled dark green hedge behind or when the salmon poppies are in full bloom and framed by *Sambucus nigra* 'Black Lace', red-leaved *Rosa glauca*, and cozied in by the pale blue flowers of *Nepeta* 'Walker's Low'. It is these flawless moments we want to record or photograph as proof we have achieved excellence as a horticulturist, designer, artist, or landscape architect.

But these moments when our visions are realized are rare for several reasons. We often design gardens to be in constant need of maintenance and

Blue catmint and *Sambucus nigra* 'Black Lace' frame salmon poppies in St. James Park, Basel, Switzerland.

adjustment by the human hand. As my work matures, I see that life and ecology do not always work according to plan. Robert E. Ulanowicz, a theoretical ecologist and author, says that order and flexibility must find a workable balance for us or any species to survive. There is an opportunity for attaining the balance described above between order and flexibility, allowance and control, through deliberately designing with substrates. Substrates are the foundation that determines plant and animal communities and each is unique to its climate and location.

Rarely do designers create or design a foundation and completely trust or allow things to unfold on their own. We are always weeding, trimming, replanting, and maintaining, all the while trying to keep our gardens as close to our ideal of excellence as we can, and it is a lot of work. I saw the chance to be proactive and create with the foundation, rather than reacting to what was happening above ground.

I believe green roofs afford designers a unique kind of freedom as there is no "ground" to react to. We can to begin to design our roof gardens and green roofs with substrates of different depths, qualities, and values, and in turn allow the corresponding plant and animal communities to follow. We can take a break from the tireless striving and establish a foundation for a spontaneous kind of beauty much grander than our human vision. ■

John Little inspecting plant communities on a roof he planted in Essex, England.

nonnative wetland species, as base substrates and discovered that each one produces a slightly different and unique plant community and ecology depending on both depth and location. For example, China reed has high water-holding capacity and, when seeded with conservation hay material, mimics the alpine meadows from which the seed was taken. There are also different results based solely on varied depths of these substrates that show a direct relationship between substrate depth increase and the density of these communities and their biomass.

When it comes to substrates, several areas influence the quality of the seedbed and ultimately determine what can happen. We'll look at a variety of options in this chapter but cannot possibly cover one for every situation or region. Instead, this information will serve as a guide. Bear in mind that what is most important is that every choice is site specific and must meet the requirements of the project.

SUBSTRATE DEPTH

Generally speaking, green roofs with a substrate depth of less than 6 inches (150 mm) are called extensive roofs, green roofs with 6 to 12 inches (150–300 mm) of depth are referred to as semi-intensive, and those with more than 12 inches (300 mm) are called intensive roofs. Research is finding that maximized biodiversity and plant growth coupled with building constraints also encourage this variation of substrates as beams can be point loaded and areas can flow between extensive, semi-intensive, and intensive depths.

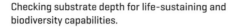
Checking substrate depth for life-sustaining and biodiversity capabilities.

Nutrient-depleted ceramic substrate produces a dwarfing effect on yarrow, asters, and grasses on a green roof in Essex, England.

Depth choices have several implications. The first is that in many cases more depth often equals greater opportunity for plant variety. Deeper substrate depths in planters and pots expand the plant palette and allow the introduction of large plants—shrubs, trees, and perennials having deep root systems. Depth is important, as is the size of the planter, to accommodate the mature growth of the specified plants. Determining substrate depth is also somewhat controversial as some people in the field think that the roots do not need to grow down to flourish. Remember, roots can grow laterally as exemplified by *Verbena bonariensis* growing in the cracks of the concrete pavers on a London roof.

Verbena bonariensis flourishes in a crack between concrete pavers on a London roof.

The second implication is that by varying between extensive, semi-intensive, and intensive depths, designers begin to construct a roof garden through substrates and create specific microclimates that host different plant and animal communities. This is interesting not only for plant performance but also for invertebrate habitat such as that of spiders, beetles, and wild bees. The Environmental Agency Green Roof Toolkit, prescribed for green roof development in the United Kingdom and written by Dusty Gedge, requires varied depths and substrates that support more diversity of species.

Stephan Brenneisen found significant changes in vegetal communities and species richness with increased depths of substrate. Just an inch or two (25–50 mm) can make it possible for a different plant ecology or performance altogether. The accepted sweet spot is between 6 and 8 inches (150–200 mm), similar to what was noticed on the Essex roof. With just a few more inches of substrate, the variety of perennials, annuals, and grasses increases. Intensive roofs have the option of adding trees in areas where depths can be built up to 24 inches (600 mm) and beyond. This type of change in plant materials is evident on a commercial roof in Germany that has several substrate depths and a plant palette that goes from low growing herbs and sedums, to iris and geraniums, to mugo pines and rose bushes.

MEDIA COMPOSITION

There are ranges of substrates composed of everything from native soils to technically engineered materials, but for each rooftop garden it is essential

to think critically about locale, what resources are available, and what makes the most sense for that specific site. Any given roof can hold one or a combination of all of these substrates, and there is no right or wrong medium. The decision depends on the ultimate goal of the roof and the purpose it is meant to serve.

Native Topsoils

Native soils deserve consideration because, even if in small amounts, they often contain mycorrhiza, a symbiotic association between a fungus and the roots of a vascular plant. Such relationships are an important component of soil life, fungi, seeds, invertebrates, and other valuable qualities of the local region.

A successful example of native soil use is the rare collection of meadow orchids found on the water treatment plant constructed over ninety years ago in Wollishofen, Zürich (see photo on page 220). Today the roof looks much as the surrounding countryside did when the soil was excavated, and the species found are a result of using this original substrate. Studies also support native soil as an important factor in supporting and promoting native endangered species.

Native topsoils can be hard to find in urban areas, as often these sites have been excavated down to subsoil and had new material or fill added. Frequently native soils are minimized due to fears about weight restrictions on existing structures and the concern that weight or saturation capacity is not a readily available calculated value. In contrast, technically engineered substrates have been designed and tested to meet international or national specifications and to avoid liability issues such as erosion and plant failure.

Technical Substrates

As the interest and market for roof gardens grow, the availability of engineered substrates is on the rise. These usually consist of lightweight drainage material such as shale and volcanic materials, particles that are often baked or put through a chemical process to mimic naturally occurring pumice. Such materials can be available locally but are often shipped long distances and blended with a bit of compost, sand, and other fillers. These engineered substrates were developed primarily to meet weight restrictions and drainage requirements, and to prevent compaction yet provide enough depth and water-holding capacity for plant life to survive. They are especially useful for extensive roofs and in combination with sedum mats and cutting plantings. The substrates drain quite quickly, but they do not always have long-lasting or ideal qualities for sustaining long-term and diverse plant communities.

Garden Soil

Most nursery centers carry garden soil or potting mixes in bulk. These mixes are often made of composted organic material, drainage material such as sand, perlite, or zeolite, and a bulking agent such as partially composted wood, coconut coir, peat, or similar material. This soil can lose fertility and performance over time, and it can reduce in volume. Often garden soil is recommended for container plantings in roof gardens and can be used in other unique situations such as in combination with China reed.

For the rooftop bar at 620 Jones, garden soil composed of perlite, sand, compost, and coconut coir was used because of the large volume of concrete planters that needed to be filled. The soil also suited the tropical garden plant palette.

Reclaimed Materials

In urban areas, the need to replace sidewalks and roads is leading to a surplus of recycled brick, fly ash, ceramic, concrete, rubble type materials, and styrofoam. These can be good, cost-effective choices; however, they can also have problems from high lead content or other contaminants, which may affect plant growth. It is important with any reclaimed material to have it tested for leaching or reacting since the origin of the material has been lost.

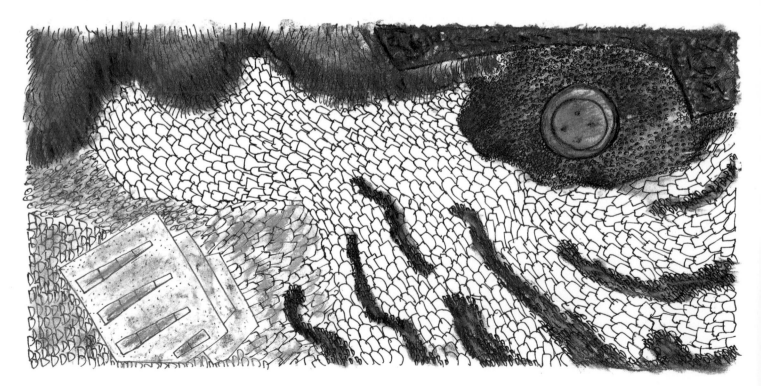

This rough sketch shows the layout of varying substrates on a roof garden designed by Annika Kruuse. Note the concrete steps (far left) and sand dune (far right) separated by waves of dark and light gravel substrate.

Some fun and unusual materials to try are broken-up recycled granites and marbles. Ceramics have a light color and low fertility, and produce excellent alpine and hardy communities of white asters and yarrows as seen on many of green roof designer John Little's roofs in Essex. There is also the ingenuity of using styrofoam as in the GaiaSoil developed by Paul Mankiewicz, plant scientist and executive director of the Gaia Institute. Incorporating styrofoam in a substrate has the benefit of reusing a waste product while providing air space and insulation.

On the Wat Tyler green roof in Essex, England, Dusty Gedge and John Little employed an array of recycled materials to design a roof for wild bees. They used old rope and timbers for habitat shelters and even colored juice straws for nesting cavities. They also used a lye tag substrate made up of pulverized and carbonized fly ash, which made room for lye tag specific lichen and is a host for a rare spider.

Organic Materials

Raw organic material including farm or forest products such as mulch and hay is yet another option. This follows basic permaculture and sustainable agriculture concepts of layering materials and slow composting. A rooftop can easily mimic the straw bale gardens on concrete developed for intensely urban areas, such as the Red Hook Community Farm has done in Brooklyn. Other materials being tested are wood mulch, leaf compost, and green wastes.

Aggregates

Aggregates serve five main functions: drainage around mechanical items, underlayer drainage, surface paving, water conserving mineral mulch, and as a substrate for invertebrate habitats. Many examples of aggregates are available, ranging from beautiful local gravels filled with seashells like the one Lisa Lee Benjamin used on the Heron's Head EcoCenter roof, to same-size white pumice utilized for drainage purposes.

In choosing aggregates, consider where they were quarried because gravel pits can be environmentally damaging if not managed correctly. Also, note that native aggregate and rock is a limited resource that cannot be grown or made. For most projects, the closer the material was quarried the better, but sometimes from an aesthetic perspective a certain color may be required that needs to be sourced from far away.

Another example that blends all these ideas is a Swedish roof garden designed by Annika Kruuse and Marten Setterblad who, utilizing principles from Dusty Gedge and Stephan Brenneisen, made a unique roof with concrete, sand, and gravel substrate.

FERTILITY

Fertility is an inherent part of soil health, but for green roofs and roof gardens where there is a limited amount of substrate, fertility can be a tricky subject. Often plant communities behave much differently on a rooftop than they do on the ground due to all the environmental factors.

On that windy roof in Essex created with a variety of substrates from typical garden soil to chopped up reclaimed ceramic bits, several areas of low fertility existed next to areas rich in compost with high fertility. It was very apparent in areas with more organic matter that plants performed much better

A rooftop garden comprised of pink columbine, yellow iris, red quince, and purple smoke bush in Pratteln, Switzerland.

than those in areas with low fertility. For example, high-fertility areas prepared with organic material and garden soil yielded tall, lush white asters with fewer blooms, while low-fertility areas produced asters that were almost an alpine version, with profuse miniature flowers and much smaller leaves.

Flowers will often proliferate under stress as the plants are trying to reproduce as quickly as possible in fear they may not make it. A roof situation that is stressed by environmental factors can create a survival-of-the-fittest competition that results in diverse and hardy plant communities in these rough situations. A case in point is John Little's Essex roof; made up of ceramic substrate and not much else, it is full of prolific wildflowers, forbs, and herbs. Contrary to what we might think, low fertility doesn't mean a lull in activity.

According to one theory, fertility in the form of organic matter or compost can be exhausted quickly. Plants get greedy, suck up excess nitrogen, and become too big before giving out early. This leaves a void the following year with nothing to follow as everything is used up. In a low-fertility situation, the soil yields nothing to start with so plants have to make due and survive, then fearlessly return the next year to do it again.

Despite the argument for low fertility, there are also valid arguments for higher fertility. Often organic material can hold more water and encourage flourishing plants. For example, a basic container garden, similar to a roof garden, essentially has four walls and a bottom, a drainage layer, and is often pumped full of nutrients to get the best possible bloom and foliage. At ground level, we know that fertility and nutrients are important for getting certain results with ornamental plants, but we have think about what we are designing a bit differently on the roof where maintenance is more difficult due to access, and climates can be harsher. Do we want our gardens to be on a continuous drip system constantly dosed with dissolved fertilizers? Alternatively, do we want to look at other ways of adding fertility or designing roofs that need very little supplement? The intended results and functions will drive many of these decisions.

BIOMASS

Another concern is biomass. Often defined as living or nonliving plant matter, biomass lies on top of the substrate, yet has a large effect on performance and function of the plant communities and biodiversity. The native meadow hay of the Swiss countryside mentioned previously often functions as a seed bank and mulch. There is also the issue of build up after a season's growth. In some cases, the biomass needs to be mowed off to maintain the health of the roof. Mowing sometimes leads to improved plant biodiversity. The decision to leave biomass or remove it may depend on the intended results or outcome, or it may not be subject to control. In blustery cities like Toronto, the wind removes nonliving matter even if the intention was to leave it over the winter months.

Plant Communities

The definition of the ecological term *plant community* is the same on the

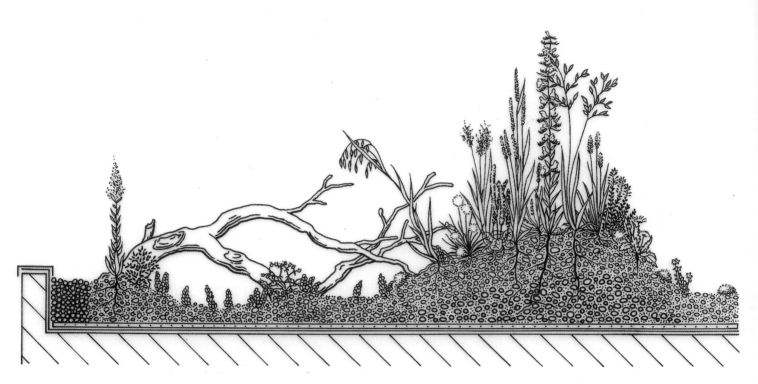

In this drawing by Sybille Erni and provided by
the Green Roof Competence Center at Zürich,
the depth of substrates illustrates varying
plant communities.

ground as it is on a roof. A community is a recognizable and complex grouping of plant species that interact with each other as well as with the elements of their environment, and is distinct from adjacent assemblages. The overall appearance of a plant community is created by the particular species present, as well as their size, abundance, and distribution relative to each other. The delicate balance of environmental factors such as soils, climate, topography, geography, fire, time, and humans and other living beings dictates community structure and distribution.

On the roof, these "choice drivers" inform plant selections and determine what kind of plants will flourish. Most cacti, for example, will thrive with very little to no organic material, while trees and shrubs need some organic material to grow. Prairie plants indigenous to western North America and requiring full sun on a roof will perform differently with a full day of sun than if planted under solar panels. On a roof, those sun-loving plants might thrive in partial shade since climatic conditions on roofs tend to be hotter, drier, and windier than those on the ground; a bit of relief from the intensified conditions might actually help these plants do better.

Hostas on a roof garden in the eastern seaboard of the United States might not do as well as on a roof in California, where the temperatures are higher and the humidity is lower. Twenty-one inches (525 mm) of precipitation in Cambridge, England, is far different in distribution and effect upon nature than the seventeen inches (425 mm) a year in Denver, Colorado, a high-altitude arid prairie.

There has been increased experimentation and research in recent years on climate appropriate plants. Richard Sutton, professor of ornamental horticulture, landscape ecology, and design at the University of Nebraska, researches the impact of growing media on native grasses and native plant assemblages on green roofs. He has discovered that native plant assemblages like the short grass prairies of Colorado thrive in conditions similar to rooftops with shallow substrates, low fertility, drought, heat and cold. Mark Simmons, director of Ecosystem Design Group at Lady Bird Johnson Wildflower Center, studies the design of sustainable vegetated roofs and native grass. His research revealed that even deep-rooted grasses like big bluestem (*Andropogon gerardii*) might do just fine in 6 inches (150 mm) of soil predicated on the theory that the roots will grow laterally instead of vertically.

In England, Nigel Dunnett, professor at the University of Sheffield, designs pictorial meadows on green roofs using perennials and annuals to provide seasonal color from early summer to late fall. Pictorial meadows create mixes of color drawn from impressionist paintings rather than exact replicas of wild flower meadows. Horticulturalist Mark Fusco developed a plant palette for the first green roof at Denver Botanic Gardens (DBG) utilizing his extensive research with native plant communities on the ground. The new garden incorporated plants from all over Colorado including alpine plant communities from approximately 14,000 feet (4270 m) above sea level. Prior to designing the green roof, Fusco created a ground level garden at DBG by placing native plants from all the biomes in Colorado in shallow concrete troughs. He determined the troughs mimicked the conditions on a roof and thus used many of the same plants on the roof.

PLANT COMMUNITY SUCCESSION

Succession is another ecological term used to describe which plants survive and how. Some species will take over and become dominant in the plant community, a factor to consider when selecting plants and setting up a maintenance plan. Manfred Köhler from the University of Applied Sciences in Neubrandenburg, Germany, studied the long-term vegetation dynamics of two extensive green roofs over twenty years. Ten plant species were sown by seed. Over that time observers counted 110 species, but only 10 to 15 of them were dominant and could be considered typical extensive green roof plants. Temperature and rainfall distribution had the greatest effect on plant diversity.

Additionally, plant communities or assemblages comprise a great amount of biodiversity from the mycorrhizae to annuals, forbs, and grasses, which in turn lead to a broader support of animal diversity. In his paper, *Media Modifications for Native Plant Assemblages on Green Roofs* written in 2008, Richard Sutton concluded that sedum overuse on extensive green roofs could present a problem in the future. He stated that monocultures generally are unstable and often susceptible to catastrophic changes, and can result in problems with insects and diseases. He noted that even when not planted in monocultures, *Sedum* species are susceptible to molds, fungi, and root rots and several species are susceptible to insects.

Based on this information, here are key questions to ask about design intention before you start:

- **What are the succession patterns and how can you design your roof to guide, inform, or control these patterns without doing harm?**

- **Are you planting with mats, plugs, or by seeds?**

- **Do annuals affect the long-term design or are perennials the show-stoppers?**

- **Who is going to duke it out with whom?**

- **What climax community are you aiming for?**

- **How do you plan for rich plant communities?**

- **How do you maintain against certain succession changes, such as invasive birch seedlings or pasture grasses blowing in?**

Lilies, alliums, and mulleins in Perdita Fenn's London roof garden.

A pear cactus in bloom on the roof at Denver Botanic Gardens.

Three questions for

Mark Fusco,

horticulturalist and green roof designer in Denver, Colorado, about native plants for arid climates.

---

1. How does your work as a horticulturist on the ground influence your work on green roofs?

My background in environmental science, landscape design, and horticulture, and my work as a horticulturist at Denver Botanic Gardens have been key to my knowledge of semi-arid and arid plant species. I have mostly worked with native North American plants from steppe communities, high alpine and subalpine communities, and desert communities from around the world, but have also experimented with plants from drier parts of the world like Iran, Iraq, and Turkey. In nature, many of these plants thrive in well-drained, shallow soils that are minimal in nutrients—conditions that mimic green roof environments.

2. How do you see your work with arid plant communities fitting into a wider context for green roofs around the world?

There is a vastly underutilized world of plant material that should be incorporated into more designs of green roofs for a multitude of reasons such as increased drought tolerance, lower maintenance, greater aesthetic appeal, broader habit creation, increased NOx (nitrogen oxide and nitrogen dioxide) sequestration and stormwater remediation.

Plants from North American and Asian steppe climates grow with very little moisture and long drought periods, high winds, low relative humidity, high temperatures, low temperatures, and long periods of exposure to the sun. Native species of grasses and forbs like *Arenaria*, *Bouteloua*, *Dalea*, *Erigeron*, *Opuntia*, *Penstemon*, and *Phlox* thrive in these climatic conditions. Although they are occasionally used in green roofs today, if even 5 percent of the species of *Artemisia*, *Erigeron*, or *Eriogonum* were deemed green roof worthy, there would be at least a dozen new green roof plants from which to choose.

Due to their native range and the diverse climatic conditions in which they thrive, well-chosen *Sedum* species can fit into almost any situation on a green roof. Almost every green roof should include sedums, but they should be accompanied by plants from other genera for genetic diversity and to give the green roof the greatest opportunity to survive regardless of weather conditions, soil conditions, and maintenance regime.

Plants from high-elevation plant communities in North America, Asia, and South America are in many cases perfectly suited for high-elevation green roofs. The mat-forming species of *Paronychia*, *Phlox*, and *Silene* can be combined with plants from the daisy and grass family, such as species of *Erigeron*, *Hymenoxys*, *Poa*, *Rhodiola*, *Sedum*, and *Trisetum*, to form a long-lived and low-maintenance, high-elevation green roof.

Sagebrush communities in the western United States are generally typified by large stands of *Artemisia tridentata* and in some areas accompanied by *Chrysothamnus nauseosus* or *Atriplex* species or *Ephedra*. These areas can look like large monocultures, but a closer

"It is very exciting to think about vegetative roofs across the world brimming with the best green roof plant species from across the globe."

inspection reveals multiple species thriving in the well-drained soils. Living within the protection of these dryland shrubs are a great number of subordinate plants like species of *Allium*, *Arenaria*, *Astragalus*, *Erigeron*, *Oxytropis*, and *Penstemon* that have the potential to do well on green roofs. The sagebrush communities are interspersed with canyons, outcrops, and rock fields, which host species of *Eriogonum*, *Oenothera*, and *Petrophytum*. Many of these same plants that fill drought-tolerant gardens throughout western North America just might do well on green roofs also.

Aside from sedums, the best green roof plants are probably cactuses, especially *Opuntia* species. Extremely adaptable to heat and cold, they thrive when grown in well-drained soils. The best part is that, in all but the hottest, driest parts of the world, they never need irrigation on a green roof.

The prairie may be the most underappreciated landscape in the world. The high steppes, riparian zones, bottomlands, arroyos, rock outcroppings, and sand hills offer a wide array of climates and microclimates. *Bouteloua gracilis*, *Buchloe dactyloides*, *Koeleria macrantha*, and *Panicum virgatum* are some of the more popular grass species. Countless others like *Aristida purpurea* and an abundance of *Muhlenbergia* species have star potential. Plains forbs like particular species of *Arenaria*, *Thelesperma*, and *Townsendia* can be unbelievably showy and reliable.

3. How do you see the role of climate appropriate plants? Do you see them as invasive or not?

None of this even touches on the idea that there are countless European, South African, and Asian plant species and desert annuals that would thrive on rooftop environments. The steppes of Asia are quite similar to the steppes and plains of North America, the Mediterranean is similar to parts of California, and South Africa has the richest and most diverse number of plant species in the temperate world. It is very exciting to think about vegetative roofs across the world brimming with the best green roof plant species from across the globe. Of course, this has to be done responsibly as to not introduce invasive plants. In urban areas, this is of less concern, but in suburban and rural areas care needs be taken to choose mostly native and noninvasive exotics. ∎

Plant Materials

Many plant possibilities are available at our fingertips to paint and shape roof garden designs. For any given situation, a multitude of choices exists for creating beauty, depth, and producing diverse ecologies as well.

Defining Color Palettes

Let's begin by looking at designing in a situation with limited substrate depth and/or resources and consider the variety of sedums, succulents, and herbaceous species that are available. These plants are often used in scattered cutting mixes, mats, or planted in random patterns, and their uniqueness and beauty can be easily lost. Upon closer observation these seemingly ordinary plants host a myriad of brilliant colors such as the deep bronzy maroons in *Sedum spurium* 'Dragon's Blood', the purply reds of *Sempervivum* 'Blood Tip', and the bold yellows that highlight the chartreuse foliage of Sedum acre. In contrast, there are the subtle gray tones of *Thymus pseudolanuginosus* and *Sedum hispanicum*.

All of these tones can be woven together to create blocks of color and mixed paintings of plants. Lovely examples of this are visible through a tiny lime-green door at the top of the stairs up among the chimney stacks on Perdita Fenn's roof in London's Bermondsey district. Shallow ceramic bowls overflow with luscious mixtures of *Acaena purpurea, Trifolium* 'Wheatfen', red sempervivums, and silver limoniums. Low, tire planters are filled with sweeping layers of Asiatic lilies and flowing feather (*Stipa* spp.) grasses and edibles, while

lavender and agapanthus give way to umbrellas of Queen Anne's lace (*Daucus carota*) and *Allium* Fireworks Mix. Rarities such as beschorneria and cacti poke through in unexpected places.

Large sweeps of a few species can also result in a dramatic geometric effect. At the Vancouver Convention Centre, plant material chosen from regional plant communities forms triangular patterns. These shapes strengthen the visual impact of the sloped roofs and overall architecture of the building.

As substrate depth on a green roof increases, so do the color and plant choices. Moving beyond sedums, succulents, and herbaceous species, it's time to introduce ornamental, or native, grasses and flowering perennials, which can accentuate each other very well. As always, remember that because of climatic factors, some plants will behave differently on the roof than on the ground. Among them are succulents, which begin bronzing as they are stressed. These reddening reactions, however, can also be part of the overall aesthetic experience.

Plant palettes can be composed of pastel or primary colors and follow a loose garden style or one of high design. For a bolder result, consider combining burgundy-leaved trifolium, mullein (*Verbascum* sp.) with its broad gray-white leaves and tall light yellow flower spikes, and golden feather grass (*Stipa pulcherrima*) with its brilliant, light-catching seed heads. These varieties mix beautifully and have similar climate tolerances and water requirements.

Colorful designs are possible with bold foliage and subtle tones of green, grays, and browns without the pop of showy flowers. On the rooftop terrace of 620 Jones in San Francisco, vibrant neon

TOP Pinks (*Dianthus* spp.) and bird's-foot trefoil (*Lotus corniculatus*) add beauty to an ecological meadow atop a transit center in St. Gallen, Switzerland.

BOTTOM Details such as sempervirens flowers and silver limonium leaves draw attention to this small London roof garden.

Sedum 'Angelina' and sparkling maroon-striped, silver-leaved *Astelia* 'Red Gem' highlight splashes of burgundy-leaved cordylines. A backdrop screen of *Ficus pumila* and *Arbutus* 'Marina' with burnt orange bark, glossy green leaves, and tiny sweet pale pink cascades of bell blossoms rounds out the palette. The only flowers are the fire red of *Leucadendron* 'Safari Sunset' and the tiny yellow eyes among the burgundy leaves of the oxalis ground cover. The colorful picture of bold foliage entices and entertains the visual senses and creates a different vision of what a garden can be.

By increasing the depth of the substrate again, much larger succulents such as slate blue- and white-striped *Agave* 'Mediopicta Alba', and colorful shrubs like the rich purple varieties of smoke bush are possible. With more depth, larger masses are possible that can offset and accentuate other efforts on the green roof. These areas of depth can also be smaller sections of the roof where the beams are point loaded and where substrates can be piled higher or can hold larger containers. The possibility of trees also comes into play, which allow the creation of even larger backdrops to hold the perennials and annuals in front. For example, on a tiny roof in Brooklyn, deep green birch trees are placed in the back of the garden where the extra weight can be supported. The trees provide a backdrop for the calm sea of green ground covers, creating a peaceful composition with this monochromatic palette.

SEASONAL COLOR AND TEXTURE

As the seasons shift, the colors and textures of plants also shift. On New

Himalayan honeysuckle and variegated cordyline at the entrance to the rooftop bar at 620 Jones in San Francisco.

Agave 'Mediopicta Alba Splenda' is one of the many interesting and climate appropriate species that expert horticulturist Sean Hogan utilizes in his green roof designs.

Three questions for
Mark Simmons,
director of the Ecosystem Design Group at the Lady Bird Johnson Center, University of Texas, Austin, about plant communities.

---

1. Where do you start when designing a plant palette or plant community?
Where the green roof is a primary component of building design and is assigned one or more performance objectives as an integral part of whole building design, specified minimum performance targets exist, and the roof must be designed accordingly and cannot be compromised. Examples are specific thermal performance, stormwater retention volume target, and species habitat design. The plant palette and/or other abiotic structural components dictate the green roof design and the build design must accommodate this.

When the green roof is not a primary component of building design, the plant palette is a product of optimizing the primary performance goals. Green roof design in this case is dictated by desired function on the one hand and structural and economic constraints on the other. In other words, you first ask the question, What do you want the green roof to do in terms of aesthetics, storm-water retention, building cooling, habitat, and so forth? Next ask, How do the other abiotic components like drainage and media depth, limited by building structure, further constrain this function? Once these have been addressed, the plant composition can be constructed by "backing-in" to the design to find plants that will fulfill these constraints.

2. How do desired ecological outcomes affect your decision making?
By definition, a roof with a living component exhibits intrinsic ecological processes. Moreover, an intelligent green roof design would consider sustainability and or regeneration characteristics, in which case ecology would play a vital part

of design. Are these plants suitable for the climate and the growing media? Will they reach a nutritional equilibrium with the growing media to minimize maintenance? Will the species reach a successional state in a short period to optimize performance?

3. How do you see grasses playing an increasing role on green roofs and biodiversity?

Many grasses are well suited to some green roof environments, particularly those roofs in climates with unpredictable fluctuations in temperatures and precipitation. Many green roof plants in temperate or more stable climates fit one particular life history strategy. For example, most succulents are obligate stress tolerators, while many perennial grasses are excellent facultative stress tolerators. That is, the latter can change physiological strategy by rapid regrowth during periods of high resource nutrient or water availability, or alternatively, in times of resource limitation by sloughing off living shoots until conditions improve. This capability is largely possible because grass shoots (tillers) are relatively easy to manufacture by the grass and at short notice. Grass tillers adapted to disturbance by grazing or fire have a relatively short life span of several months and are switched on by changes such as light quality, soil temperature, and water availability. When the environmental situation changes, the grass can simply stop growing new tillers or even go dormant altogether to wait for better times. ■

Prairie grass provides a subtle background for spent rudbeckias in Chicago's Millennium Park.

Complementary leaf shapes in a garden roof in Basel, Switzerland.

York's High Line, the summer colors are limited to mostly yellow and white flowering perennials. The restrained color palette of the blooms places more emphasis on the green textures of the shrubs, trees, and grasses, which enhance the native forest feeling. In fall, the brilliance of the grasses and seed heads begins to unfold, and in winter, the birch leaves descend and create mulch for the following spring. The auburns, golds, and taupes of autumn are a major contrast to the greens of summer, which in turn change from the brilliant colors of spring after a dormant winter. The changes and flowering times are often exaggerated on a rooftop because the climate is harsher than on the ground. So how do designers utilize these elements to best advantage?

Evergreen conifers are obvious choices for winter. A wide selection of dwarf conifers is available including broadleaf evergreens like mountain lover (*Paxistima canbyi*) and wild buckwheats (*Eriogonum* spp.), which provide contrast in color and texture to the browns of dormant grasses. Even cacti and acantholimons with their prickly skins have winter interest.

LEAF SHAPES

Large and small, narrow and slender, evergreen and semi-evergreen—not all leaves are green nor do they look the same even if they are the same height. On the lower beds of Denver's MCA green roof, cacti with their spines, shape, and momentary garishly colored blooms appear very different from acantholimons with their spines, rounded shape, and halo of pale blossoms. Yet each thrives in similar soil depths and water.

It is normal to associate less soil depth with smaller-leaved plants, but bladderpod (*Physaria bellii*), native to Boulder, Colorado, has an identical shape but larger leaves than the more easily recognizable sempervirens.

The beds at MCA showcase three simulated plant communities in substrates 1 foot (30 cm) deep. The two top beds simulate the prairie with its narrow-leaved plants, grasses, and forbs, and are meant to be seen from afar. In fact, it is not possible to look down on these beds unless you live in the adjacent building. From a distance, the soft, fine textures moving from the thin blades of grass to the huskier-shaped butterfly milkweed (*Asclepias tuberosa*) simulate the color changes of plant communities in the nearby Boulder foothills. Shifting from grassland to shrubs, the softness of this long view belies a complex ecosystem that delights the viewer upon closer inspection.

The prairie is like the desert: from far away it looks monotonous and quiet. People often bypass the prairie for the thrill and drama of the Rocky Mountains. However, the micro views of the prairie reveal an intricate weave of forbs and grasses. In the MCA prairie beds, blue grama grass (*Bouteloua gracilis*) mixes with penstemon, artemisia, pulsatilla, and liatris. In their natural environment, these plants thrive in rocky, gravelly soils without much organic material, and with very little water. One of the upper beds of the roof garden is populated with plants with blue foliage like butterfly milkweed (*Asclepias tuberosa*), glaucous hair grass (*Koeleria glauca*), Menzies' and Grand Mesa penstemons (*Penstemon davidsonii* var. *menziesii* and *P. mensarum*), and autumn moor grass (*Sesleria*

autumnalis). Another features the lighter green foliage of *Artemisia viridis*, blue grama grass, and fameflower (*Talinum calycinum*).

Despite the fact that grasses are deep rooted, blue grama grass seems to thrive in 4 or more inches (100 mm) of soil in varying climates in its native habitat from the Rockies to the California coast. The fountain grasses (*Pennisetum* spp.) require a lot of water, but they will do much better at the bottom of a sloped roof than the native desert pine muhly (*Muhlenbergia dubia*), which fails if it receives too much water. Even grasses like blue avena (*Helictotrichon sempervirens*) and blue fescue (*Festuca* spp.) will thrive in 1 foot (30 cm) of substrate.

Bulbs offer different leaf shapes, especially allium varieties, where the foliage accentuates the bloom, as seen in the large white globes on High Line Park and in the playful green *Allium vineale* 'Hair' on the roof at MCA. *Allium* also seems to do well on roofs throughout Europe and North America. The pale shades of *Scilla alba*, star of Bethlehem (*Ornithogalum* spp.) and *Nectaroscordum bulgaricum* highlight the flat beds at LAMOTH (Los Angeles Museum of the Holocaust), while the leaves fade into adjacent grasses, extending seasonal bloom from early spring through June. *Muscari* species and *Iris reticulata* are the early bloomers that dot up the gray of Dusty Gedge's roofs in England, leaving their green leaves to add color for the rest of the season.

PLANT HEIGHTS

In the past, the depth of the growing media often determined plant heights

TOP Lavender and lilies in a myriad of colors and textures fill this pot on a London roof garden.

BOTTOM Desert-adapted plants survive well in the sunny shallow soil on a roof at Denver Botanic Gardens.

on green roofs, but research by Mark Simmons reveals that some plants will tolerate less soil and still reach relatively tall heights. The Vienna roof garden of Gerald Steinbauer, president of the Austrian Association, one of the largest green roof contracting firms in Austria, proves this point. Located on the eighth floor the garden looks like a ground level shrub and perennial bed with a contorted filbert and lilacs framing a shallow pool edged with water-loving iris beneath the bronze leaves of a Japanese maple.

On the dry end of the spectrum, nothing beats the dramatic juxtaposition of a 15-foot [4.5-m] agave bloom arising out of architectural, blue leaves surrounded by ground hugging masses of *Delosperma* species and mounding dots of *Draba* species and *Dianthus anatolicus* on the green roof above the café at Denver Botanic Gardens. The middle ground relief comes from the dusty green foliage of fernbush [*Chamaebatiaria millefolium*], littleleaf mountain-mahogany [*Cercocarpus intricatus*], and butterfly milkweed [*Asclepias tuberosa*], and only the magenta blooms of the cacti in the foreground draw your eyes away from the last gasp of the agave.

VEGETABLE GARDENING

Food production on rooftops is becoming increasingly popular. At Eagle Street Rooftop Farm in Greenpoint, Brooklyn, vegetables for sale are grown on the 6000 square foot [560 sq m] roof. With so many acres on the ground to produce food, it might seem superfluous to grow food on roofs, but in a dense urban core, growing food on a roof takes you out of

the city for a moment and this experience is not to be underestimated. Imagine walking around mounded beds flush with greens while looking over the East River towards the skyline of Manhattan.

In Vancouver, growing food seems to be a shared passion. One of the city's first green roofs, the Fairmont Waterfront Hotel herb garden, boasts a 2100-square-foot [195-sq-m] garden planted with over sixty varieties of herbs, vegetables, fruits, and edible blossoms used by the hotel chefs. Blackberries tucked behind the diving board of the swimming pool adjacent to the garden thrive, and the hotel management is equally proud of the eight beehives, safely hidden below the main roof deck.

Also worth mentioning is the BMW dealership on the other side of Vancouver in Richmond, British Columbia, where the owners invested in an extensive green roof planted with alpine and regular strawberries, blueberries, red currants, banks of lavender [*Lavandula*], roses, and other herbs. They have given their beehives a special location out of the coastal winds behind the espaliered apple trees, growing in just 1 foot [30 cm] of soil.

Autumn grapes ready for harvest at the Fairmont Waterfront Hotel in Vancouver, British Columbia.

PART

TWO

Process

6

The Predesign Phase

A morning meeting to discuss green roof possibilities led by Dusty Gedge on the roof of Natural England's office in London.

During the predesign phase, designers research the often-invisible but vital components that serve as parameters for the entire design and construction of the project. These components range from the physical makeup of the structure to visible mechanical parts such as vents and air conditioning units. Considerations such as access to the roof require thinking and planning. Regulations or restrictions within the building or municipal codes, and policies and incentives that guide or encourage the process all play a part. Without these pieces of the puzzle designers cannot move on to develop creative responses.

The segue between architecture and green roof design involves in-depth information, research, and communication from and between many parties. Designers cannot just show up on site, take some photos, and design a garden. They need to follow through on due diligence before they begin.

Then there's assembling the design team that serves in a much higher technical capacity than a team working on a ground landscape. For the roof at the Museum of Contemporary Art (MCA) in Denver, because we came in after the building was designed and under construction, we hired the architect of record as well as the structural and mechanical engineers to help us connect the built environment with the green roof site. It's unlikely you'd need to hire these individuals if you came to a ground level landscape project where the building had been finished and you were just constructing a garden around it.

Roofs are not blank slates. A lot of information has to come to the surface before beginning the design. Part of sorting out the issues is calling on the consultants and experts who either were involved in the original architecture or need to be involved to move the project forward. At MCA the predesign phase was vital to the programming and conceptual development that followed. For example, point loading the beams required penetrating the waterproof membrane that the architect in conjunction with the roofing consultant had already specified. Communicating with those team members was essential before we could proceed.

Understanding What's Beneath You

The term *beneath* in this case is figurative as well as literal because there are variables such as codes, historical guidelines, and Homeowners Association (HOA) rules that are not physical but have as much relevance as the actual structure. If any one piece doesn't fit with the others, the constraints and, consequently the design of the project, could change, sometimes quite dramatically. For example, if residential clients find out that they have to spend an additional $25,000 or more to comply with building codes, they might cancel the project. Or, if additional costs are required to re-enforce the structure of a roof, a client might choose to go with a less expensive option, causing the scope of the project to shrink considerably.

Getting to this information in the beginning, and as inexpensively as possible, is critical. Be up-front early on with your clients so they are aware of unexpected hidden costs that could

Karla Considers the Options

Lisa Lee Benjamin and I encountered several surprises on top of an old concrete building with massive 12-inch (30-cm) thick walls, large exposed concrete beams running both directions across the ceiling, and a series of substantial concrete columns in the middle of the floor plan.

We anticipated that the concrete slab roof would be able to hold a lot of weight since the building was an old flour mill but chose to consult a structural engineer before proceeding. In addition to adding new decks, planters, shade structure, and vegetable beds, the client also wanted to keep an existing spa. Obstacles like limiting load factors would not only inform the overall design but also define it due to cost measures.

Along with the contractor, we convinced the client, who was not eager to spend the several hundred dollars, to devote funds to a structural analysis. The findings were unexpected and presented a challenge to what followed. Through analysis of existing drawings, x-rays of the concrete, and studies of exposed concrete and rebar where a skylight had been cut out by the previous owners, the engineer determined the concrete would not hold up to any more weight than the anticipated snow load, and she was unwilling to allow any additional weight other than the snow load factor.

The client was baffled since an old wood deck already straddled half of the roof with a large hot tub strategically placed above the line of columns. The wood decking was dried out, cupping, and splintered, and in desperate need of replacement. To make matters worse, the deck framing system sat on bricks and wood shims directly on the membrane, a huge risk to damaging the membrane. The previous occupant had obviously not contacted an engineer for help. To add to all this, membrane leaks caused water to seep through the concrete decking into the owner's loft.

Not only would the engineer not approve any work on the existing deck, she also strongly urged the removal of the deck and spa. The 100-year-old roof was designed for 30 pounds of snow load per square foot (146 kg per sq m) and no more, and the existing decking exceeded the load factors deemed to be safe, as did the spa.

However, there was room for improvement and the engineer recommended two options of supplemental structure to enhance the load factors. The first entailed building a steel frame to hold planters. The frame would hang off the parapet walls and be cantilevered out a few feet. The second option was to essentially point load or put the entire load on the structural beams with a steel framing system, much like the framing system under a traditional deck. We had to consider either of these options to have any green at all, like an intensive garden with trees to screen and vegetables to eat. The framing system would then act like a platform supported by the underlying beams and spanning the area between the beams, and we could then construct decking and planters on top of the platform.

These options ranged from $25,000 to $75,000, quite a bit of money beyond the normal costs associated with installing a landscape. Certainly, the owner did not anticipate any of this when they purchased the loft with its spectacular roof offering 360-degree views of the city, and it was a lesson for us in the role of structural analysis. We ultimately went from a full-scale garden plan with intensive beds full of apple trees and sweet peas to a reduced plan of lightweight plants and an extensive green roof. ∎

influence the project. They also need to understand that a budget is not just about substrate and plants. There are always those people who want what they want and are willing to pay for it. Then there are others who want, for example, to filter storm water to comply with incentive programs, but don't want to cover the added expense. Better to have that information from the start.

On the literal level, the critical difference between ground landscapes and green roofs or roof gardens is the structure or the built object on which the live material rests. At ground level, you only have to deal with the soil under your feet, but on a roof, whether that of a garage or a thirty-story building, a thorough analysis is required to determine whether that roof can handle the extra weight and how much it can handle. This information is a vital cost of compliance, the amount of money it takes to comply with regulations or rules, that must be determined before you and your clients can begin.

Acquiring this data for a recently constructed building may involve nothing more than a phone call to the structural engineer, but under most circumstances ascertaining this pertinent information requires a structural analysis from a structural engineer. Older structures may necessitate a much more in-depth process of testing such as examining concrete core samples from a concrete roof deck, or sheer tests of load-bearing walls. It's a good idea to forewarn a client that a more detailed analysis may be necessary and that any additional expenditure for what are essentially building x-rays could reveal crucial technical details about the structure that will save money in the long run.

A deer made of willow sticks does not exceed the load factors for this green roof in Silverthorne, Colorado.

DETERMINING LOAD FACTORS

The National Roofing Contractors Association defines structural load as a deflection or any displacement in a body from its static position or from an established direction or plane, because of forces acting on the body. A structural analysis determines load factors and the general structural integrity of a building. Several categories of load are pertinent here.

Dead loads are constant or permanent loads on a roof, like the structure itself or the existing walls and mechanicals. Live loads, also referred to as imposed loads, are temporary or moveable, and include people, planters, and pots. Environmental loads are defined by climatic conditions like wind, snow, seismic activity, and ponding. For example, local building codes may require green roofs to resist anticipated wind loads caused by the force of the wind as it hits the roof, or wind sheers created by parapet walls or the location of the building.

Wind loads vary based on geographical locale. Winds can be mitigated by the height of the parapet wall. Vegetation-free zones or borders of rock ballast at the base of parapet walls are another way to counter high winds. Wind is also a factor during the construction phase when materials like lightweight insulation can easily blow away. In high wind areas, trees or tall shrubs need to be tethered or staked to prevent them from blowing over.

In cold climates, the amount of snowfall must be calculated into the load factors, while seismic loads are determined by the anticipated parameters of an earthquake or by gravity waves of a tsunami. Ponding loads are associated with water retention on a roof, and in most circumstances, clogged drains are the culprits, but sometimes rooftops are intentionally designed to pond to create a habitat for birds, amphibians, or wetland ecosystems. Identifying all or any combination of these load factors will inform how to proceed.

The flour mill example (see box) illustrates that age is a critical variable in calculating load factors. Just because a building was built a hundred years ago doesn't mean it was built stronger. What may look like a concrete bunker won't necessarily have a roof that can support extra weight.

Likewise, new buildings may come with similar considerations. Often they are built to carry only the load specified in the original design, so if the architect did not envision a green roof on top, very likely the load factors won't accommodate one. In such cases, it is necessary to utilize structural beams and parapet walls for places to add more weight.

One simple way to estimate how load factors translate into the depth of a substrate is to use this formula: 1 inch (25 mm) of substrate weighs approximately 7 to 8 pounds per square foot (34–39 kg per sq m). The minimum depth for healthy plant communities is 3 to 4 inches (75–100 mm). Thus, to support a 3-inch (75-mm) substrate, a roof would need to be able to handle a minimum of 21 pounds per square foot (102 kg per sq m).

Make sure to ask the engineer how much weight could be added to the beams and how close to the exterior or parapet walls of the building. These are places where soil can be mounded or planters and pots with much deeper substrate can be placed. There is always the more costly option of building additional structure to hold more weight to

A roof designed for amphibians at the headquarters of Gemperle AG, Sins, Switzerland, aims to provide food for lapwings.

Four questions for

Tom Moe,

structural engineer at Martin/Martin in Denver, Colorado, about structural considerations.

1. Why is it important to calculate structural loads?

The loads from the green roof have to be taken down through the structure to the foundations just like the other permanent and transient loads of the building. In terms of the design, it is important to assure that the structure and foundations have the capacity to carry all the loads that the building will see during its lifetime. It is also necessary to understand what type of green roof system will be used to account for the loads to the structure.

2. Can you give some examples of the difference in weight of various soils and substrates?

Generally, soil weight of earth fill is figured at 120 pounds per cubic foot (1920 kg per cu m). That is, a 1-foot (300-mm) depth of soil weighs 120 pounds per cubic foot. If the material is loosely packed, its could be calculated at 90 to 110 pounds per cubic foot (1440–1760 kg per cu m), but over time the soil will compact and more could be added, thus bringing the weight up to 120 pounds per cubic foot. The weight of the roofing system excluding beams and girders and assuming no ballast is calculated at 20 to 30 pounds per cubic foot (320–460 kg per cu m) in a conventional building without a green roof.

3. What is the difference between saturated and dry weights?

A saturated weight assumes that water fills the voids between the solid granules, thus displacing the air and causing the weight to increase. For instance, a sand/gravel loose mix would be approximately 90 to 105 pounds per cubit foot dry (1440–1680 kg per cu m) and 115 to 120 pounds per cubit foot (1840–1920 kg per cu m) wet.

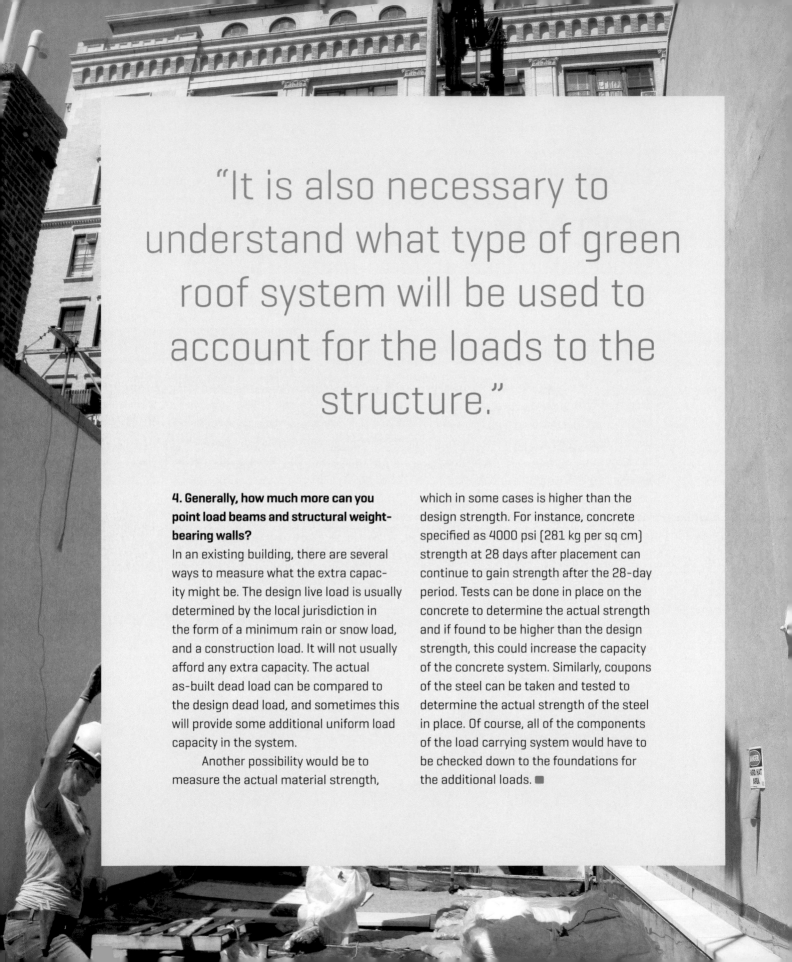

"It is also necessary to understand what type of green roof system will be used to account for the loads to the structure."

4. Generally, how much more can you point load beams and structural weight-bearing walls?

In an existing building, there are several ways to measure what the extra capacity might be. The design live load is usually determined by the local jurisdiction in the form of a minimum rain or snow load, and a construction load. It will not usually afford any extra capacity. The actual as-built dead load can be compared to the design dead load, and sometimes this will provide some additional uniform load capacity in the system.

Another possibility would be to measure the actual material strength, which in some cases is higher than the design strength. For instance, concrete specified as 4000 psi (281 kg per sq cm) strength at 28 days after placement can continue to gain strength after the 28-day period. Tests can be done in place on the concrete to determine the actual strength and if found to be higher than the design strength, this could increase the capacity of the concrete system. Similarly, coupons of the steel can be taken and tested to determine the actual strength of the steel in place. Of course, all of the components of the load carrying system would have to be checked down to the foundations for the additional loads. ■

support decking, spas, and planters.

Once the load factors are identified, utilize the information to plan the design around them because such restraints are parameters that inform and guide the design. At the flour mill, these kinds of restrictions forced us to go from a more complicated program for a dining area sheltered by an elegant, vine-covered trellis surrounded by 2-foot (60-cm) deep beds overflowing with nasturtiums interspersed with redbud and magnolia trees to a refinished deck with lightweight, aluminum planters around the parapet walls filled with upright junipers and prairie grasses.

ROOF ASSEMBLY

Because landscape architects are not trained in the roofing trade, whether they are working with an existing building or new construction, they will likely need a consultant to negotiate what those in the trade call the black arts, or roof assembly. The waterproof membrane and the extra layers on top of it are essential components of a roof assembly that someone needs to comprehend fully.

Three types of roof assemblies are known and, depending on where the insulation is placed, they are referred to as conventional, protected membrane, and cold or vented. Simply defined, a roof assembly is the layers that shed water off of (hydrodynamic) a roof or waterproof (hydrostatic) it. The assembly includes the roof deck, insulation, waterproof membrane, base flashing, counter flashing, air barrier, vapor retarder and, in the case of green roofs, root barriers.

The roof deck is the structural deck above the interior ceiling that normally

Spray foam membrane application by HB Urethane Roofing on rooftop at Heron's Head EcoCenter, San Francisco.

Flashing to protect barn wood fascia on residential roof in Steamboat Springs, Colorado.

slopes towards drains in the roof deck, and insulation is the thermal material added to roofs to reduce the flow of heat and cooling in the interior environment.

Waterproof membranes come loose-laid and bonded. Several different types exist: hot applied rubberized asphalt, thermoplastic polyvinyl chloride (PVC), thermoplastic polyolefin (TPO), modified bitumen, elastomeric ethylene propylene diene monomer (EPDM), cold fluid applied waterproofing, spray foam roofing systems, and built-up membranes. These varieties rather than those that shed water are optimal for most green roofs or roof gardens because the presence of plants means that a lot more water will be hanging around to find its way under the membrane.

When the membrane comes to the side of the roof or meets a drain or a vent, extra protection is needed to prevent water from traveling under the membrane. Flashing is the preventative system that seals the edges of the membrane, so that no water gets under the membrane. Flashing details help prevent leaks where the membrane stops, is interrupted, or is most vulnerable to water infiltrating the roof assembly.

Other layers of the roof assembly include air barriers and vapor retarders. These materials prevent or restrict the passage of air and vapor through a roof.

Finally, the root barrier layer is normally a physical barrier that prevents roots from traveling to and compromising the waterproof membrane. If roots grow into the membrane, they can cause it to leak. Some membranes (PVC, TPO, and EPDM) have the chemical capacity to keep the roots from compromising the waterproofing ability. Often

vegetation-free zones are left along the edges of the roof to keep plants away from the sides where their roots might get under the membrane at the point it stops and the flashing starts. At the Kresge Foundation in Troy, Michigan, the native grasses thriving on the roofs were migrating into the vegetation-free zone and making their way to the side of the building in search of water and nutrients. It would only have been a matter of time until their deep roots found the membrane under root barrier fabric if the membrane and subsequent layers had not been installed properly.

Beyond structural testing, existing buildings should be assessed for the state of the waterproof membrane. Several things warrant examination: membrane age and condition, details on the warranties of the membrane to ensure adding live elements will not void the warranty, and possible membrane testing. In its class on waterproofing and drainage, Green Roofs for Healthy Cities, the largest green roof organization in North America, stresses early on considerations like load capacity, wind resistance, fire resistance, accessibility, the system's track record, and how these factors affect design and selection of waterproof membranes.

DEALING WITH MECHANICALS

A roof is neither a blank slate nor an empty lot. Rather, it is a space already inhabited by all sorts of mechanicals and connections such as pipes, vents, and outlets that relate to the technology of interior environmental comfort. The placement of housing for air conditioning or swamp cooling units, and vents or flues for dryers, stoves, or ovens relates

HVAC system incorporated into a green roof in New York City.

Water hookup and irrigation box, Boulder, Colorado.

to the architectural systems of the building. The location of these mechanicals is a given and for the most part cannot be moved, so green roof designers need to figure out the best ways to work around them.

Like heating, ventilating, and air conditioning (HVAC) systems attached to a building on the ground, mechanicals on the roof are eyesores, and it is necessary to determine how they will fit into the roof landscape before designing starts. You cannot, for example, build a deck or place a planter on top of the vent for a dryer. There are, however, great design opportunities here for new construction. The right location of mechanicals can create sun traps that offer warmer areas for tender plants as well as providing protection from wind and sun.

Good design can also intentionally direct the warm air of the dryer vent into a heat collection zone that creates another climatic zone and becomes the perfect spot for a beloved Zone 6 succulent that never makes it through the winter because it is too cold. Shade plants that do not survive in direct light all day might thrive on the north side of the HVAC unit. If vents need to remain open, perhaps there is a way to use pots, benches, or water features for screening.

In the best of all possible worlds, the designer collaborates with the architect early on and intentionally arranges the mechanicals to facilitate certain microclimates or sheltered spaces that enhance the green roof or roof garden opportunities for plants, animals, and humans. For example, placing the mechanicals close to the side of the roof facing the predominant wind makes for a much more comfortable outdoor amenity space. Alternatively, solar panels can be arranged to protect and shade special

host plants for rare insects. These are some of the creative ways to turn those eyesores into solutions.

Irrigation

Another aspect of mechanicals is the location and availability of the water supply that will determine the irrigation design. Think about where the water will come from and make sure there's enough water pressure to run the irrigation system. Along that line, it is critical to figure out where the power is coming from to run the irrigation system and feed the lights, and whether it is adequate.

LEED has now understandably made potable water on green roofs a deduction in their accreditation. This poses a problem because potable water is the only source plumbed into most buildings where sewer lines go out and potable water lines go in. To get water to the roof, especially if it is several stories up, often mandates an internal delivery system. Alternative sources of nonpotable water include rainwater collection or use of reclaimed water (gray water), but these are viable solutions only if the building codes allow for them.

In Portland, where rainwater harvesting is promoted and incorporated into many municipal and residential buildings, internal rainwater lines are used to flush toilets and to re-circulate water for irrigation. Elsewhere, systems exist for collecting water released as a byproduct of running HVAC systems. Kevin Songer, a plant biologist and green roof designer in Florida, has been applying this system to irrigate his green roofs.

A Zurn drain with gravel surround for ease of access and maintenance.

Access doors are handy especially on commercial roofs needing regular mechanical maintenance.

Roof access at the Nueva School in Burlingame, California, can be tricky.

DRAINAGE

Good design starts with the architecture of the roof surface and ensuring that the surface and all the layers pitch toward the drains. Provide adequate clearance and keep all drains free of any debris or substrate that might collect around and clog them. Poorly designed pitches and slopes as well as clogged drains can cause water backing up onto the roof, resulting in unwanted ponding. This can add to the load factors and cause excessive weight and leakage of the membrane.

The practical side of drain placement involves making sure drains are easily accessible not only to deal with excess water but also for routine maintenance checks and cleaning. On the MCA roof, the deck was designed into panels that are small enough to be lifted off to easily access the drains.

Unlike new roofs, existing roofs are limited by the present drainage situation installed when the roof was constructed. The green roof design will have to work around the location of the original drains.

When designing on a new building, work with the mechanical and structural engineers to determine where you want water to go and how you want any excess to be used. With increased technology, it is now possible to design areas of ponding intentionally. Building up substrate or using driftwood can cause the pooling water to create vernal pools, temporary collections of water ideal for insect and amphibians, or permanent wet areas on a roof. Water on the roof does not have to be terrifying: it can actually be beneficial and create valuable habitats for water-loving plants. The roof at Heron's Head

EcoCenter has two vernal pools specifically for shorebird life.

ROOF ACCESS

In the green roof trade, the term *conveyance* is used to define how the contractor will transport the materials to the roof. Figuring out how to get all the plants, substrate, decking, accessories, and other materials up to the roof is not always easy. Determining the best access is a big piece of the predesign process.

Similar to structural reinforcing, access can be another large, hidden cost. It can be as simple and inexpensive as placing a ladder against a suburban residence or as costly and complicated as hiring a crane and securing permits for street closures. A range of options in between includes lifts, soil blower trucks, conveyor belts, dumbwaiters, and even freight elevators if the building management allows usage.

At the Petit Ermitage hotel in Los Angeles, the guest elevators were off limits, so all parts and pieces of the installation had to be lifted to the roof by ropes and pulleys. When installing the roof garden at MCA, the building contractor refused to allow the roof garden crew to work while the building was under the contractor's control—partly due to liability issues and because the contractor was on such a tight schedule that he did not want anyone or anything in his way. Consequently, installation was stalled until five days before the official opening when the building had a temporary certificate of occupancy. All of the steel planter beds were fabricated, waterproofed, loaded, planted, and irrigated off site

Often materials can only be delivered by crane and even this can be difficult in narrow spaces. New York City.

A green roof financed by incentives at One Union Square East, a mixed-use condominium in New York City.

before they were shipped by truck to the museum and craned over the building while utilizing radio contact between the crane operator and the assistant on the other side.

When transporting materials up an elevator or stairs, remember to protect the interior space and furnishings when carrying roofing materials, substrate, and plants. To protect floors, walls, corners, and walkways, cover them with butcher paper, using nonstick tape as necessary to keep it in place. Provide extra, cushioned protection for any corners or walls that could get damaged if large objects bump into them. This practice is common in dense urban areas where roof access is often through a client's office or apartment. Taking these precautions adds a fair amount of time to the installation but saves the cost of cleaning or repair services afterward.

Restrictions and Regulations

HOAs and co-op boards function as extralegal bodies that govern what happens in a residential building when it comes to design and construction. Homeowners as well as property managers make up the body of these groups, and in many situations, they determine what goes on a roof and how it gets there.

HOAs can also prevent the building of shade structures or the adding of planters around the parapet walls because these design moves might change the visual integrity of the original building. Co-op boards often require that a plan for the proposed design be submitted and voted on. In such cases,

allow extra time to prepare the required documentation and presentation before getting approval. Anticipating and planning for this process needs be included in the schedule and budget.

City codes cover what is allowed on a roof, so the local building department is a good first stop for research on what can and cannot be put up there. For example, a code might restrict adding structural components like shade structures and screening walls. Because the MCA building had not received its certificate of occupancy, the design team had to submit pages of structural load documentation to get a permit to install the roof garden. The city wanted to ensure that what was being placed on the roof did not exceed the designated load factors.

City codes can also encompass limitations for historic buildings. Often municipalities do not want to see additions that would interfere with the historic profile of the building. Additional codes outline maximum capacities for occupancy in commercial and public buildings.

INCENTIVES

Some cities and communities have policies that guide the implementation of green roofs or roof gardens, and others that offer incentives for including them in a building design. In Germany, a world leader in the implementation of green roofs, taxes are collected on anticipated stormwater control or usage fees, and owners of impervious roof covers are levied a 100-percent utility surcharge. Thirteen German cities allow a reduction of between 50 and 80 percent of the utility fee for installing a green roof.

Twenty-nine German cities in the 1996 ZVG (Gardening Central Association) survey provide a direct monetary subsidy to developers who use green roofs.

Another type of indirect subsidy allows developers to use green roofs as mitigation for the provision of open space. Chicago requires all projects with residential units to provide new open space or pay an open space impact fee. If a green roof is included in the project, the developer can receive a credit on the impact fee provided the green roof is accessible to the residents of the building or the public.

Copenhagen now requires that all new flat roofs with a 30-degree pitch or less, both private and public, have to be vegetated. If old roofs have to be retrofitted, the building owners may be able to receive public financial support for a green roof. In Switzerland, the cities of Basel, Zürich, and Lucerne mandate that every new flat roof be planted per building code.

In the United States, cities like New York offer property tax abatements for green roofs. The city and county of Annapolis, Maryland, provide up to a $10,000 tax credit in the form of a property tax abatement for people who try to reduce stormwater pollution on their property including green roofs. Incentive grants in Portland pay up to $5 per square foot (0.09 sq m) for new ecoroof projects on industrial, residential, commercial, or mixed-use buildings.

Chicago promotes green buildings through awards, grants, design competitions, and fairs. It provides a series of guides for homeowners renovating or rehabilitating their homes, and expedites the building permit process for approved builders of green buildings. A green roof helps a project qualify for the expedited permitting and possibly a fee waiver, if the project is aiming for a higher level of LEED certification. Since 2004, the Windy City has implemented a policy that requires green roofs and other sustainable measures for projects receiving financial or zonal assistance. This was the first policy in the United States to require private developments to include green roofs.

Elsewhere in the world, Toronto requires green roofs for new construction of over 20,000 square feet (1860 sq m), and in Singapore, the NParks program will fund up to 50 percent of installation costs of green roofs to raise the level of sky rise greenery and enhance the city's image in high activity corridors. In 2011, in a concerted effort to fight the ever-rising urban heat island, Tokyo established "The Tokyo Plan 2000," requiring new buildings greater than 10,760 square feet (1000 sq m) or over 1/4 acre (0.1 ha) to green at least 20 percent of their usable roof space.

Increasingly, independent agencies in different countries have voluntary programs that give points for green roofs. International programs include the U.S. Green Building Council (USGBC), LEED; the Green Building Council of Australia (GBCA), Green Star; the Comprehensive Assessment System for Built Environment Efficiency (CASBEE) in Japan; and the Green Rating for Integrated Habitat Assessment (GRIHA) in India.

DEALING WITH STORM WATER

Because of the decimating effect of pollution on our navigable waterways leading up to the Clean Water Act (CWA), the demand to deal with storm water on site has cities either requiring or giving incentives for using a green roof to filter storm water before it reaches the ground. The CWA, initiated in 1949 and revamped and expanded in the seventies, is monitored by the EPA. It strives to protect American waterways by overseeing surface water quality protection through the management of stormwater runoff. Green infrastructure approaches like green roofs are one method for capturing and filtering storm water to maintain or restore natural hydrologies.

There are also matters of pollution and of overwhelming the stormwater system, which causes floods and stream destruction because the stormwater system tends to concentrate the flow of water. Green roofs are part of the solution because they slow the water from a storm down and filter it of pollutants. In Portland, the city offers $5 per square foot (0.09 sq m) toward green roof construction, which would otherwise need to be paid toward stormwater fees.

To find out more about incentive programs in your area, call your local building department, use search engines on your computer, or visit Greenroofs.com.

SPECIFICATIONS

For years designers and builders in Europe and the United States have relied on the German FLL (Forschungsgesellschaft Landschaftsentwicklung Landschaftsbau)—guidelines for green roof specifications. According to Manfred Köhler, who was with FLL from the beginning and is currently at the Institute of Ecology in Berlin, the FLL was a network of people interested in green

roof technologies. Today the organization has about forty-five working groups, but the green roof group was the first with about fifty members.

Since the late 1990s, the FLL has established guidelines for the design, implementation, and maintenance of green roofs. The codes help to set up green infrastructures in a certified way. The existing guidelines were prepared for specific climate conditions and typical technical solutions. In a global sense, only the basics apply all over the world: the need for an impermeable roof layer under the green roof, wind uplift, root barriers, and the amount of water retention per square foot. Most of the other factors vary all over the world.

The FLL guidelines include substrate composition for different environments, plant communities and soil depths, plant selection, and proper drainage. The guidelines also outline specific tests for determining which waterproofing and root barrier materials resist root growth, and evaluations for the weight and water-holding capacity of substrates. The latest edition is from 2008 and is available to download on their site for a small fee.

The international standards organization, the American Society for Testing and Materials (ASTM), recently put together a green roof task force to establish green roof standards. It is imperative for anyone involved in green roof design to be familiar with these guidelines, because with few exceptions, building products must comply with accepted industry material standards. The ASTM develops and publishes voluntary consensus technical standards for a wide range of materials, products, systems, and services for the construction industry. Although these standards

are voluntary, they provide a framework for the accepted way to build green roofs and add credibility to liability issues.

Charlie Miller, president and founder of Roofmeadow, a green roof design and installation firm in Pennsylvania, has been an active member and participant in developing these green roof standards, and personally authored four of the five standards that ASTM recently published. These standards allow differentiation among similar products, demonstrate specification compliance, and establish accepted thresholds for safety and quality. The methods described establish a basis for comparing fundamental green roof properties such as maximum weight and moisture retention potential, and are designed to measure critical material properties for green roof materials under conditions similar to those encountered in the field.

The American National Standards Institute (ANSI) and the Single Ply Roofing Industry (SPRI), in cooperation with Green Roofs for Healthy Cities (GRHC), have jointly developed three standard practices for vegetative roofing systems. The wind standard provides a method of designing for wind uplift resistance of green roofs, while the fire standard provides a method for establishing external fire resistance for green roofs. The root repellant standard provides guidelines for investigating green roof resistance to root penetration.

Team Building

The next time Mayita Dinos, designer of the roof garden on Petit Ermitage hotel in Los Angeles, creates a roof garden, she is going to put team building and collaboration at the top of her list of

A meeting on the new waterproof membrane at Heron's Head EcoCenter with team members from Habitat Gardens, Evo Catalyst, and Eckman Environmental.

things to do. Looking back on the hotel project, she realizes that not having the right people on board up-front to sort out many of the technical aspects of the project was a real liability. Like many of us, she discovered that the technical considerations on rooftops are far more complicated than those on the ground. The crucial issues for her were how much weight the existing structure would allow, and how she could work around the weight restrictions.

The lesson here is that putting together the right team may be the single most important thing a green roof designer does, and it is never too early to start thinking about the best people to work with for a given project. It takes a team because the various parts of a green roof encompass many disciplines, and it is not unusual to have ten or more people involved before the design process can begin.

For example, during the predesign phase you might require the services of a structural engineer, water mitigation specialist, mechanical engineer, and roofing specialist. The architects of the Los Angeles Museum of the Holocaust (LAMOTH) designed the building for a green roof and then looked for landscape designers with expertise in that area—in this case, coauthors Karla and Lisa. Once we saw the complexity of the plan that included slopes of up to 45 degrees, we called in Charlie Miller of Roofmeadow because he had the most experience designing sloped green roofs. We also contacted John Greenlee, a California horticulturalist specializing in ornamental grasses, who had experience planting grasses on green roofs. Throughout the project, we worked directly with the architects and their consultants including engineers to complete the design.

143

The rolling complex green roof atop the California Academy of Sciences required an enormous amount of coordination and teamwork.

Liability is a major consideration in the design process. When a roof leaks, everyone points to someone else. Because of the overlapping of trades, blame is hard to pinpoint. That is why teamwork and good communication is so important. The roofing contractor does not want to be liable for a shovel or irrigation stake piercing the membrane that the landscape contractor installed. This process requires synergies between design and construction professionals beyond what is typical of traditional building projects.

ROLE CLARIFICATION

On the ground, it is obvious where the building starts and stops. Although there will be questions about where to source water and power, the delineations between the trades is drawn most often between structure and dirt. The segue between building and live material on a green roof installation is often less clear because you are adding a living layer to inert steel, concrete, or wood. In addition, the system is highly engineered even if it mimics ground ecological functions. This unlikely combination of technically engineered material coupled with the chaos of nature played out by soil, plants, air, water, and sun makes it imperative to clarify the roles that each team member plays before you begin.

Where possible use the same experts who worked on the building in the past. This includes trades like plumbing and electricity. Builders or carpenters who have done work on the structure may know more about its interior workings and consequently be more insightful about making

connections like flush deck transitions between exterior and interior areas. They might also have ideas about things like where to tie into the exterior of a building for a shade trellis.

VISION AND COMMITMENT

Every multifaceted project has to have a leader, and at LAMOTH the principal architect, Hagy Belzberg, assumed that role. He carried the vision along with the project's goals through to completion. Among other things, this meant wrangling with city council, convincing community members, and designing a striking icon within an extremely conservative budget. Moreover, none of this takes into account issues specific to the architecture.

When you establish your team, everyone needs to buy into the mission, or vision, of the project. This requires defining the mission around the design goals of the client. Start with a simple notion like low maintenance or high profile, and move to more complex conceptual ideas like "transforming the experience of the Holocaust." Similar to a mission statement a clear simple statement is a helpful tool that clarifies your goals in the beginning and can be revisited when challenges arise.

To elucidate the mission, start with word triggers that clients articulate when speaking of their values about the project. For LAMOTH, memory, movement, monument, and freedom were powerful initiators. These words generated images that gradually moved into a grander picture of providing people an opportunity to experience a physical transformation as they entered the

building through a garden of grasses silhouetted by light moving in the wind into the darkness of the exhibit space.

COMMUNICATION, COMPETENCY, AND TRUST

Set up a communication strategy and a communication protocol sooner than later. A good first step is establishing a central location for agendas, meeting notes, ideas, sketches, drawings, budgets, lists, Auto CAD documents, and photos. A blog is a great way to go because it is something all team members—even those in different parts of the country or world—can access anytime and anywhere.

For LAMOTH a blog was used to post all communication about the roof design and to keep the team current on particular pieces of the project. In addition, weekly conference calls with both the architect and general contractor kept everyone on track. Communication is the key to a successful team effort.

7

Site Analysis

A field of black-eyed Susans now covers this green roof designed by Karla Dakin.

Site analysis is one of the first steps in determining the requirements for a green roof or roof garden. Load factors, increased sun, wind and element exposure, and accessibility—all parts of site analysis—will set parameters for design and construction.

Integrating the Ecology

There are two approaches to site analysis: the first comes from an ecological design perspective and the second from a strictly design viewpoint. They can be used separately or in combination and are both important and applicable depending on a project's budget, schedule, and location.

Ian McHarg, an educator and landscape architect in the 1960s, did groundbreaking work in his approach to site analysis by incorporating ecological reference points as the drivers behind the design rather than following the accepted, more formal design perspective approach. In his book, *Design by Nature*, he encouraged looking at native plants, the natural hydrology, local weather patterns, and the native soils as a critical part of design analysis. This systematic set of ecological observations takes into account climate, geology, hydrology, soils, vegetation, and wildlife.

What may seem unusual about using McHarg as a reference for site analysis on roofs is that he started with the perspective of how humans might fit into a natural scenario. But with green roofs, cities are the starting point

and finding ways to integrate or allow nature back into these highly developed, constructed spaces is the mission. What we learn from McHarg is the importance of looking at rooftop landscapes as a part of a whole ecological system, not separate from the ground but rather as an extension of it many stories up. By doing so, we can create landscapes that are true integrations of natural and human environments.

Even though planting on roofs has many distinguishing factors, elements of this approach to site analysis take in the complete ecological picture. This whole system method was defined by Harvard professor Charles Waldheim and incorporates McHarg's theories with contemporary trends in green roof design.

Designer Kate Ancaya was inspired by Waldheim when she retrofitted a green roof for the Hamilton County Health Department Building in Chattanooga, Tennessee. The project was slated to be just a typical sedum extensive roof until Ancaya took note of the rolling mounds created by the Sequatchie River in the adjacent Cooper State Forest and crafted a roof garden meant to mimic the local topography and meandering river. After careful site analysis when she determined the load capacity of the existing roof, she introduced an expanded plant list and point loaded some areas to create green mounds similar to the ones she observed several stories below.

It is critical to become familiar with the natural surroundings to bring the ideas of conservation and ecology to the urban core, and to create landscapes that Anne Whiston Sprin, a landscape theorist who worked with McHarg, calls urban ecological design. The High Line, where considerable attention was

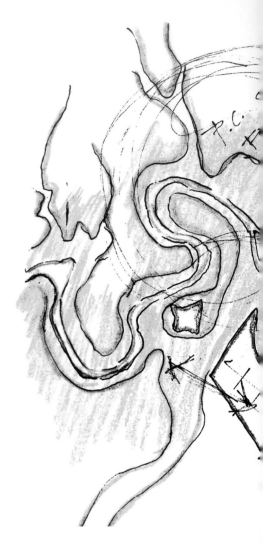

TOP A rough hand sketch illustrates the concept of topography, which inspired a green roof design by Kate Ancaya of Living Roofs.

BOTTOM A residential roof, designed by Mickey Muennig south of Carmel, California, blends into the natural environment.

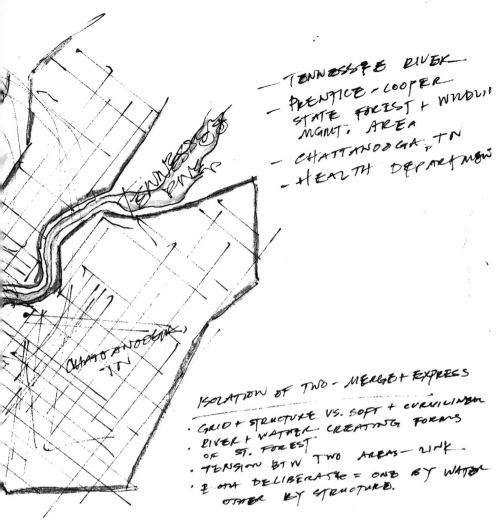

— TENNESSEE RIVER
— PRENTICE-COOPER STATE FOREST + WNDLII MGMT. AREA
— CHATTANOOGA, TN
— HEALTH DEPARTMENT

ISOLATION OF TWO - MERGE + EXPRESS
· GRID + STRUCTURE VS. SOFT + CURVILINEAR
· RIVER + WATER CREATING FORMS OF ST. FOREST
· TENSION BTW TWO AREAS — LINK.
· EOTA DELIBERATE = ONE BY WATER OTHER BY STRUCTURE.

paid to bringing in native plants, illustrates this concept. Opened in June of 2011 the High Line has a plant palette that features native shrubs and trees to create a wild, natural look on part of the elevated park.

Often designers do not have the opportunity to study the native geology or hydrology because timelines and budgets only permit them to record exactly what is on the roof, views, and access. Site analysis from a purely design perspective utilizing our skills of observation, our intuition, and our basic senses is just as valid and vital as a broader ecological view. In this case, you must observe the site closely and take pictures for further analysis back in the office. Be sure and take measurements of things that do not appear on the architectural plans, like the location of drains or gas lines.

Preliminary Planning

McHarg's students dubbed his ecological inventory the *layer cake*, and the following six factors comprise the steps, or layers, for an ecologically based roof site analysis: climate, geology, soils, hydrology, flora and fauna, social and cultural context.

CLIMATE

Weather plays a more prominent role on the roof than on the ground because rooftops are much more exposed to the extremes of normal weather, which has a direct effect on the design plan and the people who use the resulting garden. If it is windy on the ground, it will be windier on the roof. The same could be said for

Sea cliffs in Montara, California, dominate the landscape, suggesting a particular plant community (exposed maritime conditions) and color scheme (gray to rusty orange) for naturalistic green roofs in the area.

temperature extremes. Weather conditions like wind, snow, hail, tornados, and earthquakes all need to be considered.

The climate in Los Angeles figured heavily into the design of LAMOTH and created some tension during construction. Early site analysis revealed the rainy season generally runs from January to March and the city experiences a unique climatic phenomenon known as June gloom when temperatures remain cool due to the marine layer and hot inland temperatures. The planting plan and plant installation for the roof garden was determined with this information in mind, and the climatic knowledge led to plant choices pulled from similar climatic regions. With the help of grass specialist John Greenlee, the project's unique palette included *Lygeum spartum*, a cool season grass that hails from a similar Mediterranean climate of coastal Spain as well as *Bouteloua gracilis*, the underutilized western native blue grama grass whose range stretches from the Rockies to the West Coast.

Greenlee's instructions clearly stated the ideal time to plant was April through late May, factoring in June gloom. However, the roof was not ready to plant until late June. By then the June gloom had passed; the skies were clear, and the weather was very hot. The contractor proceeded to plant although the temperature reached 90 degrees Fahrenheit (32° Celsius), and many of the *Lygeum spartum* plugs that grow best in spring and fall failed to thrive in the heat. Once they were replanted in the fall, they thrived in the cooler weather and established well over the winter.

Optimally, weather, climate observations, and prescribed guidelines will be followed to ensure roof success. However, when building schedules shift,

designers need to be prepared with documentation of why these choices and schedules were made, and respond and follow up appropriately. If all else fails, it is less efficient but possible to correct these issues during maintenance.

Specific climates, microclimates, and general weather patterns will also determine the possibilities and limitations for plant and animal life. In Steamboat Springs, Colorado, winters are long, springs and falls are short, and summers are relatively hot and dry. In addition to experiencing these extreme temperature changes, it is among the snowiest places in the Northern Hemisphere. For planting purposes, Steamboat Springs is located in United States Department of Agriculture (USDA) cold hardiness zone 4a, which means the average annual lowest temperature dips below -30 degrees Fahrenheit (-34° Celsius).

These conditions are exaggerated on a rooftop. In Steamboat Springs on a south-facing roof that gets plenty of sun, is sheltered from the wind, and is insulated below, a small microclimate can be created that might allow some plants rated zone 5 to survive. The climate on the roof differs from that on the ground and can be a zone or two warmer, allowing for a wider selection of plants. In a place where plant choices are so limited, one zone makes a big difference.

It is also critical to look at the duration of the rainy and dry seasons in the region. Is the spring rainy season from April until June or February through March? This information in useful to determine planting time and will affect irrigation requirements. For example, Portland, Oregon, has a ninety-day dry season in the summer with no rain. Sean Hogan, horticulturist and

In the heat of summer, drought-tolerant blue grama grass produces horizontally held seed heads.

A native sea thrift thrives on this green roof made of local granite selected to mimic regional ecologies in Cornwall, England.

The city skyline with myriad colors and shapes can be another reference for site analysis.

owner of Cistis Nursery, considered this when he designed his roof with natives and climate appropriate succulents and cactus. They could tolerate the wet autumn, winter, and spring as well as the dry summer if given a small supplement of ½ inch (13 mm) of water every thirty days.

GEOLOGY

The second layer in this analysis cake is the regional geology. At first pass, we may only see a mass of buildings surrounding a specific site; nothing might jump out at us like a natural landmark or mountain range to let us know where we are. On closer inspection and from a geographical, geological, and historical view, the site may be situated on a delta, an old seabed, or in a river valley.

It may seem strange to start with the deep bedrock when our intention is to build in the sky, but it is these subterranean layers that provide the foundation for understanding all the other layers to follow. Depending on your location, the bedrock and strata can be volcanic, metamorphic, or sedimentary.

For the Haslam roof in Sennen, Cornwall, England, the native granite bedrock was used to determine the roof geology and topography, and answer the client's request for a seamless transition between the roof and ground landscape. The substrate was made of pulverized granite and several other ingredients from the local quarry and surrounding area. This geologic base informed the selection of the roof flora and fauna just as the surrounding granite cliffs inform their surrounding ecology. Pink sea thrifts, found in the native plant

communities, are now thriving in abundance on the roof and this is a direct result of close observation of the local geology.

SOILS

An analysis of the first layer of rock or other local geological patterns points to the native soils and aggregates that might make up the substrates. On a river delta or valley, a mixture of sedimentary rock, sands, silts, gravels, and possible clay soils may be readily available or buried deep under the tarmac/asphalt. The native soils also provide information about the minerals and micronutrients that suggest the basis for what plant life and other life the roof garden will be able to support.

In situations where access to the conditions is no longer available, detailed soil data can be obtained from sources like the Natural Resource Conversation Service (NRCS), which provides information on exactly what is beneath a given site. It does this by performing soil tests on site or by researching past soil tests used for engineering purposes during previous construction which the architect or contractor may have on hand. In urban areas, this can be an interesting treasure hunt as the soil has been often been altered from its native state or imported.

At Heron's Head Park located on San Francisco Bay just south of the city, the soil is built from the trash and debris of a reclaimed landfill, which posed an interesting challenge for soil analysis when trying to determine what type of substrate to use. In this case, a technical substrate mixed further down the peninsula and a simple pumice aggregate were chosen for the EcoCenter roof. One of the project goals was to provide an attractive habitat for native birds, coastal annuals, and perennials. Since there were no native soils on site, we did our best to mimic conditions and fertility levels of native soils specific to that region of the Bay.

The urban geology of the landfill also fed creative decisions in the parapet design, where abstract patterns of recycled materials such as pipes, beautiful old marbles, and brick rubble reference the recent history of the landfill. This layer, so much deeper than simple site and soil observations, establishes the design in an artful, metaphorical way within the geographical and historical context.

HYDROLOGY

Water is the most precious resource on this planet and one that often requires a larger perspective to design responsibly within our water limitations. Knowing how much water is received in the form of rain, sleet, and snow per year will often guide the roof requirements regarding stormwater mitigation and irrigation, and provide information about what plants, if any, will survive on the roof without irrigation. The amount will vary depending on locale because coastal locations or proximity to a large body of water can influence weather patterns, humidity levels, and annual precipitation rates. In some cases rain calculators and sensors, which can be purchased at the local irrigation supply store, will help determine the exact numbers at a specific site. Basic rates are also readily available on the Internet by region, but these are only general guidelines

Unused and waste building materials form the gabion parapet at Heron's Head EcoCenter, San Francisco.

A mountain meadow provides clues for what will work on nearby rooftops. Steamboat Springs, Colorado.

because other uncalculated sources of water have an effect as well.

Some sites may have seasonal coastal or river fog, inversions which produce heavy condensation as well as large amounts of morning dew that can be collected and used. These often overlooked sources of moisture and water can make a difference in a design. Kevin Songer, a green roof designer at Metro Verde, in Florida, has been using his permaculture background to look at new ways of capturing water from dew on green roofs, an approach that adds another layer to our basic water availability.

Water can also be collected from rooftop HVAC systems. The hotter it gets, the more water these systems give off, and one industrious homeowner in Detroit hooked up a plastic pipe to his air conditioning unit and ran it straight into planters overflowing with vegetables. When one planter got drenched, he moved the pipe onto a board that carried it to another planter nearby. The next logical step would be to set up a cistern to collect and store the water from the unit.

The watershed reveals information about a site and region's capacity during large storm events, which in turn factors into how a green roof or roof garden will need to function in relation to stormwater mitigation. It is then possible to increase or decrease the speed at which the roof releases water in accordance with these findings. Tom Liptan and Portland's stormwater team have installed several stormwater data collectors at various drains on green roofs to demonstrate how efficient they were at water detention and to test whether they were meeting requirements set by the city.

FLORA AND FAUNA

With climate, geology, soil, and hydrology considerations factored in, it is time to examine how those items affect the vegetal layer, and determine what flora and fauna existed historically, exist now, and are possible in the future. The range of plant choices also expands as we pull from similar climates globally to create palettes that may not be found on the ground landscape. The plants growing in conditions around the world that are similar to yours are referred to as climate appropriate plants, and they will thrive in your region although they are not native.

Botanic gardens and horticulturalists bring plants from similar climates back to their own gardens, subject them to research and tests, like whether they are invasive or not, and then encourage them in the nursery trade. Designers also can gather information about plant choices simply from observing what is growing and thriving locally, even if it is just the surrounding street weeds.

In his study of native spiders in Switzerland, Stephan Brenneisen illustrates how analysis of existing flora and fauna on the ground can lead to intended consequences on the roof. In an inventory along several railways, he found 154 species, 2 of which had never been found before and 40 of which were noted for being quite rare. By imitating what he witnessed on the ground level and mirroring the substrates and plant material, he was able to create a spider habitat on the roof, which in turn helped support richer ecological communities on the green roof overall.

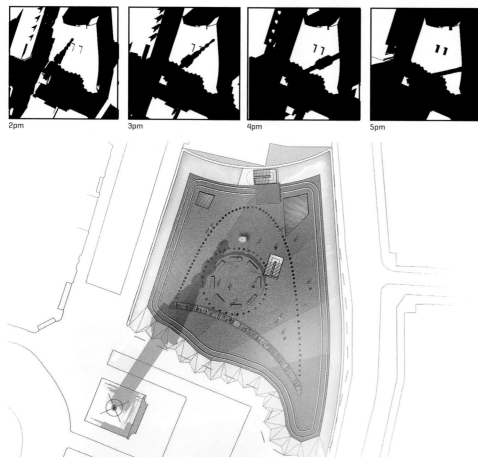

2pm   3pm   4pm   5pm

Sundial design for the roof of the Monument Building in London, by Make Architects.

SOCIAL AND CULTURAL CONTEXT

Green roofs are by their nature an integral part or derivative of a social and cultural context, and the final preliminary design layer examines what is happening in and around the potential site regarding humans and social interaction. By examining the iconography and cultural make of a neighborhood, designers can get ideas of how they may or may not want to design a green roof.

Similar to animals in an ecosystem, people have patterns and habits as well as beliefs and experiences that inform how they move through and use a space. Let's go back to LAMOTH, which is set in the heart of the highly used Pan Pacific Park. Before the project began, observations were recorded about park usage, circulation, community needs, and what would integrate best with the existing environment. This data translated into conceptual ideas that the building be sinuous with the park and be accessible during park hours. The roof defined the building's presence and became accessible to and from the ground on the east and west sides. It was imperative that the roof garden feel connected to the park, yet elevated above it. Cacti were planted strategically to reinforce the boundaries of the parapet walls and to handle building security; cameras were mounted on the roof in specific locations and a guard put on staff.

Social and historical context also played a decisive role in determining the green roof design of the Monument Building by Make Architects in London. The plans called for an accessible green roof garden to be located on top of a new building being erected in the heart of Monument Square. From an analysis standpoint, the Monument landmark was an inescapable presence, and it was important that it be respected and the historical context be integrated into the design. The concept of a sundial motif for the green roof utilizes the shadow of the Monument to tell time on the green roof, highlighting the landmark and encouraging human interaction with the sundial because the roof is accessible. The planting scheme plays into the sundial design by illustrating the time with different species.

These examples illustrate the capability of green roofs to interact with the existing culture, skylines, and ecologies. By taking the time to become familiar with a place and its history, a designer will find that designing and creating a successful roof garden project become easier.

Observation and Research

Observation and research are part of any site analysis whether you approach it from an ecological or solely design perspective. The first and most essential question for you and your client is, What do you want the roof to do for you? Do you want to reduce stormwater runoff, or does the roof need to provide a sanctuary for rest and relaxation? Will people inhabit the roof? Is this a green roof or roof garden or both? Do you want to grow food on the roof? The answers serve as a guide for observing, collecting, and analyzing the considerable data for a particular site.

When it comes to observation, there is no substitute for an on-site visit. Being there in person allows you to feel the wind, foresee limitations, notice opportunities, and think about what type of roof garden is most appropriate.

OPPOSITE Aerial view of the Los Angeles Museum of the Holocaust shows interaction with surrounding Pan Pacific Park.

WIND

Paying attention to wind will significantly influence your design and can make the difference between a successful sanctuary and a dead space that no one utilizes. Depending on the rooftop, the wind may sheet across from the west, or swirl around and eddy as it bounces off an elevator tower or high parapet. Generally speaking, the higher you go, the more intense the wind patterns and, unlike on the ground, wind responds to the urban landscape by creating canyons and gullies which create spins, twists, and intensities that don't occur down below. It is important to note the direction and force of the wind, especially when designing amenity spaces. No one enjoys Sunday brunch when napkins start blowing around.

SUN

Sun is another crucial feature. Rooftops are often fully exposed to sun with elements like air conditioning units and parapet walls providing the only shade. The sun is also capable of reflecting off glazing and even burning plants as roof temperatures in cities from Chicago to London can reach above 115 degrees Fahrenheit (46° Celsius). These high temperatures normally make it entirely too hot for any residents, human or nonhuman, but the presence of plants on a roof lowers the ambient temperature considerably, mitigating heat island effect.

Even in situations that are more temperate, sun is a major factor, and paving choices, plant selections, and design elements need to be chosen accordingly. It would not make sense

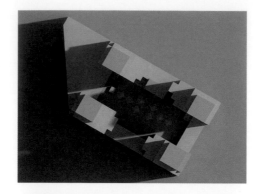

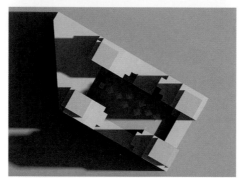

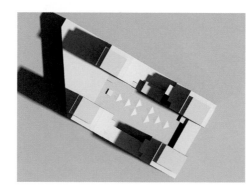

Sun studies by designer Amy Falder of New York Green Roofs show the sun and shadows throughout the day at One Union Square East in New York City.

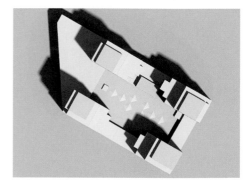

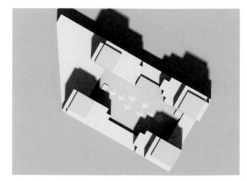

Four questions for

Dusty Gedge,

researcher, green roof activist, and co-author of Small Green Roofs: Low-Tech Options for Greener Living, about site analysis.

---

1. Where do you start when you come to analyze a site?

That's a big question and the answer starts with several more questions, What species are we looking to facilitate on the roof? What habitats are we trying to replicate? Are there constraints such as loads, waterproofing, and other architectural issues? In addition, because the roof of a single building will have varying demands on it, we tend to aim for the more garden-esque lower down and move towards more naturalistic and biodiverse roofs the higher up we go.

2. How do you incorporate the larger context of an entire city into your approach?

On a city scale, the design issues are best dealt with at a policy level. This requires clear guidelines on what a city desires from a green roof to ensure that there has been design input and not just a speci-fication, that is, an off-the-shelf solu-tion. Some attention to biodiversity is important because roof gardens should have a certain percentage of native plants as well as a particular percentage of plants of known value to wildlife. On extensive green roofs, the plants should relate to things like local and regional dry grasslands.

3. Which environmental factors do you take most seriously and why?

The creation of dry grassland green roofs for biodiversity should ensure good water storage and thermal performance (including urban heat island effect). Four- to six-inch (100- to 150-mm) green roofs will create a reasonable replication of dry grassland and this maximizes the green roof for all the other benefits.

4. How do you see the role of planned and existing mechanicals affecting site anal-ysis and big picture thinking?

Now this is an interesting question and one green roof people have been slow to grasp. Use of air conditioners, photovolta-ics, and solar thermals should be part of the design of green roofs. They can act as shading mechanisms and wind breaks. ■

A variety of sedums on one roof at the Kortright Centre for Conservation, Ontario, Canada, designed by Terry McGlade of Gardens in the Sky.

to choose black slate tile for a walkway or patio unless the space was only used in the evening. Similarly, it would be unwise to plant hostas for your bold foliage statements in the bright hot sun when a broad, cool-colored agave, white gravel, and some kind of sunshade make more sense.

The opposite situation involves rooftops located in a well of tall buildings where they suffer from a lack of sunlight. In this case, sun-loving plants will not thrive and the plant palette should be composed of ferns, anemones, and hostas. Site visits allow the designer to notice exactly what direction the wind comes from as well as when the sun is present on the roof and how the exposure will affect the overall design. You can also look for opportunities for microclimates on the sides of the structure out of the hot sun.

LOAD

While looking at a roof site also consider how the parts of the roof interact with each other. Is there a stairwell that rises above the roof slab? Is it in the middle or on the side of the floor plan? Are there parapet walls? How tall are they? Can you see beams in the slab or are they hidden?

This information will help to determine where it will be possible to mound substrate, plant trees, or build outdoor elements. Although observation will give you a feeling for a roof's constructed capabilities, it is not meant to be a substitute for structural analysis from an engineer.

Site Analysis in Action

To get a better understanding of the key areas involved in site analysis and their role throughout the design and life of a green roof, experts Terry McGlade and Emilio Ancaya agreed to walk us through two of their projects.

TERRY MCGLADE, TORONTO, ONTARIO

Green roof expert Terry McGlade has designed some of Canada's largest and most complex green roofing projects. One building, part of the Kortright Centre for Conservation, was conceived originally as a medical/rescue animal facility. It was constructed in 2003, early in North American green roof history, and it is interesting to see how the team approached site analysis initially and then was able to revisit and redesign the roof later. This project had many site-specific challenges that provide insight into the necessity for taking this stage of rooftop garden design very seriously.

Site Specifics
The project is located on 200 acres (81 ha) of forested land in the city of Vaughan in northwestern Toronto, Ontario. There are three separate roofs totaling 13,000 square feet (1200 sq m).

Social and Cultural Considerations
The roofs were meant to be viewed from adjacent office windows as an aesthetic amenity. The building was the first LEED gold building in the area, and in response to the LEED requirements, the client requested the roof have native plants and not be irrigated. At this early stage of research on green roofs, the designer relied on the expertise of a European membrane manufacturer and installer.

Local and Regional Considerations
The building is located in a clearing in the Carolinian forest, classified as an eastern temperate deciduous forest with maples, birch, beech, ash, and oak. However, German green roof standards (FLL) for the substrate were specified, and a substrate with very low organics was installed. The all sedum plant palette followed the substrate, which also worked in Germany. It was hoped that native plants such as Queen Anne's lace (*Daucus carota*), crown vetch (*Coronilla varia*), and goldenrod (*Solidago* spp.) would self-seed, but in the narrow profile with minimal organics, the designer's hopes did not materialize.

Climate Factors and Weather Patterns
The forest and site is located at latitude 43° 48' 36" north and longitude 79° 49' 47" west. This specific area is designated a Canadian climate Zone 5, which is slightly colder and harsher than the neighboring Toronto Zone 6 as it is just outside of the city and is not affected by the heat island effect or by Lake Ontario's temperature moderation.

The area around Toronto has a typical wind pattern from the northwest and most storms move in from this direction. Occasionally there are very high winds and rare tornados, although these are not typical and did not affect the design. Due to a mature forest, the site was protected so wind in this particular case was not a major factor.

The annual average rainfall is around 20 inches (500 mm) per year. Rarely do the major storms deliver more than 2 to 4 inches (50–100 mm) in twenty-four hours. This was clearly not enough to sustain sedums in such a thin substrate profile.

Slope and Existing Conditions

The three roofs have a southeast orientation so individually they did not present conditions with differing exposures and did not dictate the need for different plants for each roof. The only areas that offered microclimates with more shade were those areas very close to the edge of the building, and even then, it was minimal.

There was no visible slope on this roof, just enough to facilitate drainage, and because the project was new construction, existing site conditions on the roof were not relevant.

Structural Load Factors

The load factor was the most important item and trumped all other considerations. The building seemed to be a concrete bunker, and the designers assumed the load factors would accommodate a healthy amount of substrate allowing for a native plant community. However, the structural engineers deemed the load factors to allow only 22 to 24 pounds per square foot (107–117 kg per sq m) above dead and snow loads. This allowed for only 3 inches (75 mm) of substrate.

Because this was one of the first large commercial green roofs in Toronto and knowledge was limited, the design team was bound to use specific products that conformed to the specifications and warranty of the roof membrane. The membrane manufacturer who installed the roof specified a heavier FLL approved substrate with a high concentration of lava rock and very little organics. This limited the plant palette to sedums and chives. Clover was seeded but did not survive the first winter. The initial plant palette was a selection of seven sedum varieties: *Sedum acre*, *S. alba*, *S.* 'Blue Spruce', *S. kamtschaticum*, *S. reflexum*, *S. sexangulare*, and *S. spurium* 'John Creech'.

Site Access and Mechanical Interface

Because it was a new building under construction at the time and was only one story high, access was unlimited. After installation, however, there was no public access as the roofs were only meant to be viewed from office windows and access was limited to maintenance crews. All mechanicals were on the upper roof and did not interfere with either installation or design of the green roofs on the lower roof.

Lessons Learned

In 2009, the building program changed from an animal welfare facility to a sustainable research center with a focus on educational training. The clients wanted the look of the green roof to reflect the new program and asked McGlade to redesign the plantings. In the interim years couch grass (*Elymus* sp.) had infected most of the green roof and a serious weeding was required. The sedums had grown very slowly due to the limitations of the shallow soil depth and several dry summers with no supplemental water.

These results were not uncommon as McGlade found when he came across a research chart by Nigel Dunnett, director of the Green Roof Centre at the University of Sheffield. Dunnett found similar growth patterns of sedums in shallow depths and organized the data into a bell chart of growth that was almost identical to the results on McGlade's roof. Three years with no supplemental nutrients, the plants grew well at first and then slid backwards, shrinking to their original size at the time of planting.

In 2010 all previous substrate was stripped out and replaced with a substrate containing much more organic material that was also lighter, weighing 6 pounds per inch (420 g per sq cm), and allowing another inch or so (25 mm) of depth. This change in substrate allowed for a greater variety of plants that better matched the ecology of the surrounding forest. Sedums were not included in the second design, as McGlade wanted to give the clients a full color tilt, with native species geraniums, liatris, *Panicum virgatum*, a native grass, alliums, and coreopsis.

An automatic spray irrigation system was added, and with fertilization, the plants are establishing slowly but successfully. The maintenance crew is using a compost tea application and organic top dressing to re-energize the substrate to match the plant community requirements. A full understanding of the proposed plant ecology is essential for designing a successful rooftop garden.

EMILIO ANCAYA, ASHEVILLE, NORTH CAROLINA

Emilio Ancaya's roof analysis of a new residential project nestled in the heart of the rolling Appalachian Mountains, benefited from knowledge learned in the last decade. Smaller in scale than McGlade's project, this straightforward residential roof was designed to fit into its surroundings with high design elements that blend the broad ecological view and a pure design perspective.

Concept design, plant list, and photos of completion are illustrated in this design by Kate Ancaya of Living Roofs.

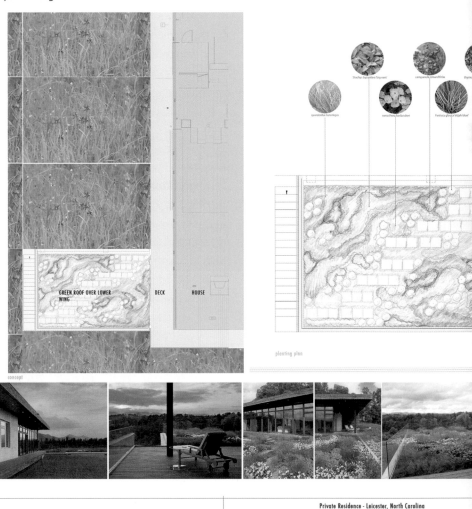

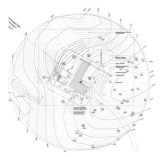

Green Roof - Leicester, North Carolina - Private Residence
Located just outside of Asheville, this contemporary residence demonstrates sensitivity to the surrounding agrarian landscape and features numerous green technologies including a geothermal field for heating and cooling, rainwater catchment for irrigation and toilet fixture use, a tankless hot water heater, and a green roof among others. The green roof is located off the main floor of the home on top of the lower guest wing and reaches out to mountain views. The green roof system chosen is a semi-intensive built up system and is planted with a variety of native and ornamental perennials and grasses to unify it with the surrounding landscape. The green roof is accessible to the owner and guests. Completed May 2009.

Details
locate: **Leicester, North Carolina**
use: **residential home**
square footage: **590 sqft**
green roof type: **semi - intensive**
growing medium depth: **4"-8"**
plant material: **native + ornamental perennials + grasses**
irrigation: **sub-surface drip connected to rainwater cistern**
our role: **green roof design + installation**
project completion: **2009**
project team: **SPG Architects, S.B Coleman Construction**

site plan by SPG Architects

Site Specifics

The site is located in western North Carolina near Asheville at latitude 35° 39′ 15″ north and longitude 82° 40′ 18″ west. The residence sits atop a hill in open pasture. The roof size is 600 square feet (56 sq m) with the measurements being 20 by 30 feet (6 by 9 m) and is 12 feet (3.6 m) off the ground.

Social and Cultural Considerations

The client purchased the property as a retreat from his hectic life in Miami. The house was to be used part-time from June through October for several years and then become a full-time residence. The client, who had grown up in Connecticut, had fond memories of the Berkshire Hills, and this property was reminiscent of that place and he felt as if he was coming home. The site was very critical and informed many of the architectural decisions on the house.

New York's SPG Architects designed the house, and Emilio and Kate Ancaya of Living Roofs, did the green roof design. The general design concept was based on the idea of infinity, highlighted by the idea of an unending connection with the rolling meadows around the house. The finished product was sleek concrete, wood, and glass. In fact, the roof was slated initially to be an infinity pool.

Local and Regional Considerations

The idea of infinite edges, which fall away and blur boundaries between the architecture and the landscape, was a big part of what determined the plant palette. The residence sits in a beautiful agrarian meadow. No official plant survey or inventory was done, but several walks through the surrounding meadows gave the designers plenty of information. Kate Ancaya observed the wind moving through the grass and the pockets of color that were woven together. From that process emerged a deliberately designed meadow on the roof.

At the time they designed this roof, the Ancayas did not look at the soils of the area, but they did use a green roof substrate mixed locally. It was comprised of compost and expanded shale with increased fines, small particulate gravel-like sand, to support native plants in the average depth of 6 inches (150 mm). Many species of fauna, mostly invertebrates that exist in the surrounding landscape, have been found on the roof such as caterpillars, butterflies, grasshoppers, and beetles. These results were expected as the green roof was designed to be a seamless extension of the landscape.

Climate Factors and Weather Patterns

Brief, heavy thunderstorms are typical throughout the summer. March is the wettest month with an average of 4 to 5 inches (100–125 mm). The average rainfall per year is about 40 inches (1000 mm). The site is located in USDA zone 6B. The weather patterns informed many design decisions to create a garden that was optimal during the time the client was in residence but also looked presentable in the rainy and snowy winter months. The wind comes from the southwest, so the site can be windy some days as the house sits on the hilltop with no forest below. The roof faces west and the garden is located on the west side of the house, so it gets full sun by late morning, which lasts the rest of the day.

Slope and Existing Conditions

One large slope has a pitch of ¼ inch per foot (20 mm per m) with some cricketing

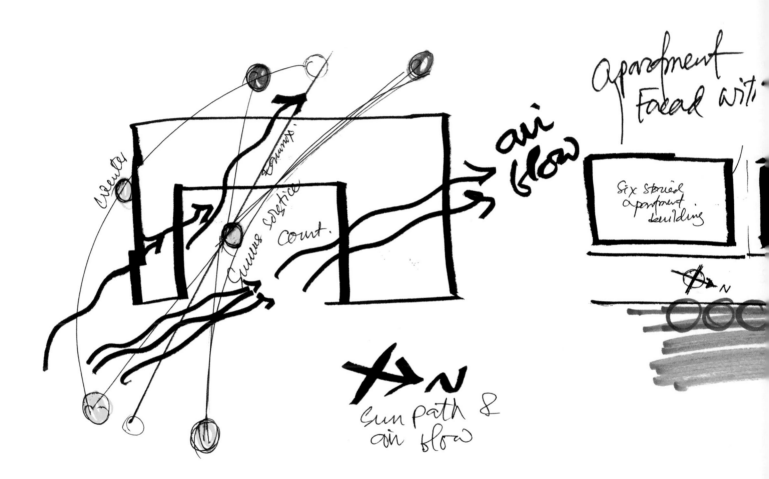

The handwritten labels in the sketch read:
- vents
- solstice (equinox)
- summer solstice
- Court.
- air flow
- ✕→N Sun path & air flow
- Apartment Facade with
- Six storied apartment building
- ✕→N

This rough site plan illustrates various aspects that need to be taken into account with a residential roof in Bangladesh, designed by Shatotto Architects.

in the corners and the drainage falls into two scupper drains. This slope affected the roof and the design as the top of the slope is usually drier than the rest of the roof. With this in mind, the growing medium is roughly 4 to 5 inches (101–125 mm) deep at the top of the slope.

The construction was new, so the only existing conditions related to the land around the site. During construction, several visits to the site were made with special attention placed on looking out from the house and in from the pasture.

Structural Load Factors

The roof is a constructed concrete slab with a load capacity of 65 pounds per square foot (317 kg per sq m). To stay well below that, the average weight of the designed green roof system was 45 pounds per square foot (220 kg per sq m). Some areas were lighter due to the slope of the roof and the desire to keep the grade level for viewing.

Site Access and Mechanicals

This was an easy site for both installation and maintenance as half of the house is built into a hill and is accessible from the ground level, the house is only one story, and the roof is only 12 feet (3.6 m) off the ground. There were no mechanicals on the roof area that required attention.

Final Analysis

This roof was a perfect example of considering the surrounding landscape and still maintaining a sense of high design all the way down to the access paths. The green roof garden matched the client's expectations of a being a maintainable, colorful meadow. The design works with the architecture and has the added benefit of functioning ecologically with its surroundings.

Documentation

Green roofs generally involve many steps from predesign to implementation, and projects can be postponed or be in process for several years. Therefore, it is important to record and organize the data you collect so it can be used effectively at any time. At ground level, most designers measure the area themselves or hire a surveyor to create a site plan of the existing landscape. It is no different on green roofs, except instead of topographical contour lines you might need spot elevations to indicate interior floor or roof slab elevations.

At this early stage, good documentation and data collection demonstrates competency and provides valuable information for all involved. For new construction, the plans for the roof garden need to be coordinated with the architect, structural engineer, and contractor because a green roof design will be integrated into the overall building plan. In retrofit, you are showing up after the architects have signed off, or in the case of an old building, are long gone.

Once a base plan is obtained all the information gathered from both the broad geographical context down to the specific structural load details needs to be recorded. A plan must then be created which contains all the above site analysis information from circulation and existing mechanicals to roof aspect. All data should be clearly demarcated on the plan, and the plan preferably stored in a location or file that everyone can view. Discuss with all involved parties how that information is to be relayed to prevent confusion.

On any green roof, the sun shadow lines and wind direction are as important to the design as where the air

conditioning unit is located, and these things need to be indicated on the plan. Notations and arrows can show directions and clarify these key observations. There are also computer tools such as Sketch Up and others like it that will map and record screen views of the sun's location during different seasons and indicate at what time the shadows will be where. This computer modeling, a great tool for measuring sun exposure, is getting much easier to use and more affordable as time goes by, but the computer should never be the definitive measuring device. It is sufficient when the design only exists on paper but nothing can replace being present on site to verify the results once the building is constructed.

For retrofit roofs, depending on the size, scale, complexity, and budget, the drill will be similar but existing documents from the construction of the building can be utilized as a base plan for recording. If the roof is simple and quite small, a photo with notations consisting of detailed notes may be adequate. In all cases, it is important to note and measure vents, penetrations, and drains through the membrane, and to identify electrical outlets, gas lines, and/or power sources. You may also need a roofing expert to confirm the health of the existing membrane but sometimes observation is enough. Anyone could confirm a membrane bulging from distortions of the insulation underneath as unhealthy.

Another thing to notice and record is any standing water, and whether the cause is a faulty or blocked drainage system or a slumping roof that could indicate structural problems. These observations let you know if adequate drainage exists for your roof garden and if any improvements or roof component replacements are necessary before you begin the design process.

Standing water present after 24 hours may indicate larger issues that need to be addressed.

8

Program

View from the rooftop terrace of the Hotel Habita in Monterrey, Mexico.

n 1986 landscape architect George Hargreaves designed Harlequin Plaza, a green roof on top of a parking structure in the Denver suburb of Greenwood Village. The design, a bold response to one of Picasso's Harlequin paintings, was metaphorically suitable for a business park that supported public art installations throughout the corporate campus, but proved to be unusable by the occupants. In fact, it was immediately apparent that none of the employees in the two adjacent buildings wanted to be in the plaza. Among the main reasons— it had no shade and was consequently too hot. The plaza had aspen (*Populus* sp.) trees, but they died or never got tall enough to offer shade in the blistering summer heat.

Although the plaza was a creative design, it was useless as a public space. Over time, it succumbed to poor maintenance, the water feature leaked too much to be salvaged, and someone else ultimately redesigned it. The new design was not as striking but proved much more accessible. Programming, the research and decision-making criteria that precede the creative process, likely would have prevented the problems at Harlequin Plaza.

Defining Program

Programming is the term for that critical juncture when a designer factors people into the equation and makes the end users stakeholders in the process. What should come out of the programming process is the merging of ideas, values, and knowledge. This process considers expectations and emphasizes communication between all the stakeholders. If the process is thorough, it will be effective in saving time and money. It will clarify the triangular priorities of budget, time, and quality. The designer must look for key words to surface that clarify ephemeral and concrete goals, and consider everything from educating the public to maintenance issues.

THE FALL AND RISE OF PROGRAMMING

For a time in the 1980s and 1990s, programming in landscape design fell prey to the tenets of Post-Modernism and Deconstructionism, where form trumped function. For that brief period, the vision of the landscape designers mattered more than the people who were going to utilize and maintain the projects; these end users had little or no voice in the process. The whole idea of programming was even dropped from some graduate design school curriculums, and the designers who believed they knew best were the sole stakeholders.

Since that time, programming has made a comeback and there has been a paradigm shift in the perspective of who should make the decisions about form and function. The current thinking has end users being more involved in the design process because it makes sense that the people who will utilize and/ or take care of the landscapes should play a role in defining the scope of work before it begins.

COST EFFICIENCY

When clients change their minds during the design process, most of them don't realize that the designer then goes back to the engineer who must recalculate load factors resulting in the designer making changes to their drawings. All of this takes time and money. The most cost-effective time for all concerned to make changes is during programming. As the developers of Harlequin Plaza discovered, it is expensive to revisit and redo a design because early programming did not include all the necessary steps or, as in their case, was eliminated.

The fundamental challenge of whole building design that involves green roofs is understanding that all building systems are interdependent and the living materials above the membrane are interacting in some way with the systems inside the building. It is essential that the owner, the occupants, and the maintenance personnel be involved to contribute their understanding of how the green roof and its systems will work for them once they occupy the building.

ESTABLISHING A PROCESS

So where do you begin? A good way to start is with the American Institute of Architects' [AIA] guidelines established to help potential clients hire an architect and understand the overall design process regardless of the size of the project. With some modification, these same principles work for green roofs and can help lay the groundwork for your project.

1. **Research the project type. Is it a green roof, roof garden, or both?**

2. **Establish goals and objectives. Consider aesthetics and environmental issues like stormwater filtration.**

3. **Gather relevant information on predesign and site analysis.**

4. **Identify strategies. An example is how to budget or phase-in projects. The latter refers to installations that take place in phases over a period from weeks to years. Sometimes phasing occurs to accommodate budget parameters.**

5. **Determine quantitative requirements. This can tie into what the needs or expectations of the client/user are.**

6. **Summarize the program. After determining the answers to one through five, it is important to document the program so you can return to it throughout the design phase.**

Sun highlights the native grasses on the roof at the Drew School in San Francisco, designed by Andrea Cochran Landscape Architecture.

Kresge Foundation Program Guidelines

In 2006, following guidelines similar to those of the AIA, the Kresge Foundation, a philanthropic organization in Troy, Michigan, finished its LEED platinum building with more than three green roofs. The Foundation went through an integrated design process that involved a highly structured team approach in planning and design. In the programming stage, the architects, contractors, Kresge staff, and other consultants came up with the following program elements:

- Purpose of the building
- Stakeholder needs
- Organizational values
- Community values
- Operating costs
- Environmental goals
- Nonnegotiable factors
- Challenges
- National/state/local requirements■

A vegetated roof at the Kresge Foundation headquarters in Troy, Michigan, connects the new office space with the original stone farmhouse on the property and replicates the grassland that once dominated the site.

Although it might seem logical to have the clients establish the program, they don't always have the experience and/or the skills to think through what they want, need, and expect from a roof garden. Designers can be the muse to the client's imagination and establish parameters for their dream garden. While programming is partly about the details and determining where the hose bibs go, it is also about helping clients identify their desires by asking specific questions about their lifestyles and priorities.

Client Expectations

By this stage, you have gathered all the site clues and examined the architectural considerations. Now client needs take center stage starting with the straightforward categories of budget, time, and quality, and followed by more illusive ideals like core values and lifestyle. Let's start with the more concrete considerations of money, scheduling, and materials. Think of them as the apexes of a triangle. Whether the triangle is equilateral, isosceles, or scalene, the individual project will determine which factor(s) is paramount.

BUDGET

Budget is a vital side of the client expectations triangle, and rare is the client who says money is no object. With clients who have never gone through a building process, it is necessary to clarify costs from the beginning because they have no previous experience and do not know what to expect. In all situations, you should know if the client has a budget number in mind. The best way to get that

information is to ask them. Until these conversations have taken place, it is dangerous to assume that all parties are on the same page in regards to budget.

On large public or corporate jobs, a formula exists for allotting a number to the landscape budget, usually a percentage of construction costs. For residential landscapes on the ground, the client can expect to pay anywhere from 10 percent or higher of the overall construction budget on landscape, but budget estimating is still a relatively new field in the green roof industry. Estimates of green roofs can range from $3 to $250 a square foot depending on the complexity of the design, but Tom Liptan in Portland and Stephan Brenneisen in Switzerland claim they can install green roofs for less than $10 a square foot.

As mentioned earlier, intangible costs associated with green roofs such as conveyance, waterproofing, and structural additions often can be equal to or more than the cost of the actual roof garden, and clients need to comprehend all aspects of the design and installation. Adding amenities like fireplaces, outdoor kitchens, and water features costs far more. It is a good idea to factor in a contingency percentage for the budget that is 10 to 20 percent higher than the established bottom line as inevitably unforeseen costs arise.

Emilio and Kate Ancaya of Living Roofs in Asheville, North Carolina, dialogue with their clients about budget in terms of the installation costs of different systems and substrate depth, which are based on the square footage of the project. Vegetated systems for green roofs such as pre-vegetated mats, pre-vegetated trays, plant plugs, seeds, and cuttings all have various predetermined square footage costs.

Trays of plant plugs filled with *Crassula radicans*, chosen for their low cost, await planting on the Los Angeles Museum of the Holocaust.

Intensive roof gardens (those with over 6 inches/150 mm of substrate) cost more because of line items like decking, shade pergolas, grills, water features, or fireplaces. By keeping themselves educated about the field and the full breadth of products available, the Ancayas are able to price what is best for a client.

TIMELINES

Clients with no building experience are unlikely to consider the costliness of changing their minds or taking too much time making decisions, and it is up to the team leader to help them understand the consequences of their actions or inaction. When a deck project with small pots morphs into a patio with aluminum planters big enough to hold apple trees, the cost goes up. Waffling, indecisiveness, and changes in direction have a ripple effect on everyone involved in the design process, which in turn bumps up the budget and extends the schedule.

Weather also affects timelines. In regions with distinct seasons, even mild ones, there are appropriate planting times. At LAMOTH, grasses planted in hot weather did not survive because they needed cold weather for a healthy start. In cold climates, plants will simply not be available in the dead of winter. New construction also factors in: if any problems cause the construction schedule to shift, that in turn pushes back the green roof installation. If the installer has to come back several times due to delayed construction or weather, conveyance costs go up.

Planting begins in one section of the Los Angeles Museum of the Holocaust roof garden.

QUALITY

Regardless of the size of the project, special order or custom design items will drive the program, cost more, and take more time to acquire than similar items that are prefabricated. When a couple living on the East River in Midtown Manhattan hired the architectural firm Graftworks to design a sitting area on their roof, what could have been a relatively simple program revolving around the client's love of pretty flowers, soon became quite complex. The couple's desire for high-quality materials and a creative design plan resulted in an expensive high concept design that required extra time and staff to complete.

Since the space was minuscule, the architects wanted to use built-in planters, seating, and shade. Using the icon of a water tower, ubiquitous on Manhattan rooftops, the architects came up with a metaphor of unfurled water towers that translated into wood ribbing in strips. This novel idea resulted in undulating strips of decking, which become shade canopies and chaise lounges, with hidden planters placed between the curled strips. This required shoring up the entire roof to accommodate the 3000-pound (1360-kg), $40,000 deck. In addition, the job was located five stories up, mandating a large crane and five workers to position the heavy, structural framing and decking. Apparently, the views are terrific and the customers felt the end more than justified the means.

DEFINING CORE VALUES

In a corporate setting, core values are the primary ideals that form the foundation of an organization. On a personal

A roof garden designed by Andrew Clements on the island of Anti Paros, Greece.

A deck designed by Graftworks in New York City.

level, these central values refer to more ethereal ideals like beauty and honesty, and to our feelings about the sacredness of nature. These essential tenets require no external justification and guide us in making decisions about what elements will define our rooftop gardens.

It might seem superfluous to ask a homeowner about core values, but sustainable and environmental are just buzzwords if there's nothing to back them up. Determining how invested someone is in these and other more abstract ideals is essential to the success of a project. A client might say they want to minimize water use but still ask for roses that require more water. Alternatively, someone could request native plants but the variety of nonnative penstemons they want requires importing plants from far away. Getting clients to define what they really mean by low maintenance, low water, and energy efficiency is just as important as their addressing abstract goals like beauty and comfort.

When it comes to identifying core values, clients need guidance, and by asking the right questions, designers can lead them to come up with their own answers. Focus on the client's motives and identify key words that begin to define how they would like to use the space. Sample questions include the following:

- **Does the use of water guide you?**

- **Is beauty important?**

- **How do you expect this garden to define you?**

- **Form versus function? Is one more important than the other?**

- **What do you want the space to provide for you?**

- **How do you like to spend your time outside?**

- **Do you like to eat outdoors?**

- **Are biodiversity and being part of a larger whole important to you?**

In the case of the New York City couple with the $40,000 deck, it became clear to the architect that quality materials and high design were among their core values and he responded in kind with a very creative and unusual design.

Sometimes the designer has deep-seated core values that require accommodation on the part of the client. For example, people who employ green roof designer/builder Andrew Clements, based in Greece, know before they work with him that they are hiring his particular vision for an ecologically based design. His clients need to embrace those same core values around the environment so they are on board from the beginning.

That vision, in Clements's words, "at the risk of sounding a bit pompous, is to allow/recreate/establish rich, complex, biodiverse Hellenic ecosystems on built surfaces." This has numerous advantages, one of them being little or no requirement for irrigation and maintenance. Clements's approach also cuts down on long-term costs—something that might tempt clients to spend the money for a green roof. However, the beauty of his work also contributes to convincing the client of his worth. His

Oblong planters accentuate this Manhattan penthouse patio designed by Ken Smith.

creations often sit on top of contemporary Greek architecture sheathed in white stucco where he juxtaposes the quiet, orthogonal forms with plant palettes that either blend seamlessly with the land beyond or jump with the brilliant colors of magenta, pink, and purple delospermas.

Sometimes designs will hinge on money versus beauty and how much clients are willing to spend on form and function. Are they okay with paying to beef up the structural load factors so they can have trees on the roof? What about costlier maintenance fees? Obtaining this high level of detail early on as well as identifying the pertinent core values will help clarify cost considerations and get to the heart of what the client wants.

OTHER PROGRAMMING CONSIDERATIONS

Understanding the technical intricacies of a green roof calls for educating all the stakeholders about what makes green roofs not only different from ground landscapes but also important. Simple items like drains, for example, can determine the long-term success of a project. If the drains don't work, the garden can fail from oversaturation and the roof will likely leak. Unlike a ground level landscape, a garden on top of a building is part of the whole building system and must be treated as such.

Other key program items might include questions about space accessibility and viewsheds. On a green roof that Ken Smith designed for a couple on their Manhattan penthouse, the owners wanted "a sense of enclosure without perimeter planting" because they didn't want to block the views of the city. Smith replied with an abstracted version of a more traditional garden utilizing huge white fiberglass forms meant to be whimsical permutations of scholar's rocks found in traditional Chinese gardens.

When horticulturalist Mark Fusco began the design process for the first green roof on top of the cafeteria at Denver Botanic Gardens (DBG), he had some obvious goals. Because DBG is a nonprofit research institute, Fusco knew he would have a lot of room to experiment with plants, substrate depth, and irrigation. The freedom of experimentation means he didn't have to worry about plants dying, a concern not lost on most designers.

A critical component of the program was factoring in the thousands of visitors who come to the gardens every year. Including a green roof and education about it was a core value that affected the design process. The need for clear and engaging didactics influenced the deliverables including beautiful drawings and explicit plant identification. Finally, the budget was so small that Fusco was forced to seek donations for didactics, materials, and installation in exchange for marketing visibility for the donors. The roof garden is a stunning success on all accounts.

HONORING THE VISION

The process of defining the program also identifies the vision. Honing the vision—being sustainable is an example—will bring you closer to clarifying how the program meshes with budget and schedule.

For the students at the Orh Torah Stone High School in Jerusalem, being able to create the first green roof on a

The agave adds strength and texture to the desert roof at Denver Botanic Gardens, designed by Mark Fusco.

public building was their primary objective, and thanks to a pilot project sponsored by the Jerusalem Municipality, they got to do just that. The budget was next to nothing but the students were undeterred and held fast to their original visions. They had plenty of energy and ideas to come up with intensive and extensive beds for testing and research, and their sketches inspired the final plans executed by Studio Landscape Architecture in Tel Aviv.

The students pitched in on the execution by building the wood deck and benches and by helping with the planting. An oval planting area in the middle is mostly for vegetables and herbs to be cultivated by the students, and maintenance is in their hands as well.

Community and Environmental Concerns

The Kresge Foundation is in the business of funding environmental programs at schools and nonprofits, so when they decided to remodel their headquarters, they wanted to practice what they preached. The integrated design team helped the Foundation to set its priorities in the context of community and environmental concerns. A brochure handed out at building tours highlights the priorities:

- **Support the health and productivity of building users.**

- **Create an appealing environment that attracts and retains Foundation employees and welcomes visitors.**

- **Remain in the current location.**

- **Preserve and utilize the farmhouse, barn, and other agricultural structures on site, allowing these original buildings to remain visually dominant.**

- **Achieve efficiencies in energy, water use, and long-term expense.**

- **Reduce water production.**

- **Obtain materials from surrounding areas to minimize transportation fuel used.**

- **Achieve LEED certification through the U.S. Green Building Council.**

The outcome of this in-depth exploration of program included several green roofs on different sides of the building. The roofs, filled with a mix of native grasses and perennials to mirror Michigan prairie ecosystems, provide fantastic viewsheds from most employee windows (see photo on page 174). Similar plants are repeated on the ground landscape around most of the campus. From inside, workers look out onto an infinite space of prairie. Last spring a mother goose built a nest, laid eggs, and hatched goslings on one roof, after which the facilities manager brought in a wildlife biologist to safely relocate the family to the ground.

In Sennen, Cornwall, England, Geoff and Julie Haslam, graduates of a green roof training course taught by Dusty Gedge and John Little, used an angled parapet gabion filled with native granite chunks placed at an angle to handle wind. This was partly due to the local planning restrictions, which called for a

Green roof garden on the Orh Torah Stone High School in Jerusalem, Israel.

The steel beds create social spaces at the Port of Portland headquarters in Oregon, designed by Mayer/Reed Landscape Architecture.

Pink sea thrift sits on the edge of a roof inspired by the granite cliffs of Cornwall, England.

low profile roof, and was inspired by the surrounding landscape. The substrate was composed of a mix of local granite gravels and some composted green waste with a bit of local demolition waste for filler. It was then seeded with native flowers and forbs such as wild pansy, kidney vetch, scarlet pimpernel, cornflower, chamomile, and sea thrift to mimic the surrounding ecology.

IMPROVING WORKING CONDITIONS

We have written about policy guiding the design process, but job creation, life cycle thinking, and working smarter can also be program components. The new headquarters for the Port of Portland at the Portland International Airport created 2500 jobs when the local unemployment rate was in the double digits. Using no state or local tax funds in the budget, 10,000 square feet (930 sq m) of ecoroofs were a large part of the equation.

Programming objectives included developing a building that would be as green as the budget could afford. The resulting building with parking garage uses 75 percent less water and 36 percent less energy thanks to the insulating properties of the ecoroof, an integral part of the whole building and site. The ecoroof reduces surge loads in storm events and improves temperature and quality of the water before the storm water reaches the central stormwater management system.

The design included a program objective to choose plants that did not attract birds or wildlife for the obvious reason that fauna would endanger the safety of airline operations on

Three questions for
Tom Liptan,
landscape architect for the City of Portland's Bureau of Environmental Services, about the role of government in the green roof movement.

---

1. What role can government play in implementing green roofs?

One role of government is to become aware of things that are likely to be beneficial to its citizens. When the city of Portland became aware of vegetated roofs and their potential usefulness with stormwater management, our next step was to get educated, prove it to ourselves, and determine how to apply it in our situation. Once that was figured out, it was time to educate the public, which was followed by building community acceptance and determining ways to move the idea forward. In some cities, the idea(s) may come from the public, in which case the city staff needs to become educated first.

2. How has your work in Portland affected your outlook on policy and the future of green roofs?

Based on the success of city-initiated pilot projects that provided us with empirical data, we began work to find and remove unnecessary barriers, and to create incentives, codes, and regulations to encourage people to design and build ecoroofs. The city council also passed a resolution in 2005 that requires all city-owned buildings to roof or reroof with ecoroofs where practical. Code incentives were created, such as the zoning floor area ratio bonus and a credit for managing storm water. In 2007, the city developed a five-year financial incentive program unlike any other in the country. The goal is to help bring about the construction of 43 additional ecoroof acres (17 ha) within that five-year period. Almost one million dollars a year is budgeted for ecoroofs of any size within the city limits. The money applies to both residential and commercial projects and

> "Our next step was to get educated, prove it to ourselves, and determine how to apply it in our situation."

has been hugely popular in furthering the vegetated roof movement in our city. To date, hundreds of projects have been approved.

3. Can you share some methods for soliciting money from the private sector for funding green roofs?
We have never solicited money from the private sector. Our incentive money comes from stormwater fees, which almost all city property owners and developers pay. Those same property owners and developers are eligible to apply for incentive money for their own green roof projects, and when their ecoroofs are completed, they receive a 35-percent reduction on their stormwater fees. When the city prepared a cost evaluation of the costs and benefits of installing ecoroofs on private and public buildings, it found that the financial returns in Portland are very promising. Currently, two developers have decided to install an ecoroof on their new building because of the extended roof life, which for them is a very important ecoroof attribute. It's moving toward a win-win for everyone. ■

the runways just feet away. Social goals included changing employment fiefdoms scattered across four offices that some thought had become too inefficient, to create a more convivial and productive work environment under one roof in a centralized headquarters. Another social goal was to design a positive feeling about the place where people live and work so part of the green roofs included areas for employees to go and enjoy the outdoors. There are places for seating and eating alongside artful steel beds filled with plants that do not attract birds.

Most importantly for a public project, it came in on time and on budget. The 4-inch (100-mm) substrate depth of the ecoroof, enough to support sedums, helped to keep the cost down and the selected sedums do not encourage habitat formation. The bonus was LEED platinum certification when the building was planned to go for gold.

Sedums in angular patterns complement the skylights on the Port of Portland headquarters in Oregon.

9

Master Planning and Conceptual Design

A residential green roof garden designed by the client, Daniel Jessen, and Jon Harrington of Alpine Gardens in Steamboat Springs, Colorado.

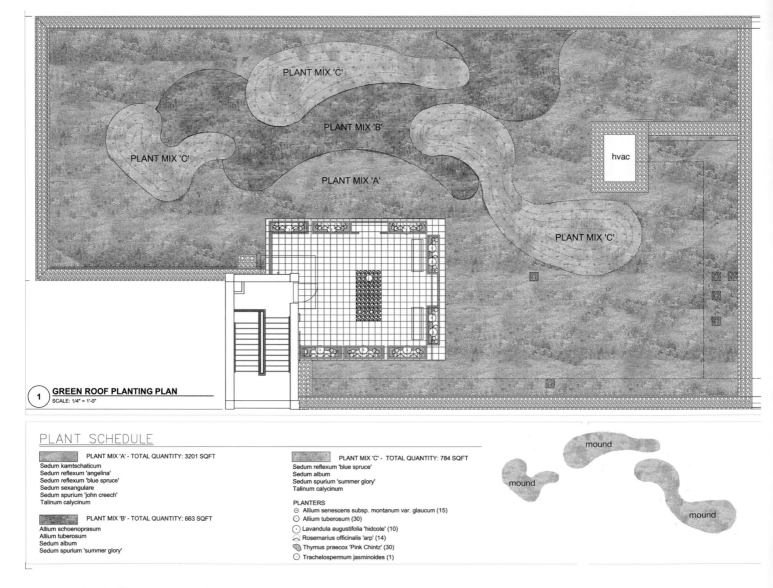

1 GREEN ROOF PLANTING PLAN
SCALE: 1/4" = 1'-0"

PLANT MIX 'C'

PLANT MIX 'B'

PLANT MIX 'C'

PLANT MIX 'A'

PLANT MIX 'C'

hvac

mound

mound

mound

PLANT SCHEDULE

PLANT MIX 'A' - TOTAL QUANTITY: 3201 SQFT

Sedum kamtschaticum
Sedum reflexum 'angelina'
Sedum reflexum 'blue spruce'
Sedum sexangulare
Sedum spurium 'john creech'
Talinum calycinum

PLANT MIX 'B' - TOTAL QUANTITY: 663 SQFT

Allium schoenoprasum
Allium tuberosum
Sedum album
Sedum spurium 'summer glory'

PLANT MIX 'C' - TOTAL QUANTITY: 784 SQFT

Sedum reflexum 'blue spruce'
Sedum album
Sedum spurium 'summer glory'
Talinum calycinum

PLANTERS

⊖ Allium senescens subsp. montanum var. glaucum (15)
⊙ Allium tuberosum (30)
⊙ Lavandula augustifolia 'hidcote' (10)
⌒ Rosemarius officinalis 'arp' (14)
🍃 Thymus praecox 'Pink Chintz' (30)
○ Trachelospermum jasminoides (1)

A concept drawing illustrates topography and
design for a North Carolina green roof by Kate
Ancaya of Living Roofs.

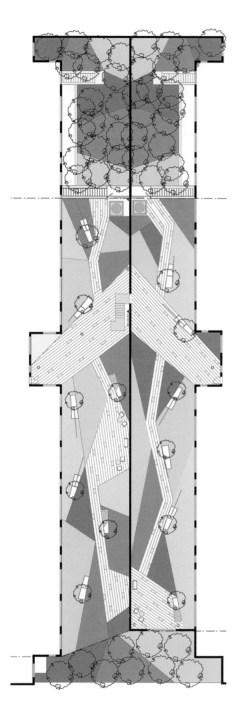

This roof plan created by Hanna Packer of Town and Gardens, New York, illustrates pathways, circulation, and planting patterns.

Master planning is the step in the process when the designer takes all the elements of predesign, site analysis, and programming and synthesizes them into an overall picture. It is essentially a visual integration of all the information that has been gathered, and the time to explore the functional relationship of one element to the other.

Establishing the Big Picture

A master plan is the first step in the formal documentation process to creating real space. While roofs might seem like leftover spaces that need little planning, they are parts of the building. Designers are realizing that the complexity, availability, and potential of roofs calls out for thoughtful design.

Going through a conceptual process helps to synthesize the site and program, making way for details in the construction documentation phase. For example, where will the pots go so they don't block circulation around a table? How will drains interact with the deck? What's the best layout for maximizing views from a hotel roof for breakfast guests and afternoon swimmers? It is during this stage that decks, vegetation-free zones, substrate mounding, the sizing of various hardscape or softscape areas, and the right place for an array of elements like dining and water begin to come together.

This phase tends to stay within a conceptual framework and is illustrated on a larger scale as the broader concepts of program are translated into visual ideas. That said, details also drive the design, so the trick is to focus on the big picture while keeping an eye on items like drain and vent positioning that will ultimately guide the location of larger issues like pathways and patios. Other variables are not controllable by the designer. The site cannot be expanded, the slope of the roof will guide drainage, and grading also depends on drainage and load factors. A detail like accessibility, identified in site analysis and predesign, will provide parameters to paint a gestural picture.

At this stage, you may have determined that the design will support 6 inches (150 mm) of substrate, but knowing exactly what the makeup of the substrate will be can come later. This is the time to figure out locations of beams so you can rough out where you will berm up substrate for trees or place planters or span deck framing, but now is not the time to specify the exact dimensions or the precise height of the planter. Your research may also have revealed that the roof will need several layers above the waterproof membrane but actual specification can wait. Instead, stay conceptual and translate key words and core values into concrete form.

Sketches normally illustrate the master planning phase and overall site plans. Eventually, you will work off a measured plan with all the doors, walls, and drains indicated, but right now, it is more important to know where the drain is rather than its exact distance from the parapet wall. This isn't the time to specify what kinds of decking the client wants but to figure out the location and size of the deck. You do this by referring back to programming to accommodate the number of people who will occupy the

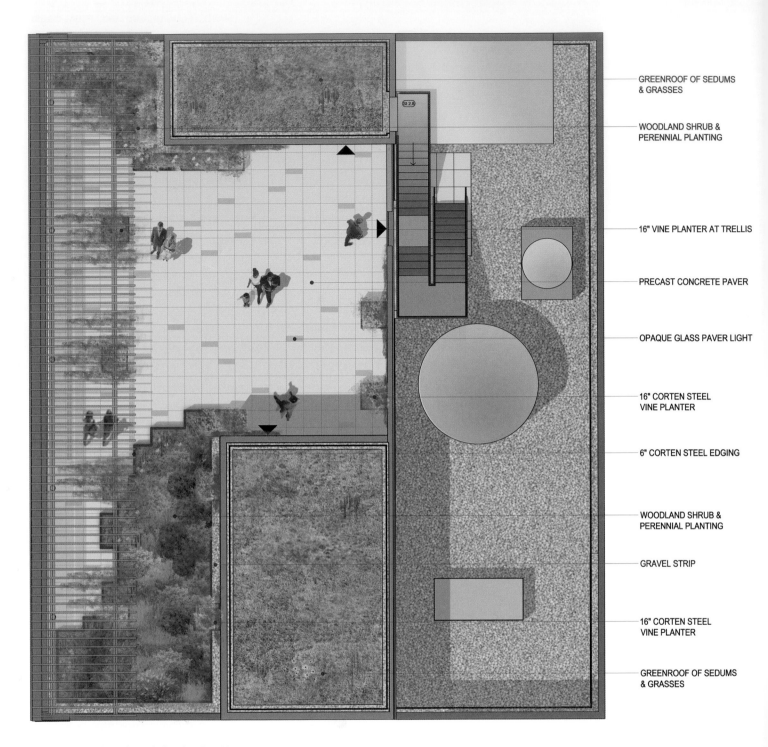

GREENROOF OF SEDUMS
& GRASSES

WOODLAND SHRUB &
PERENNIAL PLANTING

16" VINE PLANTER AT TRELLIS

PRECAST CONCRETE PAVER

OPAQUE GLASS PAVER LIGHT

16" CORTEN STEEL
VINE PLANTER

6" CORTEN STEEL EDGING

WOODLAND SHRUB &
PERENNIAL PLANTING

GRAVEL STRIP

16" CORTEN STEEL
VINE PLANTER

GREENROOF OF SEDUMS
& GRASSES

Clarifying intentions through drawing. Brooklyn
Academy of Music roof garden by Starr
Whitehouse Landscape Architects and Planners.

space and by looking to the site analysis to clarify where the best views are and where the most comfortable places out of the wind are.

Similar to ground landscape design, green roof design uses the same tools and creative process but you have to remain mindful that you are on a roof and the master planning process has to integrate these differences. Familiarity with ground level landscapes might give you confidence to repeat design moves up high, but remember sun and wind conditions, even one story up, are different. For example, perennials in 4 inches (100 mm) of substrate on a roof in Steamboat Springs surged in the first season while the ground landscape with the same plant material was slow to fill in.

Clarifying Intentions

The job of the designer is to translate both the concrete and the ethereal into spatial reality. Whether you are designing 200 square feet (19 sq m) or several acres (hectares), the intuitive process is the same, but the time spent and documentation produced grows exponentially with the size and complexity of the project. As SLA, an urban design firm in Copenhagen, discovered, when you are master planning large areas like the "City Dune" project and tying the roof of the new building headquarters of the Swedish SEB bank to the surrounding harbor area and the rest of the city, the process is going to be complicated.

The backdrop that SLA had to deal with was the harbor front of Copenhagen, a location long criticized for its low quality office buildings, introverted shopping malls, bad public infrastructure, and few public spaces worth using. SLA

hoped to create an inviting space that bank employees and the public could use, and they wanted to facilitate pedestrian mobility and encourage visitors to connect to the nearby Danish National Archives and on to Tivoli Congress Center.

Physically the site was located above an underground garage on the corner of two busy streets where the creation of a cool environment in the heat of the summer was the most important principle. The visual design emblem selected was the metaphor of the sand dunes of northern Denmark and the snow dunes of the Scandinavian winter. The soft curvilinear lines of the concrete emulate the topography of dunes, reiterated by the pillowlike beds of trees and perennials. Grade changes translate into stairs that rise and fall depending on how you move through the space. From the outside, you are gently drawn in between the large buildings. Rather than a foreboding entry with steep stairs that lift visitors up into a level interior, this entry sequence is reminiscent of walking between or around dunes, in this case green dunes with trees that provide shade on a hot summer day. Even the buildings have curved shade canopies that relate more to the ground plane rather than the vertical orthogonal lines of the bank. The result looks like a giant dune of sand or snow as the urban park slips in between the buildings.

In another example, what landscape architects Laura Starr and Stephen Whitehouse of Starr Whitehouse in New York like about the master planning process is that it is a time to combine opportunities and constraints, and transform them into built form. Their design for the roof garden at the Brooklyn Academy of Music reveals the

fall → winter

spring

summer

ease with which they translate program from abstract to concrete. For them, the constraints provided opportunities.

The client was a nonprofit organization looking to transform a tar roof into a green sanctuary with little budget for design and construction. The site was a retrofit that involved the new construction of an additional floor. The program called for flexibility for special events and private spaces for soliciting donors. The client also needed outdoor classroom space for teenagers and children, all on a fixed footprint. LEED certification was a goal. The load factors were set and wind issues were relevant as well as light and shade constraints.

To save money on fees, the landscape architect brought in New York Green Roofs, a design/build company that came to the table with extensive green roof expertise and ways to save money throughout the process. The documentation details an open space, sheltered on one side with a shade structure. The floor plan, punctuated with large planters point loaded on beams, provides both microclimates for plants and private moments for conversations.

FROM KEY WORDS OR METAPHORS TO DESIGNED SPACES

The key words that came out of the programming process at the Los Angeles Museum of the Holocaust (LAMOTH) were *freedom*, *love*, and *beauty*. These words in turn generated metaphors like light, movement, regeneration, and transformation. The master plan focused on turning these key words and metaphors into design choices around plants, color, texture, and seasonal change. For

example, the concept centered on creating a three-season garden of grasses that regenerates every spring, a metaphor for a field of transformation.

In this case, the key word *freedom* became a physical reality by translating other program needs, like low-water use, low maintenance, and durability, into a garden that thrived with little care and water, returning every year to grow up into tall grasses reflecting light and movement in the wind. *Beauty* was reflected in the plant palette that enhanced the crisp, clean concrete parapet walls. *Love* was expressed by the cycle of the entire garden that dies back annually and rejuvenates each spring with the first sign of bulbs followed by grasses.

In a residential setting, key words can relate to the personal background of the client. For a tiny green roof less than 250 square feet (23 sq m) in Boulder, Colorado, the clients wanted a modern look to match their house. They collected art, valued the creative process, and adored Japanese rock gardens. One of them was a professional jeweler. On their wish list were a low-maintenance water feature, winter interest, and lots of color throughout the growing season because the roof garden would be located just on the other side of a glass wall from their master bedroom. Finally, they wanted to connect the aesthetics of the roof with the ground landscape. That's a lot of program for such a tiny space. The load factors allowed for about 6 inches (150 mm) of soil with more load on the beams and close to the parapet wall.

Author Karla Dakin came up with two conceptual options for the master plan, both focusing on the metaphor of jewelry. For one, she used rocks as symbols of jewels and water; the rocks

A seasonal study of color for the grass palette for the Los Angeles Museum of the Holocaust: (top) fall to winter, (middle) summer, (bottom) spring. Designed by Karla Dakin and Lisa Lee Benjamin, illustrated by Karla Dakin.

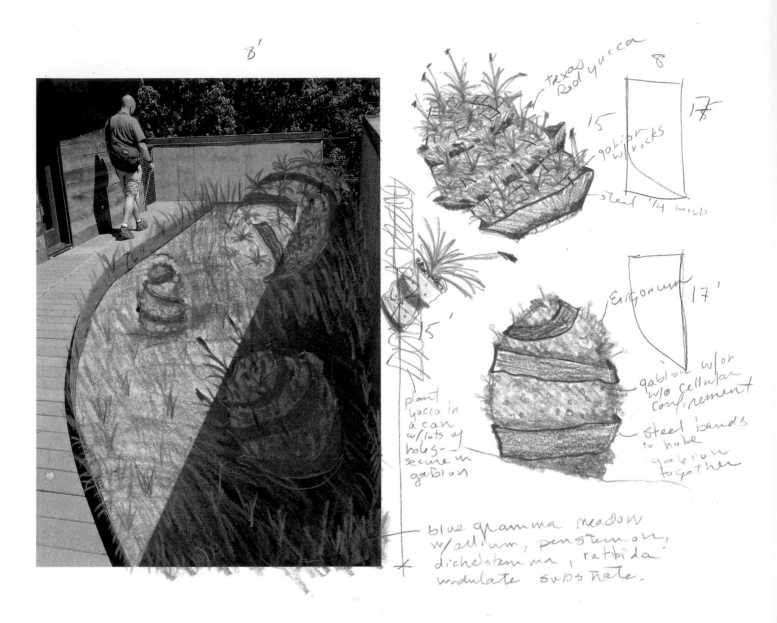

8'

texas Red yucca

8

15

17

gabion w/rocks

steel '/4 mild

Erigonum 17'

plant
yucca in
a can
w/lots of
holes—
secure in
gabion

gabion w/or
w/o cellular
confinement

steel bands
to hole
gabion
together

blue gramma meadow
w/allium, penstemon,
dichelstemma, ratibida.
undulate substrate.

on this roof would have to fly or float. To fly, rocks would be strung like gems in a necklace on cable from the corner of the deck across a parapet wall that extended in front of the house to the entry door. This necklace would provide the connection between roof and ground as it stretched in sections a few feet down along the parapet wall on the roof deck. Then the necklace extended along the top of the concrete wall hanging down in long sections one story to the ground in the front entry.

Laid like the scales of a fish, the same rock material could also be a metaphor for water and serve as a maintenance access path through the garden. This stone path would complement a simple water feature made from a livestock trough meant to be reminiscent of Scandinavia where the other client grew up.

The second concept was to mimic jewel-encrusted Fabergé eggs by making egg forms of wire circled by bands of steel or copper filled with soil and planted with colorful perennials that sparkled like gems. Throughout the growing season, the eggs would be covered in flowering plants nestled in a bed of evergreen ground covers. The clients loved this idea but went for the first option because it had the water element.

At Forum Homini, a boutique hotel in South Africa designed by Activate Architects, the historical context prompted key words like *spiritual*, *renewal*, and *reconciliation*, which resulted in the form of a resolution between the landscape and architecture. In this case, the architecture embraces the landscape as the site of spiritual meaning and renewal, created by literally blurring the boundaries between the two. Like the disappearing edge of an

Two conceptual designs by Karla Dakin for a residential roof in Boulder, Colorado: (this page) rock "necklace" and trough water feature, (opposite page) flowering Fabergé eggs.

Green roofs at Forum Homini hotel on Letamo
Wildlife Estate in Gauteng, South Africa, designed
by Activate Architects.

infinity pool, the green roofs look like the South African prairie far beyond and are planted with the same native grasses and perennials. A good part of the building is submerged under concrete roofs covered in native veldt grasses. Visitors enter the hotel through a metaphorical cleft in the rock, and many of the walls of the hotel are faced with stone gathered from the site itself.

This Utopian vision contrasts sharply with the stereotypical image of South African landscape as violent, dangerous, and threatening, and often designed against structures of closure and interiority, the latter referring to the house closing in on itself with little connection to the outside. This project explores the new relationships with the land that the end of the politics of racial division has opened up in post-apartheid South Africa.

CREATING A MASTER PLAN

At Uncommon Ground, a restaurant in Chicago, the owners knew from the start that a roof garden situated at the top of the program list would drive the entire renovation of the building. Core values of public accessibility and organic certification also played out in the master planning process. To integrate the roof, structural details required thinking about the entire existing building down to reinforcing the original creaky foundation.

While the details emerged later in the process, the conceptual ideas affected everything else. Because Uncommon Ground has a high-end vegetable garden with a focus on aesthetics, the 2500-square-foot (230-sq-m) deck made from post-consumer recycled materials was not only a sleek version of

A productive vegetable garden on the roof was a key part of the master plan for Uncommon Ground, a Chicago restaurant.

Shelter options at Petit Ermitage in Los Angeles protect from the sun's rays during the day and provide private enclaves at night.

Thyme covers the flagstone steppers of this rooftop patio in Boulder, Colorado.

rooftop farming but also it was meant to be an extension of the restaurant with weekly tours offered for a small fee.

Annual flowers along with herbs and vegetables went on the wish list, and conceptual planning included laying out locations of raised boxes. Activity zones for seating areas, workstations, and the utility closet were mapped out around the perimeter. For the interior area of the deck, ten planter boxes, each 10 by 4 feet (3 by 1.2 m), were laid out for maximum capacity but planned on casters for ultimate flexibility to rearrange as necessary. The Uncommon Ground roof is an extension physically and philosophically of the restaurant below, and the owners were able to develop the building as one cohesive aesthetic statement that also carried out sustainable practices like using recycled wood and saving used cooking oil for biodiesel fuel.

CONCEPTUALIZING SHELTER

The master planning process is also the time to think about whether architectural elements of shade and shelter are on the program list. For a residential project, once you have figured out in the predesign phase whether the roof can hold a pergola and if the homeowners association (HOA) allows it, incorporate the shade shelter with the rest of the program by locating it on the plan. You might be able to size it roughly, but locating it is good enough. Shade and shelter usually go hand in hand with dining or sitting outside and protection from the sun.

Look for clues on the existing architecture to see if possibilities exist for attaching a shade structure. If not, your only option may be temporary

shade such as umbrellas. The architecture of the building should help with the shade structure attachment on one side of the house. If this is the case, structural considerations might drive where the seating area goes.

For a roof garden located adjacent to a wall on the west side of a home in Denver, hot afternoon sun necessitated a shade structure but one that did not block the spectacular Rocky Mountain views. The structure was such that it could be attached to the house with a metal frame that extends out over the entire seating arrangement with retractable shades on the top and west side, giving the owner options for managing shade depending on the time of day.

For the exposed, hot roof at the Museum of Contemporary Art (MCA) in Denver, Karla Dakin conceptualized shade based on her love of the sod roofs found in novelist Willa Cather's descriptions of prairie homes. In the final concept plan, a large bed filled with prairie grasses shades a cafe table with four chairs where the employees like to sit for lunch as opposed to eating in a sitting area on the southern side of the building that has great views of the city but no shade.

Preliminary Layout and Flow Patterns

Site analysis provides strong clues about establishing the preliminary layout. All that information about access, circulation, and mechanicals can now be incorporated into the master plan. It might be as simple as establishing vegetation-free zones around parapet walls, vents, and HVAC units or a more complicated scenario involving access for

maintenance. This is the time to lay out ideas for pathways around plants so they don't get stepped on, choosing plants that do not mind foot traffic, or settling on an aggregate to go between plants. Andy Creath, owner of Green Roofs of Colorado in Boulder, usually proposes path options like steppers, gravel, or mulch depending on the wind conditions and/or to provide his clients with different price points. Circulation is just as important to Creath as it is to the client because he is the one normally maintaining the roof after installation.

DECK SIZE AND ERGONOMIC CONSIDERATIONS

What is important at this stage is to ascertain how the clients intend to use the roof. If they are planning to utilize their roof gardens for dining and entertaining, now is the time to determine how big the deck or patio area needs to be. Will there be seating for two, four, or eight? Is there room for eight on the limited roof space? The ergonomics that normally apply on the ground need to be rethought on a roof because circulation areas will be much less.

Since many roof gardens tend to be on the small side, consider rectilinear tables because they seat more people in smaller areas than circular or square tables do. To get a sense of the space, sketch up a table with chairs on the plan. Perhaps a narrow rectangular table is the best solution or a table with leaves that can be extended. It might be unnecessary to have eight chairs on the roof at all times, but is there a place to store them? Sometimes you don't have a choice because the size of the roof is what it is and will determine how many

This rooftop designed by Hannah Packer of Town and Gardens, although narrow, still provides access for a variety of activities.

people it can support at one time, and that in turn will influence the design.

There are main drivers for making decking size and location decisions aside from how many people your client wants to seat. There are views to consider or to block. There are areas with less wind or more shade that naturally make attractive places to sit. Perhaps the windiest area has the best view. Is there a way to temper the wind so you can sit and enjoy the vista? If that's the case, make visual or written notations on the page that table and chairs must be accompanied by wind screening. There will probably be several design directions. Choose the best two or three and sketch them up.

CIRCULATION

Circulation largely depends on who is using the roof, and most of the time the focus is on humans. The space might be so small that there is very little to consider but then again you don't want to put pots in front of the staircase. It might seem that it is too early to consider a detail like pots but if the space is tight with a budget to match, it's a good idea to rough out areas where pots might go and even size them to see how many you might propose.

When the space is larger, as at the Xcel Energy roof in Denver designed by RNL Landscape Architecture, the design needs to incorporate an array of potential users. To accommodate socializing and break-time requirements, the roof is separated into different areas by large planted beds, which either are raised or flush with the decking. There are tables to sit at and open areas in which to stroll around. The placement of the open areas shows sensitivity to the site, and

it's possible to see across the roof to the city beyond from just about anywhere. Despite being two stories above street level, the Xcel roof gives users a sense of where they are situated in the urban grid. It feels very much like a public park, and how people move through that kind of space influenced the conceptual planning around circulation.

Activity Zones

When it comes to establishing activity zones, a garden on the roof is not very different from one on the ground, and now is the time to prioritize space. Even with limited square footage it's possible to designate areas for different activities, so asking about pets and children, even if they are future considerations, is very important. Pets can destroy gardens easily by walking back and forth and lying in planted beds. Mapping out specific areas for the pets with dog-resistant plant material is one solution. Designing raised beds out of reach is another possibility.

The same can be said of children. Will they run roughshod through the planting beds? Is it possible to make play spaces that some day could be used to grow vegetables? If the design incorporates areas for toddlers, can it be flexible enough to adapt for teenagers in years to come? Other ways of satisfying kid needs include a water feature or spa.

Safety issues are very different on a rooftop and need to be worked out especially when children are concerned. Municipal codes normally dictate built responses to safety needs regarding the height of parapet walls or the design of railings; however, it is important to consider how kids will occupy a space. Is

there a designated area for them where they cannot interact with vents that might be hot to the touch?

Commercial ventures generally afford more square footage and consequently greater possibilities for activity zones. At Vancouver's Fairmont Waterfront Hotel, formal gardens flank a swimming pool and a spa. Guests can walk among edible plants surrounded by boxwood hedges reminiscent of the English countryside. It is only when visitors wander close to the parapet edge to take in expansive views of the water and the Convention Centre with its huge green roof across the street that they are reminded where they are.

COOKING ON THE ROOFTOP

Whether the activity is a corner for the hibachi or a full-blown outdoor kitchen, it must be located on the plan now. Where the gas line comes out of the building will determine where cooking takes place, and a grill can be used to block unsightly views. Airflow needs to be checked to avoid smoke traveling through windows.

It's at this stage that it must be decided whether to treat the roof as one whole space where activity zones merge together—kind of like a studio apartment—or whether to divide it into several distinct areas. For the latter, think about how the zones will be separated. Will you use flexible elements like pots and planters or more permanent fixtures like trellises or pergolas?

If the footprint is large enough, you can divide food prep from lounging like landscape designer Rebecca Cole did in a roof garden in the Tribeca section of New York City. Using a wide selection of

Boxwood hedges surround herb gardens at the Fairmont Waterfront Hotel roof garden in Vancouver, British Columbia.

A retreat designed by Rebecca Cole on a New York City rooftop.

different pots in various sizes and shapes planted with annuals like chartreuse sweet potato vine and trees like birches, she created different living areas on one roof. Lounging is separated from dining. Clusters of pots hover along the parapet, opening at spots to frame vistas. Several gathering places make the roof feel larger than it is. The clusters of vessels enhance privacy and create an unfolding of the garden as you move through it.

GROWING YOUR OWN

If your clients say they want to grow food on the roof, you need to find out what exactly that means to them. Depending on the size of the roof, vegetable gardens can range from herbs in pots to large farms. Pots and shallow substrates dry out rapidly in hot weather, but since vegetables can grow in very little soil, they could be planted in an extensive tray system. Water is the lifeblood of vegetables, and irrigation in some form must be considered. Because irrigation is necessary if low- or no-water use is an important program item, the client needs to know growing food is an area for exemption.

Utilities and Access

Among the early details to confirm in the master plan process is making sure you have power, how much power, and where it is located. Water sources should be located as well. Document your master plan on a base plan with dimensions and locations of all utilities.

There are several ways to source a base plan: get one from the owner, architect, or builder; take the measurements yourself and prepare an as-built plan; or the client can hire a surveyor or civil engineer to map it out. This base plan will give you enough details to make broad conceptual strokes without having to go back later and change your plan to match existing site conditions. The plan should also include details like water, gas, and power sources, and show access points for installation and operation. If you do not have this kind of information, it will affect how you proceed later on.

Due to the short and hectic schedule Karla Dakin was given when the MCA roof garden was designed (building construction was almost done when green roof construction began), this information was not secured until the construction documentation phase. It was only when communication was set up with the mechanical engineer that she was able to establish that the site actually had enough power for the irrigation system, water feature mechanicals, and lights. The point is that if, in this late stage of the process, Karla had discovered that the power was insufficient to run irrigation to all the beds, the design would have had to revert to an earlier conceptual stage to rework the configuration of the planted beds.

It is not advisable to plan a patio near a HVAC box unless you also plan ways to screen and soften the mechanical because most clients will want to block that view. The southwest corner of the space might be perfect for the grill, but if the gas line comes out of the northeast corner around the other side of an elevated stairwell that breaks the plane of the roof surface, it will cost a fair amount of money to run the gas line around and across the site. Similarly, locating a deck adjacent to the electrical

Skylights adorn a green roof at One Union Square
East in New York City, designed by New York
Green Roofs.

Amenities such as decking, power, and water are easily incorporated on this Denver roof.

outlets means you might not have to walk through plants to plug something in.

Sometimes in the master planning process you realize that it's the mechanicals and building details that drive the design. This was the case with New York Green Roofs' master plan for a building in Union Square in New York City. Instead of trying to screen or soften the skylights and elevated stairwell, the design accentuated and celebrated these elements by proposing that the green be a foil around them.

Although the details for installation and maintenance get refined later in the process, at this early conceptual phase you need to identify options for installation. It might be obvious that a crane won't work and that you will have to use the freight elevator, but are there also stairs? Is there room on the roof to store materials before and during the construction process, or do you have to preload everything and carry the pots up already planted? Are there elements of maintenance in the future that should be considered now, like access?

On small suburban residential jobs, ladders are often the only way up to install and maintain. Does the owner have ladders? Are they stored on site? The answers to all these questions will be flushed out later, but it is important to notate them on the plan now because they can become line items for preliminary pricing.

Budget Guesstimates

With the master plan in place, it's time to match items up with rough numbers to give the client an overall picture to respond to for the next phase. It is very helpful to the client to see guesstimates attributed to clearly defined line items like conveyance so you can begin a conversation about the cost of daily crane rentals or labor costs to carry materials up stairs.

Unless you are working on a large project with experienced team members, the client will not know what to expect in terms of budget. Even on a large project without prior experience, budget estimates sometimes do not take into account the complexities and resulting costs behind green roofs or roof gardens. The additional line items around installation, drainage, and roofing components are the hidden costs that can significantly alter a project. Just as there are professional cost estimators for ground level projects, there are professional cost estimators for roof gardens who can assist you with this part of the process.

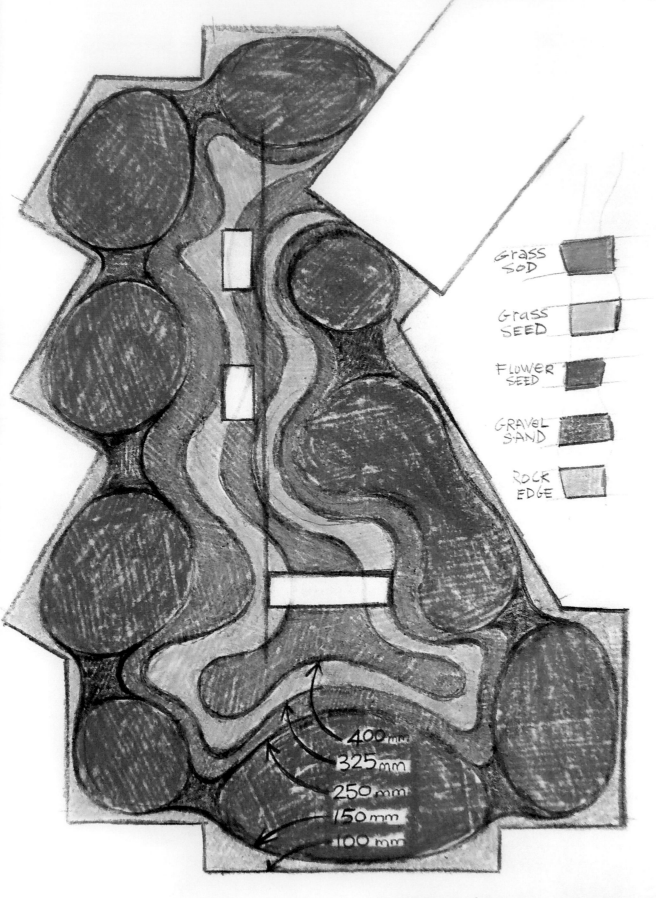

GRASS
SOD

GRASS
SEED

FLOWER
SEED

GRAVEL
SAND

ROCK
EDGE

400 mm
325 mm
250 mm
150 mm
100 mm

2011.

10

Design Development and Construction Documents

A simple yet detailed layout of planting scheme and substrate depth for Sean Corcoran's Irish seaside roof.

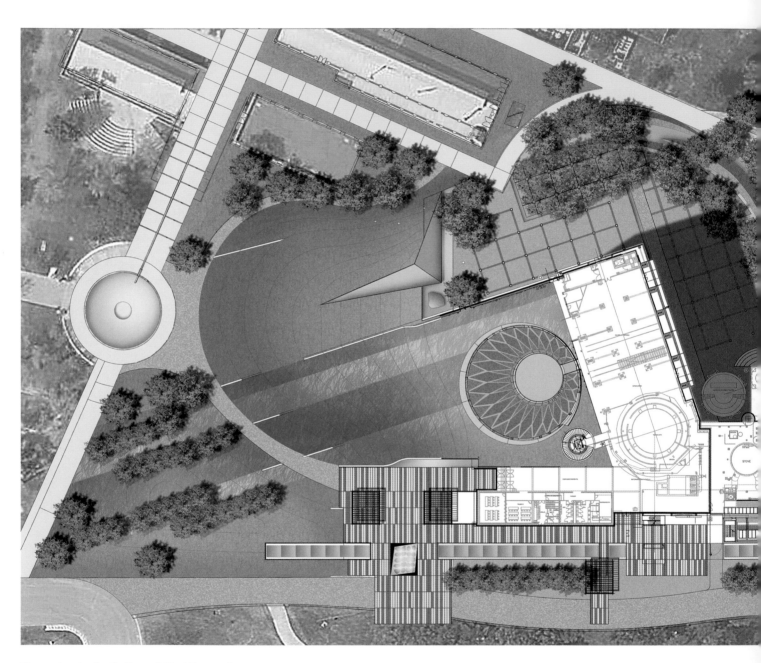

The master plan for the Horno 3 Steel Museum in
Monterrey, Mexico, designed by Claudia Harari.

T he purpose of developing design is to create construction documents. By now, thanks to master planning, all the ideas are on the table and all of the general concepts and key values have become three-dimensional. During design development ideas become refined and are simplified into very clear drawings and written specifications for bidding and construction. This phase is about distilling information, getting into the details, and creating documentation to explain exactly how to construct the intended design.

Many plan categories make up a set of construction documents including demolition, roofing, drainage, grading, mechanicals, layout, paving, planting, irrigation, lighting, and furniture. The number of documents will vary based on the scope of the job, and a variety of approaches can be taken.

For one small residential space, Karla Dakin's main job was to specify plants while her team member, Andy Creath of Green Roofs of Colorado, provided expertise on the layers above the membrane and irrigation details. For that job, Dakin only produced a planting plan. More complex projects, such as the Horno 3 Steel Museum in Monterrey designed by Claudia Harari, required many more documents and the level of detail escalated as well. Harari's plan outlined a planting scheme that delineated the formal design of patterns inspired by the architecture of the building.

Another key reason for construction documents is clarification. This is accomplished through plan, section, elevation, and details and written specifications. Being clear is exceedingly important because contractors aren't mind readers and designers should not expect them to remember a conversation about the exact percentages of organic material to lightweight pumice. Because so many technical details go into constructing a green roof, this is the time to work through the master plan to distill and clarify details for construction.

Layout Plan

Similar to the layout plan for a ground level landscape, the layout plan on a roof details the shape and size of decks, planted areas, vegetation-free zones, circulation paths, locations of shade structures, outdoor kitchens, water features, or play areas. In this phase, the designer determines exactly the size and materials of all the required program elements.

With roofs, it's also necessary to incorporate all the elements of predesign, such as the interface of the building into the design. If there is access, where does it occur? Roof gardens by their nature imply occupation by people so paths need to be incorporated that lead visitors out onto central spaces.

Unlike roof gardens, many green roofs will not be occupied by people and may have limited access for upkeep of vegetated components and checking to make sure the green roof is performing as specified. If that's the case, be sure to incorporate into the construction documents any requirements for maintenance and other related issues such as where window washers hook into the parapet for cleaning the windows.

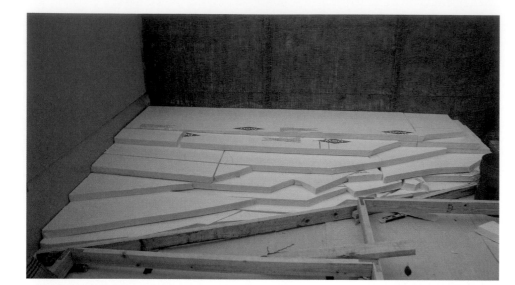

Layers of foam create beautiful forestlike topography for a roof in Brooklyn.

Chris Brunner of New York City Green Roofs carefully removes the capillary mat from around a roof vent in Brooklyn.

Roof Composition

The composition of roofs encompasses all of the layers on top of the roof slab including the waterproof membrane. Depending on the situation, the architect or roofing consultant may select the membrane, and the green roof team will specify the remaining layers.

SELECTING THE WATERPROOFING MEMBRANE

Design details associated with waterproofing come up in both retrofits and new construction projects. If the project is a retrofit, start by assessing the state of the existing membrane. Because manufacturers only guarantee membranes for a certain number of years, it is extremely important to know where the membrane is in its life cycle. If you are about to place extensive decking or hundreds of square feet of green roof on a membrane with only two years left on its warranty, you might want to consider including a new membrane to the scope of the project.

There are several ways to get an accurate assessment of an existing membrane. Consult with an architect who specializes in roofing systems or contact the installer who put the membrane on. If you know the make of the existing membrane, the manufacturer could be helpful in recommending someone to assess the state of the material.

Whether the project is a new one or a retrofit, it's the designer's job to see that the entire surface drains well and is well sealed. Most drainage problems come from penetrations in the membrane, whether intended like a drain, or unforeseen like a puncture from a sharp object. If you are involved in a project where it is your job to specify the membrane, keep in mind that in addition to the price of the membrane there are costs that vary depending on the type of membrane you specify, and warranties to consider. Also, be mindful whether the membrane is adequate to hold a green roof for a determined period.

Today's waterproof fabricators are well entrenched in the green roof industry, offering their own specifications as to layers above the membrane, substrates, and even plant material. Prior to purchasing and installing the membrane, ascertain whether deviating from the manufacturer's recommended specifications will affect the warranty of the membrane itself.

THE LAYERS ABOVE WATERPROOFING

Always have a section in the construction documents that describes exactly what layers you want to include. This section could be applicable to planters or an intensive or deep substrate situation. The layers need to be illustrated or described in written specifications so it is clear to the contractors how to bid and install.

Any conversation about layers has to start with a look at industry history. Because much of the green roof technology emanates from Europe, the current technology was developed to support plant material—predominantly sedums—and green roof materials have been developed around how sedums will thrive. These plants do great in Europe and moist climates like the Midwest and certain parts of the East Coast of the United States, and layers like drainage

Vernal pool on the roof of Heron's Head EcoCenter,
San Francisco, designed by Lisa Lee Benjamin.

boards and moisture mats are meant to accommodate the water needs of sedums. What we are seeing now in the industry is a branching out and exploration of other plant material that is both native and climate appropriate. The water needs for any given plant palette must be the driver behind layer design.

Another piece of the conversation centers around the fear that green roofs will cause a roof to leak, making getting water off the roof as quickly as possible a critical design objective. To that end, layers serve different purposes. The root barrier membrane, generally furnished and installed by the roofing installer, prevents roots from growing into the waterproof membrane, and compromising its waterproof capacity. Moisture mats help to slow the water down by holding water in the mat. The drainage board, another layer, also deters water while giving supplemental moisture to shallow-rooted plants.

Experiments are being conducted with substrates and traditional drainage layer components as well as testing new materials for roof layers above the membrane, all of which retain water for longer periods. Researchers, product developers, and designers such as Lee Glaslow of Conservation Technology in Baltimore, Maryland, and Dusty Gedge of London are testing the use of wool capillary mats instead of drainage boards to retain water below the substrate. The wool capillary mat acts similarly by holding water and allowing it to wick through the soil when necessary.

Concurrent with the rise in popularity of green roofs is the increased research about membrane performance below living systems that is helping decrease concerns about water on the roof being a scary concept. As long

as the roof drains and has a sufficient load to hold the weight of the water, the benefit of retaining water can exceed the anxiety of getting it off the roof as quickly as possible. The debate goes on about whether drainage boards support plants or actually hurt them by killing them when the cups are empty or causing root rot when they are full for too long.

Holding water on a roof is similar to the concept of bioswales and rain gardens in ground landscapes where the designer strategically plans to hold or detain water on site for irrigation purposes. There are also situations other than irrigation when it's desirable to have water pool on a roof such as the vernal and permanent pools like those specified by Stephan Brenneisen and Lisa Lee Benjamin to encourage better habitat and a wider variety of plant material. At Heron's Head EcoCenter, two designed pools have proven to add habitat value by attracting birds for bathing and drinking.

Alternatives to Plastic

A counterproductive by-product of green roof design is the amount of plastic that goes into the layers above the waterproof membrane. The layers that go below the substrate are often fabricated out of plastics—sometimes recycled, sometimes not—a technology borrowed from civil engineering and the agriculture industry. Consequently, designers continue to look for ways to simplify the layers and reduce the amount of plastic used.

Some designers, like Andy Creath, turn to gravel as the drainage layer instead of drainage boards if the load factors allow for more weight. Creath likes to substitute aggregate for drainage board products by using a moisture

Native rare orchids colonize the roof of
Seewasserwerk Moos in Wollishofen, Switzerland.

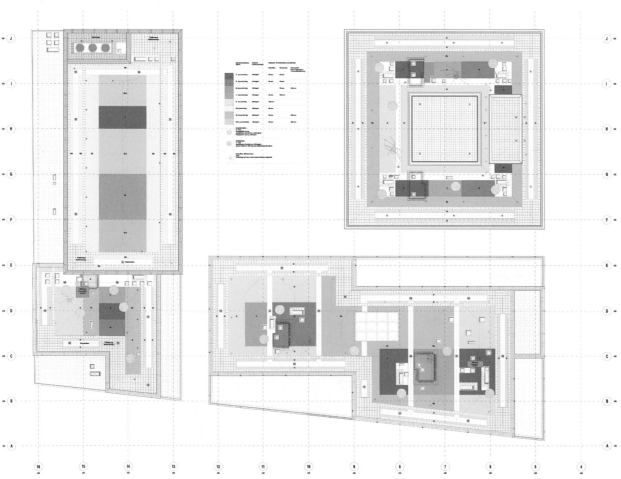

mat, then 2 inches (50 mm) of gravel topped with filter fabric. His method results in an extra 2 inches of space for the plants where roots will thrive in a highly oxygenated space. Essentially, this system increases the potential substrate depth from 5 to 7 inches (125–175 mm), and most of the time aggregate is less expensive.

Some substrate materials, such as expanded shale or pumice, act as drainage. At Heron's Head EcoCenter, Lisa Lee Benjamin and green roof designer Fredrick Ballerini installed a capillary mat and a pumice drainage layer to move excess water into two 3,200-gallon (12,000-liter) rainwater catchment tanks for reuse in the irrigation of the plants on the roof.

During the design phase think about what can you do to reduce the amount of products while still maintaining the same performance over time. Long-standing roofs such as the one at Seewasserwerk Moos, a water treatment plant in Wollishofen, Switzerland, have endured with few manufactured materials. Constructed in 1914, this roof was one of the first ferro-cement buildings built in Zürich. The ceiling of slab beams is 3 inches (75 mm) thick, finished with ¾ inch (20 mm) of mastic asphalt. The substrate consists of 2 inches (50 mm) of sand and gravel as a drainage layer and 6 to 8 inches (150–200 mm) of topsoil from surrounding farmland. Ninety years later the layers have combined with no adverse effects. The only restoration has had to be on the edges. The farmland topsoil has acted as a seed bank, enabling rare native orchids to colonize. This project also illustrates that designing a simple system that is easy to understand and install leaves less chance for error.

According to Andy Creath, the key factor to determining the layers above the waterproof membrane is plant selection. Until recently, thanks in large part to the prevalence of sedum mats, most clients request the popular mat, or carpet, form because it provides instant gratification much like turf sod. It's also readily available. This presents a dilemma for Creath who designs in the dry Colorado climate, which is not necessarily optimal for sedum mats, and he's faced with designing systems that increase the retention of moisture on the roof so the sedums will survive in a dry climate.

In this instance, ground level gardens, where native grasses and climate appropriate plants are increasingly popular, are ahead of the curve because green roof designers are just beginning to introduce native or climate appropriate material to a larger extent. If a client wants drought-tolerant native grasses or cacti planted, it will require a different layering system beneath the substrate and the onus is on the designer to make modifications accordingly.

Specifying Substrates

In the trade, substrates are an engineered material often called out by a written specification. Each substrate is a combination of mineral and organic components that satisfies the exact specifications the designer is looking for. The composition of this mixture depends on load factors, and plant and habitat requirements.

The trend in substrate depth is moving away from shallow systems of 3 or even 4 inches (75–100 mm) because it doesn't hold water and plants need more depth to expand their root systems. Many designers are asking for a

A substrate plan created by architect Max Dudler for a rooftop in Zürich, Switzerland.

Detailed sections of various components on the
Los Angeles Museum of the Holocaust, drawn by
Roofmeadow.

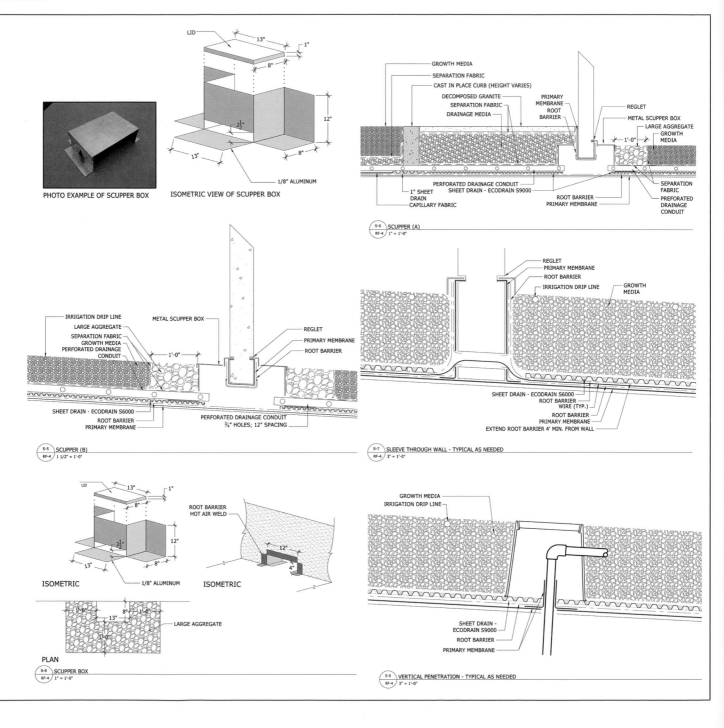

PHOTO EXAMPLE OF SCUPPER BOX

ISOMETRIC VIEW OF SCUPPER BOX

LID
13"
1"
8"
12"
2 1/2"
13"
8"
1/8" ALUMINUM

GROWTH MEDIA
SEPARATION FABRIC
CAST IN PLACE CURB (HEIGHT VARIES)
DECOMPOSED GRANITE
SEPARATION FABRIC
DRAINAGE MEDIA
PRIMARY MEMBRANE
ROOT BARRIER
REGLET
METAL SCUPPER BOX
LARGE AGGREGATE
GROWTH MEDIA
1'-0"
PERFORATED DRAINAGE CONDUIT
SHEET DRAIN - ECODRAIN S9000
1" SHEET DRAIN
CAPILLARY FABRIC
ROOT BARRIER
PRIMARY MEMBRANE
SEPARATION FABRIC
PREFORATED DRAINAGE CONDUIT

S-6 / RF-4   SCUPPER (A)   1" = 1'-0"

IRRIGATION DRIP LINE
LARGE AGGREGATE
SEPARATION FABRIC
GROWTH MEDIA
PERFORATED DRAINAGE CONDUIT
METAL SCUPPER BOX
1'-0"
REGLET
PRIMARY MEMBRANE
ROOT BARRIER
SHEET DRAIN - ECODRAIN S6000
ROOT BARRIER
PRIMARY MEMBRANE
PERFORATED DRAINAGE CONDUIT
3/4" HOLES; 12" SPACING

S-5 / RF-4   SCUPPER (B)   1 1/2" = 1'-0"

REGLET
PRIMARY MEMBRANE
ROOT BARRIER
IRRIGATION DRIP LINE
GROWTH MEDIA
SHEET DRAIN - ECODRAIN S6000
ROOT BARRIER
WIRE (TYP.)
ROOT BARRIER
PRIMARY MEMBRANE
EXTEND ROOT BARRIER 4' MIN. FROM WALL

S-7 / RF-4   SLEEVE THROUGH WALL - TYPICAL AS NEEDED   3" = 1'-0"

LID
13"
1"
8"
12"
2 1/2"
13"
8"
ISOMETRIC
1/8" ALUMINUM

ROOT BARRIER
HOT AIR WELD
12"
4"
ISOMETRIC

8"
1'-0"
13"
1'-0"
LARGE AGGREGATE
PLAN

S-8 / RF-4   SCUPPER BOX   1" = 1'-0"

GROWTH MEDIA
IRRIGATION DRIP LINE
SHEET DRAIN - ECODRAIN S9000
ROOT BARRIER
PRIMARY MEMBRANE

S-9 / RF-4   VERTICAL PENETRATION - TYPICAL AS NEEDED   3" = 1'-0"

minimum of 5 inches [12 mm]. Research is showing that 6 inches [150 mm] is the sweet spot to support plant material outside of shrubs and trees.

The substrate should have maximum water capacity, density, and air-filled porosity when fully saturated. The specifications should call for specific grain size distribution of the mineral content, and the chemical analysis should be balanced between nitrogen, phosphorus, and potassium. The combination needs to be thoroughly blended and samples should be tested and sent to the designer for approval.

Specifying Hardscape

The hardscape possibilities for the roof garden have already been discussed [see chapter 3], and now we consider exactly what kind of paving works best for the project. On the roof, this decision boils down to weight, cost, and what holds the hardscape above the waterproof membrane. Recent technology provides ample choices for decking from module to full-scale materials that can be cut to fit. There is also movement towards integrating different types of hardscapes, like aggregates used for flat surfaces to vary the typography, all of which increase useable spaces for everyone. Section details in the construction documents need to illustrate exactly how the decking is to be constructed and installed.

On the roof at the Museum of Contemporary Art in Denver, the deck was designed to match the rest of the decking on the roof. In this case, smaller sections were incorporated that could be removed to access drains and irrigation pipes. No deck section could be too heavy to lift.

On the roof of the Los Angeles Museum of the Holocaust [LAMOTH], the paths were designed out of decomposed granite to save money. Part of the construction documents included sections of the paths with drainage gravel underneath to allow water to flow under the walkways. It was necessary to specify a binder and grain size distribution to ensure the material would not erode. We also specified reinforcing mesh for the edges, separation fabric from the drainage layer, border containment systems, and geocomposite sheet drain on top of the waterproof membrane. PVC sleeves for irrigation and electrical lighting conduit were also included. This information appears as detailed sections on the construction documents.

How materials are sourced depends on the designer's initial research followed by close communication with the contractor. If you specify native grasses, you need to ensure they are available in the trade or can be contract-grown by willing nurseries. For the three grasses on the LAMOTH roof, we worked closely with the green roof contractors to make sure the growers could get grasses like *Lygeum spartum*, not readily available in the trade, and grow them in time for the installation. Growing time was an integral part of the scheduling of the installation as the client needed to approve the species in time for the growers to begin propagation to adhere to the deadline of the museum opening. Additionally, the contractor needed to submit samples for the designer's approval so nothing is left to chance.

Value engineering is to be expected, and in these instances a designer may have to alter the design or come up with alternative measures like using a different decking material or substituting seed for grown plants.

Any decking or hardscape material must essentially float above the water-proof membrane, and elevations need to show how high the decking has to be above the membrane to accommodate any transition between deck and doors or deck and extensive green areas. At this point, you'll find the deck jack to be a useful tool. Commonly known on the ground as shims, these lightweight plastic jacks can be adjusted to various heights and can accommodate heavy loads. Deck jacks should be used even with planters that would otherwise come in contact with the roofing membrane. Insulation can also be used to raise the level of decking or substrates.

Plant Selection and Planting Plans

Landscape architect Sue Amos of Moss-space from London gets involved in every detail of a roof garden. She believes that designing includes everything from the simplicity of how a single plant shapes the space to the highly complex and exquisite combination of plants that highlight plant structure and texture. Amos's prime focus is plants, and her love and curiosity about them has taken her to many countries to explore how various species grow in their natural habitat. Based on her findings she specifies super tough selections from places like New Zealand, Chile, and Tasmania because they can survive adverse climate conditions.

Amos's full-season planting plans emanate from her studies and reflect her desire to reinvent the wildness of the natural habitat; and her plant lists tend to focus not on flowers but on

Newly planted meadow roof in Brooklyn, designed by Amy Falder of New York Green Roofs.

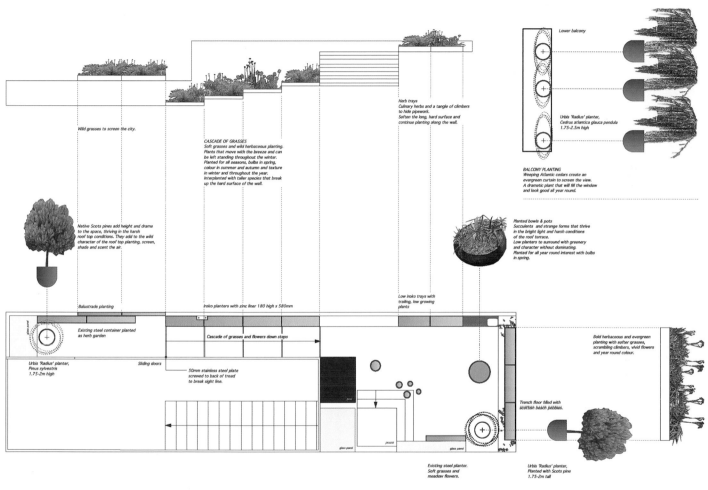

Lower balcony

Urbis 'Radius' planter,
Cedrus atlantica glauca pendula
1.75-2.5m high

BALCONY PLANTING
Weeping Atlantic cedars create an
evergreen curtain to screen the view.
A dramatic plant that will fill the window
and look good all year round.

Wild grasses to screen the city.

Herb trays
Culinary herbs and a tangle of climbers
to hide pipework.
Soften the long, hard surface and
continue planting along the wall.

CASCADE OF GRASSES
Soft grasses and wild herbaceous planting.
Plants that move with the breeze and can
be left standing throughout the winter.
Planted for all seasons, bulbs in spring,
colour in summer and autumn and texture
in winter and throughout the year.
Interplanted with taller species that break
up the hard surface of the wall.

Native Scots pines add height and drama
to the space, thriving in the harsh
roof top conditions. They add to the wild
character of the roof top planting, screen,
shade and scent the air.

Planted bowls & pots
Succulents and strange forms that thrive
in the bright light and harsh conditions
of the roof terrace.
Low planters to surround with greenery
and character without dominating.
Planted for all year round interest with bulbs
in spring.

Balustrade planting

Iroko planters with zinc liner 180 high x 580mm

Low iroko trays with
trailing, low growing
plants

Existing steel container planted
as herb garden

Cascade of grasses and flowers down steps

Bold herbaceous and evergreen
planting with softer grasses,
scrambling climbers, vivid flowers
and year round colour.

Urbis 'Radius' planter,
Pinus sylvestris
1.75-2m high

Sliding doors

50mm stainless steel plate
screwed to back of tread
to break sight line.

Trench floor filled with
Scottish beach pebbles.

glass panel

glass panel

Existing steel planter.
Soft grasses and
meadow flowers.

Urbis 'Radius' planter,
Planted with Scots pine
1.75-2m tall

Roof terrace
Shoreditch
SCALE 1.100@A3

mossspace landscape design
www.mossspace.co.uk

Simple planting plan for a rooftop garden in
Shoreditch, an area in London. Designed
by Sue Amos of Mossspace.

texture and movement. For a client in Shoreditch, she designed the planters on a balcony and roof to showcase a wild mix of deep burgundy hollyhocks, russet-colored alliums, and pale orange lilies combined with finely bladed fountain grasses and the hefty leaves of New Zealand burgundy cordylines to contrast and soften the hard edges of the city.

Factoring in weight considerations, Amos takes the engineer's data on load factors and specifies appropriate containers. She selects lightweight soil from a company that specializes in green roof soils as well as including a drainage layer or lightweight drainage material at the bottom of the pot. Amos understands that weight is not the only detail to consider when picking the soil. Because she works organically and wants to create a healthy garden that will thrive over the years, she pays attention to the makeup of percentages of what goes into the soil. Amos also knows that, despite the rainy climate of London, planters dry out quickly so she opts for irrigation systems that use drip lines or a soaker (leaky) hose.

Plant specification depends on the look and feel of the vegetated areas that you have developed in the master plan and are now refining in the design development phase to put into a planting plan. At the Museum of Contemporary Art (MCA) in Denver, Karla Dakin proposed early on that native and climate appropriate plant material be used, and the various beds were divided into different plant communities. The upper beds represented metaphorical prairies of blue and chartreuse greens while the design for the lower beds called for plants seemingly uninteresting from afar but intriguing up close. These selections of acantholimons from the steppes

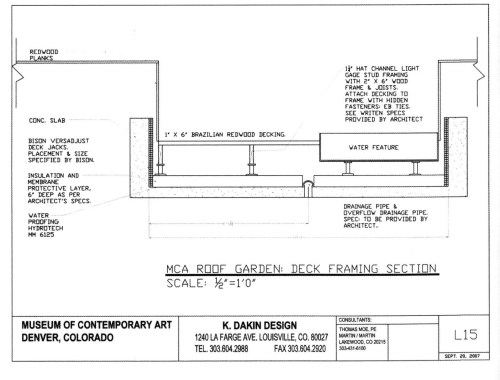

A section of the MCA roof illustrating decking details and specifications by Karla Dakin.

Three questions for

Amy Falder and Chris Brunner,

founding partners of New York Green Roofs, about making construction documents.

---

1. What are the benefits of design/build in the construction documentation process?

Amy: If clients feel comfortable with us as both designers and contractors (and most of the time we are hired to do the maintenance as well), they don't require detailed construction drawings. In this case, after the approval of the concept and a design development, we submit a formal proposal for installation. This process eliminates the need to submit shop drawings and typically saves the client time and money. We are happy to do construction drawings if the client requires the design be sent out to bid.

Chris: Skipping the construction documentation process is going to be less and less a reality. New York City is now promoting green roofs as a Best Management Practice, and the Department of Buildings requires a licensed architect or engineer to file the documents in order

to process permits and tax abatements. Landscape architects and green roof professionals are not allowed to file.

2. Do you normally create full-scale construction documents on your own, or do you collaborate with the landscape architect or architect of record?

Amy: We have worked in both capacities, although our drawings and specifications are simple. When we do full-scale construction documents, we always make a disclaimer that we are not registered landscape architects, architects, or engineers. We always collaborate with structural engineers to start the project, as buildings in the city are old and our first question is always, What is the weight load restriction on this roof? Many times an architect is already on board and we team up with them. When we need to come up with a complicated design that requires more hours than we can handle and/or a level of expertise we don't have,

"Many standard plant specifications developed in other parts of the country or on another continent won't thrive in our environment."

we invite landscape architects to collaborate with us. For the most part, we tend to stay true to the design/build model. With the shift in the economy, we've started doing lots more bid build work recently. This has afforded us the opportunity to appreciate the intensity or lack thereof of construction documents put forth by others. Consequently, we've witnessed firsthand many crosshatches on a plan view and specifications that are cut and pasted without regard for the project nuances. We think the experience of actually building and maintaining makes us better designers.

3. How do you customize standard product specifications for each roof?
Chris: Different products have different performance characteristics. There is no "standard" in that regard; there are just products. A performance-based green roof design that is intended to perform either an aesthetic or an environmental outcome should incorporate the best products available to achieve that within budget.

Amy: No two roofs are alike. We redraw and adjust standard specifications and incorporate them into our drawings for each roof, taking into consideration the type of decking, the type of membrane, the type of flashing, weight load restriction, height of building and parapet walls, client needs, and so forth. We also do many sun studies to make sure we choose the right plants for New York City sites. Many standard plant specifications developed in other parts of the country or on another continent won't thrive in our environment. ■

of China, alpine daphnes from Colorado, and dianthus from high altitudes in the Caucasus were further vetted for their rounded form or ball-shaped blossoms.

The MCA roof garden also needed seasonal interest starting with species tulips and alliums in warm weather months, the rust foliage of *Eriogonum umbellatum* in fall, and finishing with the winter brown profile of *Bouteloua gracilis*, a prairie selection native to the Rocky Mountains. Dakin culled her conceptual ideas from the master plan with the help of horticulturalist Mark Fusco. Most of the plant material came from specialty nurseries in the Rocky Mountain region. After selecting the plants, Dakin and Fusco clearly delineated the choices in a planting plan with specific sizes sourced from nurseries.

Irrigation and Drainage Plans

Aesthetics may drive design decisions, but in the end, the availability and use of water will have a greater effect on things like plant selection. The irrigation plan determines how plants are watered—whether through drip or spray irrigation—and may be provided by the landscape architect or the installer. Regardless, it is vital to identify the point of connection for the water along with the flow rate. Like ground systems, roof systems require a backflow preventer to ensure that irrigation water does not flow backwards into the main water system of the building. If auxiliary water systems are tied into condensate components or dew collectors, the designer must provide details on how the irrigation system works.

Even with an array of possibilities, irrigation is far from an exact science.

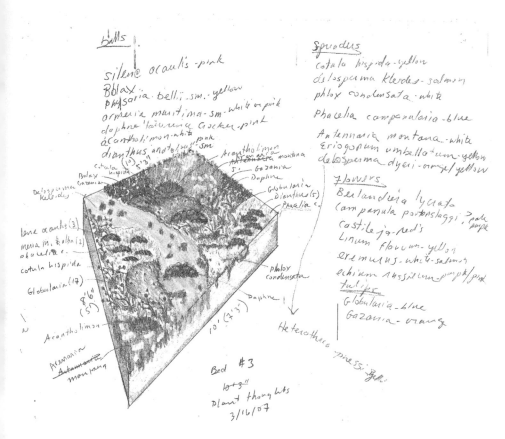

Detailed layout of plants on the MCA roof by Karla Dakin, showing the growth habits of plants.

The mature meadow with a flood irrigation system designed by Roofmeadow at the Oaklyn Branch Library in Evansville, Indiana.

In places where substrates drain quickly, drip irrigation must be strategically placed to reach all the plants especially when they are young and their root systems are shallow. Because drip irrigation often misses the roots of young plants, one alternative is spray but then you are fighting the higher winds and evapotranspiration rate on a roof.

Despite the expense, some designers advocate installing a dual system that accommodates new plantings with spray—handheld or via irrigation spray heads—and long term where drip will satisfy the needs of mature plants whose roots reach down to meet the drip lines. Andy Creath is switching over to a technology developed years ago in Australia: drip tape lined with a capillary mat fabric, which wicks the water across the fabric for a more even distribution. Capillary mats have been used in the greenhouse industry for decades.

Charlie Miller of Roofmeadow has employed flood irrigation design on six projects in the United States. Mimicking perched water tables found in nature, this same technology is used in Europe with intensive green roofs. The technique calls for blocking the drains and releasing water in an effort to saturate everything evenly while not losing water to wind and heat. The system relies on a piece of stainless steel in the drain, which operates like a highly engineered toilet float. The existing drains are outfitted with a sliding internal tube that opens or closes a certain amount depending how much water is needed. On a flat roof, you need to keep the water level constant and low, normally within ¼ inch (6 mm) of the desired level. With sloped roofs, check dams are installed to allow the water to spread.

Materials

Bluestone Aggregate

Fountain Option 1:
Font O' Fire Pedestal
1/4" thick steel plate, rust patina
30" diameter x 15" high x 6" deep

Fountain Option 2:
X-Large Obleeek
Poured concrete
16" diameter x 7.5" high x 6.5" deep

Fountain Option 3:
Low Zen Bowl
Cast stone
39.5" diameter x 9.75" high

Fountain
Short Ha
Light we
20" diam

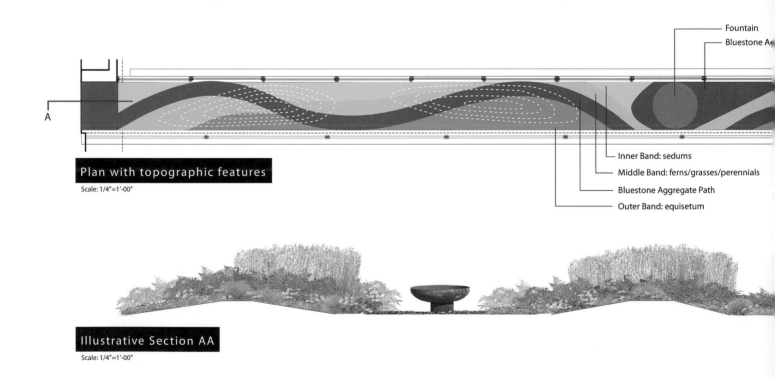

Fountain
Bluestone A

Inner Band: sedums
Middle Band: ferns/grasses/perennials
Bluestone Aggregate Path
Outer Band: equisetum

A

Plan with topographic features
Scale: 1/4"=1'-00"

Illustrative Section AA
Scale: 1/4"=1'-00"

This detail of planters, topography, and planting
helps Amy Falder of New York Green Roofs to
create the roof desired.

The flooding creates a perched water table in the drainage layer while the surface stays dry. In this scenario, the planting design can have dry meadow plants on a surface that can't access water, and larger perennials with deeper roots that can access water. The technology is simple and not prone to long-term maintenance problems typically associated with irrigation systems. Also on the plus side, there aren't lots of valves or sensors to monitor.

Miller never tries to persuade his clients to use his flood irrigation system because he claims they are either immediately seduced by the simple technology or so put off by standing water on their roof that they won't go there. The system can be run electronically off photo cells or mechanically, and typically costs about $2000 per drain covering 5,000 to 10,000 square feet (465 to 930 sq m), which is less than most conventional irrigation systems.

Here again, the issue of drainage comes up because where water goes to irrigate it also needs to drain off the roof. This is where drains, scupper access, and inspection chambers are a critical part of the construction documentation and must be documented through sections and written specifications.

for the architect to incorporate into the comprehensive building set. Other times she reviews the architect's drawings and writes specifications.

In her consulting work, Falder has witnessed more than a few architects cutting and pasting details from green roof manufacturers. This is a problem because often the manufacturers have cookie cutter approaches that only work with sedum mats and 4 inches (100 mm) of substrate, and as soon as you vary your substrate and plant material, all of the layers underneath need to change accordingly.

Falder's combined experience with bidding projects from cut-and-paste documents gives her broad exposure to a lot of construction drawings and specifications, especially ones that don't work. Not all situations in the green roof and roof garden world lend themselves to typical specifications no matter how broad the descriptions might be.

Falder knows that documenting details plays a critical role, and you have to be constantly mindful of integrating with the building. For example, make sure different substrate depths are spelled out in cross sections that define and illustrate the necessary steps for interfacing with the roof.

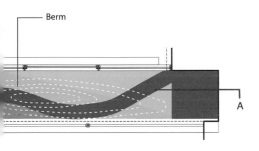

Fountain Option 5:
River Rock Planter
Light weight fiberglass
22" x 21" x 12" high

Berm

A

It's in the Details

At the forefront of the field of developing plans and specifications, Amy Falder of New York Green Roofs, is considered to be on the cutting edge. Falder often acts as a consultant for architects working on construction documents for green roofs. Sometimes she draws construction details such as a layering system on top of the membrane and passes them along

FLASHING AND LEAK DETECTION

Because flashing occurs in all green roof situations around any penetration or termination of the waterproof membrane, it is imperative to include sections that describe how flashing should be installed. Leak detection as well is a unique component of green roof construction, and there are electronic mapping devices that are installed with the green roof layers to make detecting leaks much easier over the life of the roof. These are often called out in the written specifications.

EDGING, PLANTERS, AND CONTAINERS

Similar to its role in ground level landscapes, edging in green roofs separates planting areas and/or holds gravel paths in place. Unlike in ground landscapes, you cannot use stakes or anything sharp to hold edging in place because it might pierce the membrane. There are applications fabricated specifically for green roofs that produce the same effect such as the aluminum border units specifically fabricated for green roofs. Do not leave this up to the contractor to figure out.

Planters can be prefabricated or custom made. If they are custom made, details in plan, section, and/or elevation must be drawn up to describe the desired result. Prefabricated planters can also be shown as images on the page.

ACCESSORIES

All accessories must be specified at a minimum with cut sheets defining all the details. It is also a good idea when developing the layout plan to drop in furniture with the exact sizes as every square foot on a roof counts and you should account for all the extras that will live there. Along with furniture, there are also grills, play equipment, or water features that should not only be located on the plan but also specified from the manufacturer and distributor.

This decomposed granite path is contained with poured-in-place concrete edging at the Los Angeles Museum of the Holocaust.

Four questions for

Charlie Miller,

founder of Roofmeadow, Philadelphia, Pennsylvania, about clarity of specification on construction documents.

1. What is your collaboration process when you interface with landscape architects?

The best outcomes occur when we are consulted during the schematic design phase. Then we can present a range of green roof types suited to the design intent of the architect and set preliminary pricing based on our experience with similar projects. Decisions made at this stage set the client's expectations for appearance, function, and maintenance requirements. We can also identify roof areas that pose special engineering challenges such as shade, slopes, run-off from tributary roof areas, exposed conditions, and cornice overhangs. In most cases, some combination of green roof assembly types and media thicknesses will achieve the best balance between cost and performance.

The next step is preparing performance specifications to ensure the project is built as designed. To the extent possible, we work to minimize the total number of discrete component materials. This reduces cost and simplifies construction. Roofmeadow certifies material suppliers who produce products that will satisfy the performance specifications and contractors that are qualified to install the systems.

2. How do you communicate to your clients the importance of some details such as drainage scuppers and ease of access?

We emphasize that the green roof cover assembly is the best protection the waterproofing will have. To realize this benefit all membranes must receive the same level of protection from sunlight, temperature variations, and abuse. In addition, green roofs are a natural filtration measure that results in clear water discharge at the drain. Common problems such as accumulation of leaves and icing associated with conventional roofs will not be a problem on green roofs where the drains are covered with an access/inspection chamber.

3. Can you give us a specific example of how you translate specifications to reality?

Due to the variable conditions on most roofs, including pitch, parapet height, method of ingress or egress, and so on, specifications cannot address every condition that will occur. It is important that the installation contractor review both shop drawings prepared by the roofing installer that address a myriad of conditions, and carefully investigate the finished waterproofing prior to beginning work. In many projects, conditions will arise that will require some adjustments to the standard waterproofing details and also field adjustments and we are occasionally called upon to resolve and work through field conditions with the roofer and/or contractors in a way that will preserve the design intent and leave the budget unaffected. This is most frequently accomplished through our quality assurance program provided through a certified contractor, but may also be provided as a construction administration service to the architect.

Regardless, it is very important that the specifications anticipate that close and on-going coordination between the roofing applicator and the green roof contractor will be required. Specific requirements for the mutual review and approval of shop drawings, and joint inspection of the finished waterproofing are essential. It is not uncommon to encounter topographic conflicts as roofing surfaces, parapet and threshold elevations, and green roof landscape topographies combine. The result should conform to the design intent, be pleasing to the eye, and avoid problematic access or drainage issues.

4. How have you simplified your use of technological materials since you first began working on rooftops? For example, has there been a shift in gravel drainage versus drain boards?

Roofmeadow's design philosophy is grounded in the German style in which reliance on synthetic materials is minimized and emphasis is placed on building up the green roof assembly using two or more media types with specific physical properties. As green roofs become lighter and thinner, and multiple-layered assemblies become impractical, value is attached to using synthetic components to manage moisture and drainage. Nonetheless, a decade of experience has convinced us that most geocomposite drainage layers are excessively transmissive—that is, they have an unnecessarily high horizontal drainage capacity. The result is that green roofs that rely on these components will tend to be less effective in reducing runoff peak rates and more prone to drought stress. ■

LIGHTING PLAN

When putting a lighting plan together take into account the mechanical loads available on the roof that spell out exactly how much power you have and affect how many and what kind of lights you can specify. Determining where switches and junction boxes are located is critical in the confined space of a roof. For low voltage, the location of transformer boxes should be carefully thought out and a plan needs to be developed to show their location, and where the lights will be installed. Supply cut sheets from lighting manufacturers to specify and price the exact fixtures.

When space is limited, creativity comes into play. For example, on the upper east side of New York City, Town and Gardens constructed and installed curved green roof planters using aluminum edging, fitting into the terrace perfectly. The lighting fixtures softly light the planted beds, allowing nighttime visitors to sit and enjoy the aromatic herbs, grasses, and flowering perennials.

WRITTEN SPECIFICATIONS

Written specifications are a component of the construction documentation package that normally appears in projects larger in scope and budget. These specifications provide boilerplate descriptions for the contractor and are separated into the areas of design and performance requirements.

Design requirements elucidate exactly what everything should look like, and delineate things like the planted areas and hardscape areas, including the depth(s) of the media and the exact components of the paved areas.

Undulating planters float above Manhattan.
Designed by Hanna Packer, Town and Gardens.

Performance requirements illustrate how the vegetated system should support plant growth, drainage, protection of waterproofing materials, load factors, and warranty requirements of the waterproof membrane.

The landscape contractor or green roof installer should provide the designer with submittals including technical literature showing that all the components of the green roof comply with the written and drawn requirements of the design. It should be clear in the submittals that the installer has reviewed and approved the details for the waterproofing system, including deck drains, flashings, penetrations, and coping. The samples of the submittals should include the synthetic sheet components like fabrics, sheet drains, and root barrier, as well as drainage conduit, substrate, hardscape materials, and capillary fabric.

On the steep roof slopes of LAMOTH, it was necessary to specify a method to keep the green roof system from sliding downhill. In the end, it took considerable back and forth with the structural engineer to develop details for anchors to be placed in the concrete roof before the waterproof membrane was applied. Then a cellular confinement system was called for with a certain height and cell size to hold the substrate in place.

Written specifications should also cover where all the materials are coming from, how they will be delivered, handled, and stored if necessary. This is especially important on a roof where there is generally not enough room for storage of materials, and where everything must be conveyed up by whatever means necessary. Most importantly, provisions need to be made to protect the waterproof membrane during installation, and the building during conveyance of materials. Finally, written specifications should cover quality assurance like maintenance, if included, and warranties.

Regardless of the circumstances, green roofs and roofs gardens always result in a hornet's nest of building trades coming together. There is plenty of room for confusion about scope of work and in the end a lot riding on defining the roles of who is responsible for what. When something goes wrong, not to say it will, but if it does, you as the designer want to be clear that what you specified in the documentation was not part of the failure. Especially in the United States where liability plays a huge role in the construction industry, you need to have more than errors and omissions insurance to cover your design.

11

Contracts, Construction, and Maintenance

Habitat Gardens installing a vernal pool for wildlife on Heron's Head EcoCenter in San Francisco.

During the construction phase, several differences between ground and roof landscapes play a huge role not only in the design aspect but also in bidding and construction. These differences—sequencing, conveyance, and storage—completely shift the terrain to a make or break situation, and differentiate planting on the roof from planting on the ground. In terms of getting the project installed, the budget can rise astronomically due to the costs of these elements.

Contracts

It is not unusual to reach this phase with just the architect and/or landscape designer calling the shots, but its time to put out bids for contractors, roof installers, and a maintenance team. Regardless of the scope of the project, it is likely the designer will be involved in a competitive bidding process between several parties with contract negotiation as a part of that. Rarely will a client who receives a bid just say go for it, so being a good negotiator is just another hat that designers need to feel comfortable wearing.

PROBLEMS WITH INEXPERIENCE

Bidding can be a tricky process especially with the number of people who are not green roof experts taking on green roof installations. For example, roofing contractors know all the complexities of membrane installation, drainage, and flashing, but they tend to lack knowledge about plant viability, long-term health

of the vegetation, and maintenance. With the growth of the green roof industry, roofers are stepping up to take a piece of the installation pie. Sometimes these contractors bring in horticultural and landscape experts, but they generally stay on the safe side to avoid liability issues.

Roofers tend to be risk adverse and while this is not bad, it does not push development in the field as roofers default to what is prevalent in the industry and accepted in the trade. They also take a systems approach to installation where generalized details and specifications apply to every project. However, their conservative approach often lands them in harm's way when they choose substrates that don't match plant requirements or specify plants that don't thrive in a given climate.

There is also the perennial debate over cost versus experience. In the LAMOTH project, three different landscape contractors bid on the roof. Our top choice was an experienced green roof installer recommended by green roof expert Charlie Miller, who consulted with us to find the best candidate. Also in contention were a local contractor recommended by a membrane manufacturer in the area, and a large national contractor who had done a lot of ground landscape work in the region but with very little green roof experience. During the bidding process, we did our utmost to convince the client to go with an experienced installer even though their bid was higher. The client didn't take our advice and the result was a construction process with more complications and misunderstandings. For example, in response to a written specification for the substrate, the contractor submitted an inappropriate product several times without regard to the specifications and testing requirements. A contractor with green roof experience would know the substrate products, where to source them, and perhaps be willing to work with the designer to save money.

Some waterproof membrane manufacturers will refuse to warranty their membrane unless you sign up for their complete system installations through one of their certified installers. Be aware that this option gives very little room for flexibility in design decisions. Make sure to speak with the membrane manufacturer to clarify its warranty before soliciting bids from their certified installers. That said, the general contractor might end up hiring a roof installer as a subcontractor without much negotiation because currently there simply are not enough experienced green roof installers in the industry. That is likely to change in the near future.

There are also landscape contractors long accustomed to installing ground landscapes who think installing green roofs will be an easy step to expanding their market. This naivety leads to recommending products that are not applicable to green roof situations like border units with sharp stakes that could puncture the waterproof membrane or overwatering to ensure the roof has 80 percent plant or vegetation coverage in two years. Then, if they also have the maintenance contract, they may not be willing to deal with the weed problem that results from overwatering.

Once again, the point is that, when possible, hire a contractor with green roof experience. Such individuals are more likely knowledgeable about various materials not only for green roof layers but also for irrigation and substrates. They will also have pricing readily

Karla Dakin surveys the planting plan at the Los Angeles Museum of the Holocaust before installation.

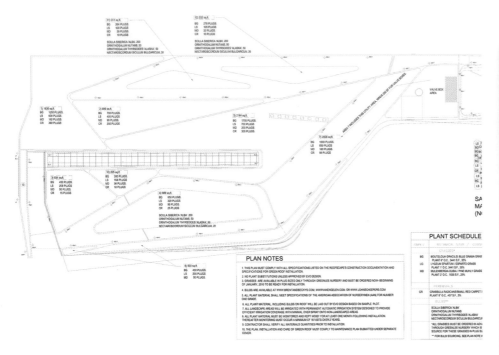

Karla Dakin and Lisa Lee Benjamin's planting plan for the Los Angeles Museum of the Holocaust.

Substrate materials are stored on the structural beam until they can be spread out on this Brooklyn Heights roof.

available to help with value engineering if need be. When this isn't an option, it is critical that the team include people with some green roof experience. Those with no experience in the industry who want to get involved should consider enrolling in courses like those being offered by Green Roofs for Healthy Cities in North America or by Green Roof Training in the United Kingdom. When that's not the possible, adding a green roof consultant to your team will be money well spent.

Construction and Construction Administration

Installation contractors deal directly with the issues of sequencing, conveyance, and storage, but it is the green roof designer who must account for the impact of these elements on the design and budget. For example, during construction you might have to preload all of the pots going on the roof garden or the section railings around the parapet will have to be short because the budget has no money for a crane and everything must be carried up twelve flights of stairs.

In the traditional ground level scenario, the designer oversees the installation as project administrator to keep an eye on the design intent and is on site regularly to ensure that the construction is proceeding according to plan. Project administrators also respond to site conditions and any idiosyncrasies that arise and necessitate adjustments to the design.

For example, at LAMOTH the planting plan called for three types of grass which included *Bouteloua gracilis*,

Lygeum spartum, and *Muhlenbergia dubia* with an underlayment of *Crassula radicans*, a fast-growing succulent ground cover. However, a certain percentage of each grass was designated based on whether the planting area was sloped, steeply sloped, flat, or by a parapet wall. To delineate every grass on a plan would have taken hours of design time not in the design budget. Nor would a sample planting suffice because of the complexities of the slopes on the roof changing every few feet and falling away in compound grades. It was much more efficient for the landscape designers to estimate the amount of grasses needed for the proposed coverage and lay the grasses out on site according to each area's needs. The same example held true for the three varieties of Mediterranean bulbs specified for the flat areas on the roof.

SEQUENCING AND CONVEYANCE

Sequencing is a distinguishing factor on a roof because all of the typical phases of installation like demolition, grading or placing substrate on the surface, deck construction, to name a few, must occur through the filter of the building. If construction on the building is happening at the same time, then the green roof installation usually must wait at least until the waterproof membrane and all flashing details have been installed. In Greece, Andrew Clements tries to install as soon as he has a roof surface to work with so that by the time the building is complete the roof is well on its way to ecosystem establishment. This process usually takes about two years on average in Greece. Establishment of plant

Planting at the Los Angeles Museum of the Holocaust.

Irrigation lines are distributed evenly on the roof of the Lichtenstein Foundation, New York.

Sean Corcoran and his team utilized native sod, which is abundant on the Irish coast, for the initial roof coverage of his seaside cottage. It produced great results.

material varies considerably depending on where the project is located in the world, but plant warranties normally set the establishment period to two years.

Sequencing shines a spotlight on role clarification and team communication because who does what and when is especially critical with roof construction. The client may balk at the extra cost of crane rental and street closures, but hauling decking components up a freight or a pedestrian elevator will hold up elevator use by the building occupants all day. Issues of sequencing and material storage are predicated by what goes on inside the building; if the building is under construction, this will hold up installation. If all of the waterproofing components are completed, then it might be possible to gain early access to a roof for installation but this will not be possible unless the electricians and plumbers have completed sourcing water and power and both are turned on.

To state the obvious, roofs are above ground, which means that 99 percent of the time how materials are conveyed to the actual site is limited to stairs, ladders, elevators, lifts, or cranes. Some questions to ask in advance include, Is there a freight elevator or alternate staircase that will provide access? What do you need to do to reserve these things? Will you need to adjust the sizes of things to fit in the elevator? Do you need to rent a crane? In most places if you are working in a busy part of town, you will need to rent a crane on a weekend or at night in order to get a street closure permit.

Conveyance plays a critical role in the timing of sequencing. It is much easier and less expensive to hire a crane and obtain permits for street closures once. Similarly, if you have to protect

elevators and stairwells, securing brown paper and carpets to vulnerable surfaces is something you'd rather not have to do twice.

STORAGE

Dense urban cores or tight suburban lots generally do not have extra storage room so deciding where to store materials ahead of time is important. Some designers, like Amy Falder who works in New York City, only allow delivery of materials on the day of installation. The size of the roof will determine if and how you can store materials. Materials cannot be stored even temporarily directly on top of the membrane so the contractor must provide protection of the membrane at all times. Wind also presents a problem because materials like insulation and moisture mats can be blown off a roof. If the wind is high, piles of substrate can drift off. Figuring out ahead of time the person with whom you or the installer will coordinate any storage issues will save many headaches.

REVISITING TEAM VALUE

The reason we are revisiting team building is that in many situations early team formation does not include a contractor or maintenance personnel, but when construction comes into play it becomes necessary to add team members. In addition, often clients will prefer to go through the design process before putting out bid documents to contractors. If you are just now adding installers to the team, their suggestions might shape or influence certain specifications once the actual numbers roll in.

Fifth-floor swimming pool and green roof garden
atop a private residence in Dhaka, Bangladesh,
designed by Shatotto Architects.

For example, if there's a steep slope and specified subsurface drip line, the contractor might recommend a drip line wrapped in capillary fabric to disperse the water more evenly and horizontally. This option might drive up costs but is worth incorporating into the specifications for the long-term success of the project. If the contractor who is awarded the bid is good at critical thinking and problem solving, then they know what products are available so they will be able to help make trade-offs in other areas such as plant sizing or exchanging plants in larger sizes for plugs.

You may end up relying on a green roof contractor to serve as the general contractor and handle the relationships with subcontractors like plumbers and electricians, and the necessary liability insurance. At the end of the day having a general contractor who knows their way around crane operators, street closure permits, electrical hookups for fountains and lights, and so forth is invaluable.

On very large projects, professional cost estimators put together budgets from the early phases of design development. Because of value engineering the pricing will change as the design develops, and designers need to be creative in coming up with solutions to maintain the integrity of the design. For example, seeds and cuttings are much less expensive than potted plants.

It is extremely valuable during this phase to communicate to the bidding parties the mission of the project so they can gear their bids to the common goal. Rest assured issues will arise that affect the design whether over budget or limited availability of materials, especially plants. These issues will need to be evaluated based on the mission so the original intent is not lost.

The Pacific Ocean is the backdrop for this green roof at the Post Ranch Inn, Big Sur, California.

This healthy ecosystem thrives with no maintenance on a dairy barn roof designed by Stephan Brenneisen, Pratteln, Switzerland.

Amy Falder tends to a residential green roof in Brooklyn Heights.

An experienced team will facilitate the construction process, working well together to establish sequencing, scheduling, and the actual installation. Experience in the green roof trade will help to build trust among the team members and go a long way to ensure good work and a successful outcome.

In Dhaka, Bangladesh, architect Rafiq Azam of Shatotto has garnered experience over the years in designing projects like the Meghna residence, a home with roof gardens on more than three levels, including several water features and a pool on the top floor. The firm consults with architects, landscape architects, structural engineers, plumbers, and gardeners who work as a team to implement the project's established standards and specific details. Before starting any construction, Azam conducts a seminar/workshop to motivate his team members and to allow all to contribute and share their own experience for the betterment of the project. This time together goes a long way to ensure the successful construction of complicated projects like the multilevel greening experience of the Meghna residence.

Maintenance

To maintain or not to maintain, this is a big question in the green roof industry. There are different schools of thought on this topic, divided between the complete absence of care to limited upkeep to weekly visits. These schools of thought develop from the design intent of the green roof or roof garden and vary tremendously.

For roofs that require ongoing attention, maintenance plans fall into two categories: the establishment period of up to two years and 80 percent coverage, and the post establishment period. The best-case scenario is to stay with the same company for both phases because they will have historical knowledge of the project, know what issues have arisen, and more likely ensure better performance out of the roof.

If a different company takes over the maintenance after the initial contract expires, there should be a handoff of the maintenance manual, or at least documentation, to describe the plants and plan including the fertilization schedule and the irrigation layout and schedule. Also included should be the green roof system with descriptions of the layers installed, a roof plan describing layout and access, and maintenance records to date.

DIFFERENT APPROACHES

Green roof facilitators like Dusty Gedge and Andrew Clements assert that ecosystems are inherently closed systems sustainable without external input. They believe that once they install an ecological system on a roof, nature will take its course and they can walk away because they are recreating ecosystems on a roof that should mimic an ecosystem on the ground.

The other camp, usually occupied by landscape architects and designers, believes the design they envisioned should stay intact and carry forth the initial message. What good is a formal design if it is not going to be weeded and the garden succumbs to natural succession obliterating the original intent? These designers believe that certain forms or design moves deserve to be preserved and are consequently strong advocates of ongoing maintenance programs. Claudia Harari included gravel borders between beds of sedums on the Horno 3 Steel Museum to help mitigate maintenance (see photo on pages 26–27) and there was very little care on the roof for the first several years. However, she advocates ongoing maintenance for this formal, patterned section of the museum roof to preserve the iconography of the original shapes.

CLIENT PARTICIPATION

Charlie Miller of Roofmeadow in Pennsylvania has vast experience in large extensive green roofs and thinks clients should take a more active role in their projects because one component of maintenance involves reintroducing plants every three to four years. He has seen many alpine plants wither after several years and encourages reseeding and/or replanting small quantities of plants on a three-year cycle. Another of his suggestions for a good payoff with little investment is to overseed roofs with annuals so that there will be a big presence one year; they will self-sow and then come back.

Miller claims that maintaining sedum roofs in the United States differs from practices in places like Germany where plant loss is not as great because the climate, which is not a continental one, allows more varieties of sedums to survive. In the United States, he sees a steady decline of biodiversity among sedums. If the East Coast experiences a brutal hot summer with drought conditions, sedums die. A solution to this problem would be to specify plants that thrive in a given region along with the sedums.

Fountain grass embraces the edge of this Manhattan rooftop garden designed by Hanna Packer of Town and Gardens.

Three questions for

Jeffrey L. Bruce,

landscape architect and owner of Jeffrey L. Bruce & Company, North Kansas City, Missouri, about troubleshooting.

---

1. What is the most difficult situation you have encountered during installation and how did you fix it?

The task that requires the most diligence and effort to ensure a successful green roof installation is the quality assurance and testing of the growing media. Within the North American green roof industry, there is no consensus on engineered soil standards. Coupled with limited public understanding of growing media performance requirements, the growing media materials can vary widely as can the proportions of the ingredients from batch to batch. We invest significant resources in managing the manufacturing process of engineered soils to ensure the growing media will perform within expected ranges while producing desired results.

The single most difficult situation in a green roof installation is when a growing media, which does not meet the specification, is delivered and placed on the roof. It becomes virtually impossible to convince the project team to remove it, regardless of how detrimental it might be to the plants or the performance of the green roof. The best way to prevent this from occurring is to prohibit on-site blending and manufacturing of the growing media. Soils should be blended off site where a rigorous testing process approves the growing media prior to shipment to the project.

2. How do construction specifications and sourcing materials affect the sustainability of the industry?

Green roof assemblies are incredible tools to enhance sustainability currently, but the industry is continuing to invest in ways to improve the sustainability of the products and processes. In the near future, we will begin to see green roofs function more as living machines that accomplish work such as water treatment, stormwater management, biodiverse habitat, thermal energy conditioners, and even urban agriculture. This shift in green roof function will be paralleled by shifts away from exotic imported plants toward naturally adapted local native ecologies, from high-embodied energy materials to new natural or recycled materials, which have a smaller environmental footprint.

The future role of green roofs in sustainability is not only the sum of its components and materials, which will continue to evolve toward more sensitive products and processes, but more importantly it is how these assemblies are used as sustainable tools in a large urban context. Green roofs will not be isolated islands of green but have limitless opportunity to become the connective tissue in a wider network of integrated green infrastructure that links these optimized green engines into regional systems. As all living plants reach for the sky for sustenance, can we reach for the sky and envision a world with green roofs reconnecting all humanity to nature in the core of our cities?

3. What two tips can you suggest that will help result in a successful installation?

Green roofs are layered systems with each layer contributing a specific performance value to the assembly. Green roofs are also intimately connected to the structure on which they reside. My best advice for a successful installation is to seek out guidance from an independently trained or accredited professional with experience in the design, installation, and maintenance of green roofs to assist you with the selection process of an assembly. These professionals can guide informed discussions with manufacturers and installers concerning assembly options while representing the best interests of the owner.

Another tip for a successful green roof installation is as simple as a single word *communication*. Green roof design and installation can cut across many disciplines such as architects, structural engineers, roofing consultants, general contractors, landscape architects, and landscape contractors. As a result, success is measured in terms of constant and continuous communication between team members so that expectations and responsibilities are known and understood by each team member. The most critical communication begins at the start of the project with the owner. The team leader's job is to work closely with the owner to fully describe the processes, visual expressions, and operational needs and program utilization so that the owner's expectation of the project is clearly aligned with the project that is delivered. Communication is a tool to uncover misunderstandings, eliminate ambiguity, cross train team members, and reinforce quality assurance. Clear expectations understood collectively by all team members foster an environment of collaboration, innovation, and excellence, which are all built on the foundation of communication. ■

As designer/builders in New York City, Amy Falder of New York Green Roofs and Hanna Packer of Town and Gardens each offer ongoing maintenance as part of the scope of services to their various clients. In their separate experiences, planted roofs are always evolving and every site is different with its own microclimates. Extreme summers make a difference and so does routine personalized care. Nothing replaces a person going out to check on irrigation, drains, and weeds.

For the purposes of this book and the advancement of green roof design, we advocate setting your intention early, clarifying client expectation, and looking to the long view.

Devising a Plan

Devise a strategy for maintenance when you are developing the program for the project. Normally the simpler the structure and components—for example, a sedum extensive roof in 4 to 5 inches (100–125 mm) of substrate—the less maintenance needed. More plants plus more substrate equals more complexity, which equals more maintenance.

Client expectations around what the finished product will look like and how it will perform over the years is one of the most critical aspects of green roof design. When you sit down with the client and review the proposed vision for the project, describe your intentions not only for the immediate vision, but also for the long view. Let your client know that maintenance continues long after the establishment of the initial planting and may include much more than weeding.

Most green roof installers include a maintenance contract for the first two

A colorful and low-maintenance palette of climate appropriate sedums on San Juan Island designed by Warick Hubber.

years to cover their warranty around plants and irrigation. Maintenance on a roof garden typically requires more time and attention if the plants range from annuals to trees. Additional program items that might be included in the maintenance plan are sweeping the decking and cleaning water features and pools.

If you establish the long view in the early design phase, the client can anticipate operating costs. On residential projects, ask the client if they expect to maintain the garden themselves. If not, do they need help seasonally in spring and fall, or do they need help weekly? You can also design for low maintenance, specifying plants that require less care like grasses that only need to be cut down once a season.

Part of your plan may have to include considerations like compliance with requirements for insurance or certification programs like LEED. Some cities like Toronto require a maintenance plan to obtain a permit. There also needs to be something in the maintenance plan in place to protect warranties around the waterproofing and to provide for the vegetated systems. For example, if the warranty calls for a certain percentage of plant coverage, then the maintenance plan must call for replanting or filling in with plants to achieve the desired coverage.

Requiring regular care and parameters around irrigation, weeding, and fertilizing are also essential components. If the vegetation is there to do more than just look pretty, and functional aspects like stormwater filtration are important, making sure you have adequate coverage is an operational goal for the life of the roof.

The benefit of long-term maintenance is protection of your client's initial

A survey is done of this meadow roof in Brooklyn to ensure proper maintenance.

Three questions for

Andy Creath,

owner of Green Roofs of Colorado, Boulder, about maintenance contracts.

1. As an installer when you establish a maintenance contract with your clients, what are typical specifications for the number of visits and their length?
Depending on the system that was installed most system manufacturers have a required maintenance schedule to follow to keep their warranty in place. Even if it is not required by the warranty, maintenance is a necessity. Typically, it is front-loaded after the installation with five visits the first month. Then visits will gradually decrease during the roof plants' establishment. Biweekly visits are typical during the first year, once a month during the second year, and the third year, if it all is going well, visits will become quarterly. The duration of time spent on site will depend on the size of the job and the maintenance needed, but it will most likely be less than a full day of work unless major repairs are required.

2. What happens during a typical maintenance visit?
A typical maintenance visit begins with a documented walk-around site assessment to look for proper plant growth, weed infiltration, signs of over- or underwatering, leaks in the irrigation system, clogged drains, signs of wear or tear in the exposed waterproofing, signs of pests (birds and others), erosion from wind or water, and collection of media for lab testing.

After the walk-around, the necessary tasks are performed to correct any issues related to weeding, fertilizing, debris removal, planting, trimming, and irrigation repair and testing. I also contact the owner's representative to discuss issues outside of the maintenance professional's scope of work. Taking pictures and documenting findings in a maintenance manual are required tasks to ensure all involved have current information.

3. What are some of the safety constraints of maintaining green roofs?
You are on a roof where falls can be fatal. Tie-offs, safety railings, or spotters are required for work around roof edges, and it is necessary to comply with OSHA standards for this work. Also, while on a roof you need to be aware of weather. Lightning, wind, rain, heat, and snow can create a dangerous environment very rapidly.

Getting to the roof can be difficult at times, so when accessing these areas, proper and safe use of ladders and other climbing aids is essential. ▪

Among other things, maintenance crews need training on the proper use of tools on a green roof and in identifying weeds versus plants.

investment. This strategy also enhances the roof by adapting the materials over time to what works best. This is most clearly demonstrated with plants like grasses that need to be cut back or thinned, but wood decking also needs care like staining. In winters without much precipitation, watering during the cold months when planters and shallow substrates dry out quickly will make a big difference come spring.

Warwick Hubber, or Wocka, as he is commonly known, of Garden Artisan landscapes in coastal Washington, designs and builds green roofs based on the knowledge that they will evolve but with very little care. Wocka's low-maintenance approach is successful because he uses sterile, engineered substrate; has little to no blow-in of seeds from surrounding land since all his projects are on the water; and employs climate appropriate plants for the plant palette.

At the other end of the spectrum is the roof garden of the Mordecai Children's Center at Denver Botanic Gardens where the emphasis is on plant education and display of a myriad of possible plant varieties for roofs in the high altitude arid prairie climate of the Front Range. The ground covers, perennials, grasses, shrubs, and trees require regular care from annual trimming to monthly deadheading of spent blooms. Maintenance like this costs money, in perpetuity, and operational budgets vary in cost depending on where you are in the world. The client must be made aware and agree to what the green roof means in terms of long-term operation budget. With larger projects, especially if they are nonprofit, it may be possible to secure funding for a maintenance endowment.

The Maintenance Crew

Pulling the maintenance people in early to discuss details could spell the long-term success of the roof, and teams unaccustomed to working on rooftops will benefit from some on-the-job training. For starters, they need to know they can't use sharp objects to eradicate weeds, and similarly when checking and cleaning drains under scupper boxes, sharp tools are out of the question as well because waterproof membranes are easily punctured.

Make sure the crew knows what plants are intended and what plants are weeds so the wrong plants aren't pulled or replaced. They also need to understand the water and fertilization requirements of the plants initially and over the long course to adjust and adapt giving the plants what they need. This is very different from on the ground because the substrate is so porous that water and fertilizer schedules have to be assigned accordingly.

Additionally, the problem with weeds on a roof is that they can take over and drive out the original plants so the roof performs differently in terms of stormwater filtration. Also some weeds can be much more aggressive, clogging drains and finding their way into the vegetation-free zones.

While ground crews are well versed in weeding and servicing the irrigation, they will not be familiar with checking the membrane, flashing, drains, and all else specifically related to green roofs. It is worth the time investment to bring crew members with little or no green roof experience up to speed on the following areas: checking to make sure the drains are flowing freely, and checking points where there are membrane

Flats of annuals, which will ensure adequate coverage on the green roof and provide seasonal interest, await planting.

Bachelors button (*Centaurea cyanus*), red salvia, and corn poppy (*Papaver rhoeas*) thrive on this Boulder green roof installed by Andy Creath of Green Roofs of Colorado.

penetrations like at HVAC units or at the edge of the parapet walls, to make sure water isn't penetrating the waterproof membrane.

While these tasks are normally associated with roofers, landscape maintenance crews have to be trained to not only address the plants, irrigation, and soil but also the roofing components. Remember, if the filter fabrics beneath the substrate get clogged and the roof does not drain freely to the drains, and the plants drown, blame will normally fall on the designer or installer. Both are held responsible.

Maintenance needs and actions may change annually and seasonally. On the High Line, long summer grasses are cut back selectively after the seed heads have been eaten by resident birds.

Maintenance Contracts

Maintenance contracts look different depending on the type of project. What they cover can vary from plant care and irrigation inspection to encompassing the waterproofing system. Your client should also make sure the maintenance company has the appropriate insurance for working in a roof.

Regardless of the size of the job, four items should be a covered in every maintenance contract:

1. Irrigation schedule outlining times, amount, and control of watering.

2. Fertilization schedule including type, amount, and timing of application.

3. Weed management schedule and, if possible, which weeds to eradicate.

4. Inspection of edging, drains, flashings, roof penetrations, and hardscape areas based on an established periodic schedule.

Additional items might include replanting specifications, ways to minimize the impact of foot traffic in the planted areas, and assigning someone to remove the vegetated cover in case of a leak.

In the interest of total clarity, Charlie Miller includes the following statement in his maintenance agreements:

Maintenance of a healthy foliage cover is essential to the long-term performance of the Green Roof. Failure to maintain a robust foliage cover may result in loss of media to wind scour, reduction in runoff management function, or deterioration of components due to UV exposure. Preservation of a robust foliage cover will require ongoing and regular maintenance.

Additionally, the appearance of the Green Roof should be expected to change over the years. A process of natural succession will result in the botanical evolution of the vegetated cover; consequently, the future distribution of plants species cannot be accurately predicted.

Necessary Analysis and Management

When planning for the long-term health and performance of the roof, it is important to set up goals or milestones. What are the desired results? What is the expected plant growth? How does one measure the performance of green roofs? Is there a chance to collaborate

with an educational or research institute to collect data? Is data available to help determine benchmarks along the way? If data is available, it is usually collected by the person who is studying it, like Jennifer Bousselot, a doctoral student who did several studies on the roof of the Environmental Protection Agency green roof in Denver. This research was published as part of her dissertation through Colorado State University in Fort Collins and is available to the public.

Pat Cullina, vice president of Horticulture and Park Operation for Friends of the High Line, currently consults on the project. His approach to maintenance is to work on changes that respond to something that could be improved or something that was lost and need to be replaced. Part of his philosophy is to be patient so he typically waits more than three months before replacing plants. Gardeners become observers of the landscape and form ongoing partnerships with the landscape designers. Piet Oudolf, a Dutch planting designer and master of grasses who also designed the Lurie Grass Garden at Millennium Park, is still involved, visits when he is in town, and wants to talk about things.

Maintenance Manual

A critical piece of the operational process of a vegetated roof is to establish a detailed manual that lays out elements of maintenance like checking drains and inspecting the working capacity of irrigation. Plant maintenance and inspection of membrane flashing points and structural elements that interface with the live system are regularly required. Also included in the manual is the schedule of visits necessary for establishment and on-going care.

At the Los Angeles Museum of the Holocaust, the maintenance contract was written up to include 80 percent coverage within two years. The components to be maintained included the roof membrane system, drainage inspection, surrounds and rooftop structures, and plant care. The latter encompassed weeding, watering, fertilizing (organic only), trimming, thinning, and pruning.

The manual also included instructions for reporting after maintenance visits and training, all the original drawings and design narrative, written specifications, and cut sheets for the accepted product specifications, including detailed descriptions of the plant material installed.

MAINTENANCE REPORTS

Documentation is an important part of the maintenance process because sometimes a warranty will not be honored unless documentation is in place. These routine maintenance reports need to cover categories for each plant and each nonliving component of the roof like drains that need to be checked. The reports should be filed every time a maintenance visit occurs and should be sent to the client. Visits need to be coordinated with the client and depend on the complexity of the project and design intentions.

Cleaning the basketball court on a roof garden in downtown Denver.

12

The Evolving Frontier of Landscape Design

An edible garden covers the roof of this bright blue building in central London.

From the beginning, it was our intent to write about green roofs from a design perspective, and we believe that is what makes this book unique. Our goal has been to share both the beauty and the challenges of green roofs and roof gardens as we presented the avenues to possibility. By encouraging designers to explore the importance of integrating humans and nature, we hope that the future of urban design will result in innovative ways of thinking about cities, and that green roofs will be an integral part of that vision.

If you believe as we do that compared to ground level landscapes, which offer a historical depth of information and examples to emulate, the green roof movement is merely in its infancy, then you can't help but feel incredible excitement about what the future holds for this evolving frontier of landscape design. Rather than theorize on those possibilities on our own, we asked the movers and shakers of the green roof world to join us at a virtual roundtable and discuss key issues affecting the future of green roof design and technology, and what those might look like in the coming decades. Their responses were both insightful and thought provoking.

Virtual Roundtable Participants

- **Stephan Brenneisen, PhD**, Zürich University, biodiversity and ecology research scientist and head of the Green Roof Competence Center.

- **Colleen Butler, PhD**, Tufts University, plant ecologist specializing in ecology and physiology of plant communities on green roofs.

- **Andrew Clements**, founder of Oikosteges in Athens, Greece, develops natural oikosystems (ecosystems) for the man-made, built environment with emphasis on extreme seismic areas and weather conditions.

- **Amy Falder**, founding partner of New York Green Roofs, a design/build green roof company.

- **Dorthe Rømø**, MA Biology, project manager on the City of Copenhagen's wastewater plan and lecturer at the University of Copenhagen about green roofs as a part of future urban design and planning.

- **Dusty Gedge**, researcher, green roof activist, co-author of *Small Green Roofs Low-Tech Options for Greener Living*, and co-founder of Living Roofs in the United Kingdom

- **Claudia Harari**, co-founder of Harari Landscape Architecture and designer of the Horno 3 Steel Museum in Monterrey, Mexico

- **Mark Simmons, PhD**, ecologist and director of Ecosystem Design Group at Lady Bird Johnson Center, University of Texas, Austin.

Plant selection is a critical element to green roof design.

The Earth House Estate, a housing development in Dietikon, Switzerland, illustrates a balance between aesthetics and ecology.

The Role of Aesthetics

Accepting the premise that the role of function on green roofs is fairly established, we wondered what the role of aesthetics might be in years to come. For one thing, how a roof looks is often a key selling feature and in order to engage the design community and their clients, a visually pleasing result is necessary. If we acknowledge that education plays a major part in the overall acceptance of the idea of green roofs, then public response becomes very important.

Colleen Butler admits that scientists tend to downplay the importance of aesthetics, but when she designed and installed a green roof where everything died, the reaction was less than optimal. "I got useful data but thanks to a terrible drought, it was ugly and I got bad attention from it," she shares. "Regardless of the function, if it is visible and accessible it needs to be good looking because that's what people are going to cue off of."

Claudia Harari envisions a merging of function and aesthetics. "I see continuous green membranes going indoors and out, and food production being incorporated into aesthetics," she says. "And actually right now, there's a huge investigation about vegetal concrete and photo bioreactors in walls that produce energy."

Then there are those like Andrew Clements who insist it will be a long time before aesthetics have any real role in green roof design, and until green roofs cover most of the world, how they look doesn't matter. "I am a lover of nature, ecosystems, and the natural look so I think human design aesthetics take a very back seat to functionality and all of the benefits that a green roof provides,"

he says. "Right now I think the most important thing is to get them up and the most effective way is to by following the ecosystem idea."

It seems only natural that designers and scientists will come from opposite viewpoints on this topic but those on the design side will likely find themselves bowing to the dictates of project developers. As Amy Falder noted, it depends on who is in charge. "When the city is driving the project, it is just interested in function whereas the private sector is more interested in the aesthetics," she says.

Dorthe Rømø sees the combination of nature and science as aesthetic partners. "The Vancouver Convention Centre, the Exhibition Hall in Basel, and the Waldspirale in Darmstadt show that nature and the city can coexist with the right mix of landscape architecture and engineering and construction," she says. "The Danish National Archive was inspired by the patterns on the buildings expressing the function of the building, and the garden was created with a choice of natural plants and different depths to support biodiversity."

And finally, in some places like Southeast Asia, the role of aesthetics is going to expand simply because the aesthetics may trump the other benefits. According to Mark Simmons, the less the built-up green infrastructure in a city, the more the demand for aesthetics on a green roof. "It's great if the green roof absorbs water or has other environmental benefits, but in many instances people will just want a place where they can go and sit down," he says.

A group of students looks at the microecology of a roof with Stephan Brenneisen in Basel, Switzerland.

Drought-tolerant plantings of ornamental grasses and euphorbia thrive on a roof in Oakland, California.

Ecology

Green roofs mean that nature is coming into the city, and nature is going to have to adapt to this new urban ecosystem. Ultimately, the ecology will provide us with the knowledge we need because green roofs and green walls are going to become laboratories for experimenting with these new urban ecosystems.

If you accept the premise that the best landscape architect is nature and that the whole purpose of a green roof is to create an ecosystem, then you also have to accept that bringing nature back into the city will solve an array of problems. That's certainly the position of Andrew Clements and his colleague Dusty Gedge. According to Clements, the notion championed by the ecology movement that the world needs saving is ridiculous. "The world has been here a lot longer than humanity and it will survive," he says. "What needs saving is humanity and I think the reason why we are passionate about this is because if you spend time doing green roofs you begin to realize that it is a very powerful, multilevel solution to the mess that humanity is in."

Gedge, who has done a lot of ecosystems training, believes the ecosystems services approach is about stewardship and restorative behavior within the urban realm. "One of the things about green roofs is that engineers can hijack them, and we are looking at how sustainable it is, how much water it holds, and how much energy it produces, which are very reductive in their process," he says. "With a realistic ecological green roof you can have a more holistic approach."

In much of Europe where people are more accepting of the fact that you give something back to nature if you make a green roof, this concept is the main driver. As Stephan Brenneisen explains, "Aesthetics is not very important in my world. In Switzerland we put nature on our buildings and we don't need to explain that, even if it doesn't look nice."

Water

With the ongoing concerns about water availability we couldn't help but examine the role that water would play in the future of green roof design. Not surprisingly, responses varied based on the geographical locales of our participants. In places like Mexico where many parts of the country are feeling the adverse effects of low rainfall, it has already had a strong impact. "It's making us very careful about things like selecting plants with low water requirements and designing substrates that are able to hold humidity in a very strong way," says Claudia Harari, who also stressed the necessity for irrigation systems to evolve and adapt to the climate. "We are looking forward to green roofs that can hold and store water and act as containers and retainers of storm water and be able to have a reservoir also."

In the northeastern United States, where water is plentiful, a week or two may pass without rain which rules out certain non-sedum plants on a roof. In response to that, Colleen Butler said she'd like to see more reuse of rainwater. "Cisterns are a way to keep green roofs alive and looking pretty without potable water," she says.

Despite residing in rainy London, Dusty Gedge claims the trouble with green roofs is the expectation that they be green all the time when that

John Little pulls weeds from the pump house roof
of a London housing estate.

simply isn't possible. "We all have to be very clever about how we design green roofs and take it away from a horticultural, ecological viewpoint to how we can incorporate technologies like air conditioning that wastes large amounts of water or photovoltaics that will produce shade," he says.

In Greece with its weather extremes, Andrew Clements believes the primary goal is zero irrigation. "We have found that an ecosystem if left to its own devices will find a way to produce water, and I wouldn't intervene and start putting in an irrigation system," he says. "We believe nature can deal with it and so we like to encourage nature to get on with it."

Maintenance

When landscape professions install a ground level garden no one expects them to do it with no maintenance, but for some reason on green roofs there's an expectation that zero maintenance is the norm. As we have learned, not only are green roofs more difficult than a ground landscape, but also now and in the future it is going to fall on the shoulders of the designers to make sure the client understands the effort it will take to maintain them.

"We've all seen roofs fail and everybody loses when that happens," says Mark Simmons. "Europeans have a lot of experience with extensive sedum roofs but when you drift into other types of extensive ones or even intensive meadow or prairie ones, maintenance is very different. Everything is on a knife-edge of survival depending on the type of roof you have. Unless you have that maintenance built in for at least the first few

years and everyone trained properly, you're going to run into trouble."

No conversation about maintenance can take place without factoring in cost, which according to Stephan Brenneisen is a major factor and possible future deterrent. In Switzerland, it is an important issue for developers and owners just to decide if they want to have a green roof or not, he says. "If you say they have to do a lot of maintenance, they may not do the roof because they don't want to have costs later on."

The kind of roof and its role is very much a part of the conversation. At the Horno 3 Steel Museum the circular main roof, considered an icon for the building, is routinely photographed so ongoing maintenance is critical. Meanwhile the other intensive roof has wild grasses and nobody takes care of it. "It depends on the role," insists Claudia Harari. "We are taking nature out of its natural environment to become part of a building, so it's not only the ecosystem; it is now part of your furniture, part of your decoration."

Learning from Our Mistakes

To date, green roof design has involved a fair amount of experimentation on the part of designers, and often those mistakes inform how we will design in the future. Colleen Butler learned the hard way about succession. After putting soil on the roof to see which plants would establish, she ended up with tons of weeds that made seeds and more weeds. "I guess if I'd left it for a hundred years I would have seen some interesting succession, but after letting it go for two years my maintenance ended up much worse than it should have been,"

she says. "The take home message was green roofs are not natural systems. You can use some things you learned from nature, but a green roof is not a completely-untouched-by-human-beings kind of a system."

The real point may be you can't apply horticulture to a green roof, and you have to think as much with ecology as with engineering. After considerable experimentation in Austin, Texas, Mark Simmons realized the one thing about a green roof that is not replicated at grade is the soil media. The two are very different. "Unless you are growing on a lava flow in Hawaii, there was nothing similar to these standard mixes that we were testing. The problem was simply air temperature, which was going well above 100 degrees Fahrenheit (38° Celsius) during the day and every day," he says. "In the end it wasn't the water, it was the roof temperature that was a major factor."

Similarly, in Switzerland many of Stephan Brenneisen's mistakes involved the use of ordinary soil instead of technical substrates. "I found out if you have very shallow substrate situations, regular soil gets too dense and is not as effective in plant production of biomass and in habitat creation compared to using technical substrates," he says. "Now we try to combine natural soil with some lava pumice and other lightweight substrates to get the good part of both systems together."

In Greece, Andrew Clements aha moment involved being over-involved. "For six years nothing whatsoever I did worked in terms of the viability of the substrates of the plants. I think the biggest mistake I made was, and I think this is quite a radical position, the more that I did, the less success I had," he

says. "The more that I got out of the way and allowed things to happen naturally, the more success I had."

Imagining

Assuming green roofs continue to be a growing and integral part of the urban landscape, we couldn't help but take a moment to reflect on what our cities and countries might look like ten, twenty, or thirty years from now. Stephan Brenneisen didn't hesitate to say that in twenty years Switzerland will likely be 50 percent green, and that in thirty or forty years all the roofs will be green. "Green roofing companies now say 90 percent of their contracts are green roofs, which is very different from the States," he says. "In the end it is very simple how to get there; it is a question of the price. You need to find very easy cheap systems to green the roof and then you can get into the building codes and force developers to do it."

Dusty Gedge envisioned London at least 40 percent green in the next twenty years, and Dorthe Rømø optimistically imagined that in thirty years cities will be outlining a green roof infrastructure, and maybe we'll actually start seeing green hot spots on Google maps. Amy Falder hoped New York would look more like Europe in that they will have more green roofs, and both she and Colleen Butler saw sewage and stormwater management playing critical roles in the future. "I like green roofs for their functionality, and in New York we have to reduce our combined sewage overflows," says Falder. "This is happening in cities all across the United States and in the next fifteen years there's going to be $182 million spent in New York alone on best

Plantings mix with the facade of the BIZ (Bank for International Settlements) building in Basel, Switzerland.

The green rooftop of the Squamish Lil'wat Cultural Center sits among the wilds of British Columbia, Canada.

management practices for green infrastructure, and green roofs are a huge part of that discussion."

Mark Simmons believes more greening of cities is dependent on education and a project like the High Line is a perfect example. "People think of the countryside as something you have to go to, and by bringing an ecologically functioning system into the city you don't just bring in something green, you bring the butterflies, the bees, and all the things we heard that make people understand more about function, and that raises expectations," he says. "So in some ways green roofs are a way to catalyze greater change looking decades down the line."

Claudia Harari concurs. "In the beginning whether green roofs need maintenance or irrigation, a little bit or none, doesn't matter because as a cultural issue it is very important that we educate people first," she says.

Andrew Clements imagined flying over Athens and observing an endless meadow where the city once was, filled with beautiful colors and smells from aromatic plants, and butterflies, robins and ladybugs. "It's basically doing all the things we know green roofs can do," he says. "We're reducing the amount of energy, and we are holding much more water in the urban environment rather than having it all run off into the sea. Basically, the city has returned to what it once looked like before we built it. That's the vision."

Conclusion

It takes creative risks to push the envelope of what is acceptable, and currently in the green roof world, the risks are paying off as the number and diversity of vegetated spaces above ground are growing. Along with that idea, we discovered that green roof design can lead to a change in our aesthetic, and projects like Millennium Park and the High Line have resulted in broad acceptance of the woodland meadow concept. The evolution of green roof design has also forced us to pay attention to the importance of contextualism and the need for incorporating climate appropriate plants into our designs.

One unexpected finding was the extent to which limitations push the design boundaries. Immutable parameters like load, wind, sun, and water consistently inspired workable, intriguing solutions. We believe this kind of creativity will continue to shift the paradigm of green roofs regardless of whether the ideas came from ecologists, landscape architects, engineers, or horticulturalists. Along with that, we have also been astounded and gratified by the ongoing research being conducted by our colleagues, who tirelessly search for the next discovery and willingly share their knowledge with anyone who expresses an interest. In the end, regardless of our role, we are all focused on the same thing—more coverage—and we believe that synergistic activity will make it happen more quickly.

Crushing environmental issues like the need for clean water are key drivers in the green roof movement and it is up to us to push for the implementation of more green on our buildings. We have an obligation to move past just our design interests and work with government agencies to further the cause of green rooftops from an environmental viewpoint. In addition, the ever-expanding possibilities for utilizing rooftops as delivery systems for feeding the poor are another shared obligation.

We realize the incredible projects and design ingenuity we have highlighted in this book merely scratch the surface and only hint at the potential of what is yet to come. We share a vision of a world where adding a green roof will be commonplace. We also imagine an enjoyment of rooftops that cuts across cultural and economic lines, and approximates the sentiments written almost a century ago by renowned Swiss architect Le Corbusier in his book *Une Petite Maison*:

> We climb up on to the roof—a pleasure known to some civilizations in former centuries. The reinforced concrete forms the terrace roof and, with 20 or 30 centimeters of earth, the "roof garden." Here we are on top! We are in the middle of the dog-days; the grass is parched. What does it matter, for each tiny leaf gives shade and the compact roots insulate from heat and cold. . . . Pay attention! It is towards the end of September. The autumn flowers are blossoming and the roof is green once more, for a thick carpet of wild geraniums has over grown everything. It is a wonderful sight. In spring, the young grass sprouts up with its wild flowers; it is high and luxuriant. The roof garden lives independently, tended by the sun, the rain, the winds, and the birds which bring the seeds.

Bibliography

Balmori, Diana, and Joel Sanders. 2011. *Groundwork: Between Landscape and Architecture*. New York: Monacelli Press.

Bousselot, Jennifer McGuire. 2010. *Extensive Green Roofs in Colorado*. PhD Thesis, Colorado State University, Department of Horticulture and Landscape Architecture.

Christopher, Thomas, ed. 2011. *The New American Landscape: Leading Voices on the Future of Sustainable Gardening*. Portland, Oregon: Timber Press.

Church, Thomas D. 1995. *Gardens are for People*. 3d ed. New York: Reinhold Publishing Company, 1955. Reprint, Berkeley: University of California Press.

Dunnett, Nigel, and Andy Clayden. 2007. *Rain Gardens: Managing Water Sustainably in the Garden and Designated Landscape*. Portland, Oregon: Timber Press.

Dunnett, Nigel, Dusty Gedge, John Little, and Edmund C. Snodgrass. 2011. *Small Green Roofs: Low-Tech Options for Greener Living*. Portland, Oregon: Timber Press.

Dunnett, Nigel, and Noël Kingsbury. 2008. *Planting Green Roofs and Living Walls*. Rev. ed. Portland, Oregon: Timber Press.

Earth Pledge. 2007. *Green Roofs: Ecological Design and Construction*. Atglen, Pennsylvania: Schiffer.

Friends of the High Line, ed. 2011. *Designing the High Line: Gansevoort Street to 30th Street*. New York: Friends of the High Line.

Greenlee, John. 2009. *The American Meadow Garden: Creating a Natural Alternative to the Traditional Lawn*. Portland, Oregon: Timber Press.

Green Roofs for Healthy Cities. 2008. Participants' Manual for Green Roof Waterproofing and Drainage 201, Course Material. Toronto, Canada: Green Roofs for Healthy Cities.

Green Roofs for Healthy Cities. 2011. Participants' Manual for Advanced Green Roof Maintenance, Course Material. Toronto, Canada: Green Roofs for Healthy Cities.

Larson, Douglas, Uta Matthes, Peter E. Kelly, Jeremy Lundholm, and John Gerrath. 2006. *The Urban Cliff Revolution: Origins and Evolution of Human Habitats*. Ontario, Canada: Fitzhenry and Whiteside.

Le Corbusier. 1923. *Une petite maison*. Reprint. Boston, Massachusetts: Birkhäuser Architecture, 1989.

Louv, Richard. 2008. *The Last Child in the Woods: Saving Our Children from Nature-Deficit Disorder*. Chapel Hill, North Carolina: Algonquin Books.

Martin, Agnes, Edward Hirsch, and Ned Rifkin. 2002. *The Nineties and Beyond*. Ostfildern, Germany: Hatje Cantz Verlag.

McHarg, Ian L. 1969. *Design with Nature*. Hoboken, New Jersey: John Wiley & Sons.

Nielson, Signe. 2004. *Sky Gardens: Rooftops, Balconies, and Terraces*. Atglen, Pennsylvania: Schiffer.

Osmundson, Theodore H. 1999. R*oof Gardens: History, Design, and Construction*. New York: W.W. Norton and Company.

Orr, David W. 2002. *The Nature of Design: Ecology, Culture, and Human Intention*. New York: Oxford University Press.

Orr, Stephen. 2011. *Tomorrow's Garden: Design and Inspiration for a New Age of Sustainable Gardening*. New York: Rodale Books.

Oudolf, Piet, and Noël Kingsbury. 2005. *Planting Design: Gardens in Time and Space*. Portland, Oregon: Timber Press.

Oudolf, Piet, and Noël Kingsbury. 2011. *Landscapes in Landscapes*. New York: Monacelli Press.

Pearson, Dan. 2009. Spirit: *Garden Inspiration*. London: Murray & Sorrell FUEL.

Richardson, Tim. 2011. *Futurescapes: Designers for Tomorrow's Outdoor Spaces*. London: Thames & Hudson.

Sarté, S. Bry. 2010. *Sustainable Infrastructure: The Guide to Green Engineering and Design*. Hoboken, New Jersey: John Wiley & Sons.

Shepherd, Matthew, and Edward Shearman Ross. 2003. *Pollinator Conservation Handbook*. Portland, Oregon: The Xerces Society.

Smith, W. Gary. 2010. *From Art to Landscape: Unleashing Creativity in Garden Design*. Portland, Oregon: Timber Press.

Snodgrass, Edmund C., and Lucie L. Snodgrass. 2006. *Green Roof Plants: A Resource and Planting Guide*. Portland, Oregon: Timber Press.

Snodgrass, Edmund C., and Linda McIntyre. 2010. The Green Roof Manual. Portland, Oregon: Timber Press.

Ulanowicz, Robert E. 2009. *A Third Window: Natural Life beyond Newton and Darwin*. West Conshohocken, Pennsylvania, Templeton Press.

Van Sweden, James, and Tom Christopher. 2011. *The Artful Garden: Creative Inspiration for Landscape Design*. New York: Random House.

Waldheim, Charles, ed. 2006. *The Landscape Urbanism Reader*. New York: Princeton Architectural Press.

Weiler, Susan K., and Katrin Scholz-Barth. 2009. *Green Roof Systems: A Guide to the Planning, Design, and Construction of Landscapes over Structure*. Hoboken, New Jersey: John Wiley & Sons.

Xerces Society, The. 2011. *Attracting Native Pollinators: The Xerces Society Guide to Conserving North American Bees and Butterflies and Their Habitat*. North Adams, Massachusetts: Storey Publishing.

Websites

ArchDaily. News/Media. *http://www.facebook.com/ArchDaily*

Archello.com. Society/Culture. *http://www.facebook.com/archellocom*

ArchiLovers. Social network for architects and designers. *http://www.facebook.com/archilovers*

ArchiPortale. Home/Garden. *http://www.facebook.com/archiportale*

Architizer.com. *http://www.architizer.com/en_us/*

Design-d'Autore magazine. *http://www.facebook.com/designdautore*

Dezeen magazine. *http://www.dezeen.com/*

Fachvereinigung Bauwerksbegrunung e.V. German Professional Green Roof Association. *http://www.fbb.de/*

Green Roof. Scandinavian Green Roof Association. *http://greenroof.se/*

Green Roof Alliance. *http://greenalliance.com/*

Green Roof Guide. *http://greenroofguide.co.uk/*

Green Roof Training. Green roofs training, workshops and information. *http://www.greenrooftraining.co.uk/*

Greenroofs.com. News/Media. *http://www.greenroofs.com/*

Green Roofs Australisia. *http://www.greenroofsaustralasia.com.au/*

Green Roofs for Healthy Cities. *http://greenroofs.org/*

Growers Austin. *http://growersaustin.com/*

Inhabitat.com. *http://www.facebook.com/Inhabitat*

International Green Roof Association. *http://igra-world.com/*

Livingroofs.org. Advice, research, and promotion of green roof systems for environmental urban regeneration. *http://livingroofs.org/*

Urban Hedgerow. *http://urbanhedgerow.com/*

Xerces Society. *http://xercessociety.org/*

Acknowledgments

No book is written in isolation. In addition to the authors, usually a long list of friends, colleagues, family members, and others contribute to getting you through the process. Each of us would like to take this opportunity to express our gratitude to those individuals.

Karla Dakin

My first level of gratitude goes out to my partners in this endeavor, Lisa and Mindy, without whom I would still be dreaming of writing a book some day. The next level of thanks goes to Juree Sondker, Linda Willms, and Andrew Beckman at Timber Press for gingerly holding our hands, constantly offering guidance and support. The third acknowledgement goes to all of our colleagues and friends who generously and kindly gave of their time and effort to provide all the jewels in this book. My family and friends, all of whom listened unfailingly while I chewed each and every bite of the elephant, must be included in my gratitude. Lastly, to Ajume Wingo who told me about his grandmother, and repeatedly reminded me that writing a book was a very honorable thing to do.

Lisa Lee Benjamin

Thanks to Flora, for my introduction to the possibility; to my sister, Julie, and the other three B's, for reminding me of the possibility; and to my two brave compatriots, Karla and Mindy, for realizing the possibility. A very special thank you to Marisa Aragona who was instrumental in the photography editing process, and to Miss Perdita Fenn, for loving her roof garden like no other and for the countless nights on her Bermondsey couch.

Mindy Pantiel

First, my thanks to Karla and Lisa for inviting me to go on this incredible journey with them. Next, I'd like to extend my gratitude to the dedicated individuals who champion the cause of green roofs every day and were gracious enough to share their time and expertise with us. Finally, I wish to thank Robert Kittilä who provided me with support and humor throughout this entire process, and who never doubted I would get the job done.

ALL OF OUR SPECIAL THANKS to Michael Berkshire for contributing the foreword, and to each person and organization that provided access to locations, photographs, and illustrations for this book:

620 Jones
Frank Alameda
Sue Amos
Emilio and Kate Ancaya
Marisa Aragona
Caitlin Atkinson
Fred Ballerini
Cath Basilio
Belzberg Architects
Dick Bernauer
Jeremy Bittermann
Jennifer Bousselet
Stephan Brenneisen
Jeffrey Bruce
Chris Brunner
Colleen Butler
Hassan Saufuddin
    Chandan
Andrew Clements
Andrea Cochran
Rebecca Cole
Sean Corcoran
Andy Creath
Patrick Cullina
Departure
Max Dudler Architects
Nigel Dunnett
Esalen
Amy Falder

Perdita Fenn
Natalia Ferńandez
Mark Fusco
Dusty Gedge
Alan Good
Graftworks
John Greenlee
Grupo Habita
Flora Grubb
Habitat Gardens
Geoff Haslam
Claudia Harari
Kendra Hauser
Sean Hogan
Warwick Hubber
David Joseph
Robert Kittilä
Husein Kruavac
Annika Kruse
Tom Liptan
John Little
Pam Locker
Los Angeles Museum of
    the Holocaust
Anthony Lynn
Casey Lyon
J. Scott MacIvor
David Magner
Peter Mauss

Ian McDonald
Terry McGlade
Charlie Miller
Tom Moe
Beth Mullins
Morag Myerscough
New York Green Roofs
Roy Noy
Zoran Orlic
Gut Othmar
Hanna Packer
Petit Ermitage
Post Ranch Inn
Julien Regnier
Dorthe Rømø
Roofmeadow
Patrick Rump
Doug Schaible
Marten Setterblad
Shatotto Architecture for
    Green Living
Mark Simmons
Ken Smith
Starr Whitehouse
    Landscape Architects
    and Planners
Town and Gardens
Xcel

USDA Zone Numbers and Their Corresponding Temperatures

Temp °F	Zone	Temp °C
-60 to -55	1a	-51 to -48
-55 to -50	1b	-48 to 46
-50 to -45	2a	-46 to -43
-45 to -40	2b	-43 to -40
-40 to -35	3a	-40 to -37
-35 to -30	3b	-37 to -34
-30 to -25	4a	-34 to -32
-25 to -20	4b	-32 to -29
-20 to -15	5a	-29 to -26
-15 to -10	5b	-26 to -23
-10 to -5	6a	-23 to -21
-5 to 0	6b	-21 to -18
0 to 5	7a	-18 to -15
5 to 10	7b	-15 to -12
10 to 15	8a	-12 to -9
15 to 20	8b	-9 to -7
20 to 25	9a	-7 to -4
25 to 30	9b	-4 to -1
30 to 35	10a	-1 to 2
35 to 40	10b	2 to 4
40 to 45	11a	4 to 7
45 to 50	11b	7 to 10
50 to 55	12a	10 to 13
55 to 60	12b	13 to 16
60 to 65	13a	16 to 18
65 to 70	13b	18 to 21

Photo and Illustration Credits

All photos by Lisa Lee Benjamin except as listed below.

Sue Amos, page 54 top, 225

Emilio Ancaya / Living Roofs, page 76 top right and bottom

Kate Ancaya / Living Roofs, pages 148 top, 164–165, 192

Marisa Aragona, page 22

Caitlin Atkinson, pages 62, 88 top

Cath Basilio, page 20 below

Belzberg Architects, page 156 top

Jeremy Bittermann, page 52 top

Stephan Brenneisen, pages 88 bottom, 104, (Sybille Erni), 220 top

Andrew Clements, page 178 top

Rebecca Cole Design, pages 34, 64–65, 208–209

© Sean Corcoran, The Art Hand, Ireland, 2011, pages 212, 246 bottom

Karla Dakin, pages 196–197, 198, 199, 226, 229, 244 top

Max Dudler Architects, page 220 bottom

Amy Falder / New York Green Roofs, pages 54 bottom, 63, 158, 216 top and bottom, 224 top, 232, 244 bottom

Natalia M. Ferńandez /Grupo Habita, pages 170–171

Dusty Gedge, page 20 top

John Greenlee, pages 35 top, 234

Geoff Haslam, pages 152 top and bottom, 185

Claudia Harari, pages 26–27, 214–215

Warwick Hubber, page 256

David Joseph, page 178 bottom

Robert Kittilä, page 18 background

Pam Locker, pages 230–231

Make Architects, page 156 bottom

David Magner, page 200

Peter Mauss / Esto, pages 31, 180–181

Ian Mcdonald, page 28 left

Terry McGlade, pages 160–161

Beth Mullins, page 55

New York Green Roofs, page 250 bottom (Chris Brunner)

Rov Noy, page 183

Zoran Orlic / Uncommon Ground, page 201

Gut Othmar, page 56 left

Hanna Packer / Town and Gardens, pages 193, 204, 238, 252

Petit Ermitage, pages 66–67, 202 top

Julien Regnier, page 48 top and bottom

Roofmeadow, page 222

Doug Schaible, page 174

Sempergreen, page 20 left (Dick Bernauer)

Marten Setterblad, page 100

Shatotto Architecture for Green Living, pages 166–167, 248–249

Starr Whitehouse Architects, page 194

Index